The Education of a Graphic Designer

Edited by Steven Heller

ALLWORTH PRESS
NEW YORK

School of
VISUAL ARTS

5 4 3   02 01 00

Published by Allworth Press
An imprint of Allworth Communications
10 East 23rd Street, New York, NY 10010

Copublished with the School of Visual Arts

Cover and book design by James Victore, New York, New York

Page composition by Sharp Des!gns, Lansing, Michigan

ISBN: 1-880559-99-4

Library of Congress Catalog Card Number: 98-70414

Printed in Canada

To Silas Rhodes
for his many contributions to design education

Contents

1. How We Learn What We Learn

2. How I Learned What I Learned

3. How We Teach What We Teach

Acknowledgments

I would like to thank David Rhodes, president of the School of Visual Arts and Tad Crawford, publisher of Allworth Press, for their support and encouragement; Ted Gachot, editor at Allworth Press, for his hard work in shaping this book; James Victore, designer, for producing a beautiful package; and all the participants for their generous contributions, not only to this book, but to design education as a whole.

—*Steven Heller*

Introduction

Steven Heller

Before "isms," "ologies," and "otics," before the Chicago Bauhaus, Yale, RISD, Cranbrook, CalArts, and the School of Visual Arts, the correspondence school was the leading academy of what we now call graphic design. When advertising became a viable industry in America at the turn of the century, commercial artists—including illustrators, boardmen, and letterers—were in great demand. Advertisements for home schooling offered aspirants a chance to earn "$65, $80, and more a week" in "a pleasant, profitable art career." And while these ads shared space in pulp magazines and comic books with schemes to learn dentistry and brain surgery, they nonetheless provided a legitimate way for anyone with a modicum of talent to learn a new profession in their spare time.

The most successful institutions included the International Correspondence Schools in Scranton, Pennsylvania; Washington School of Art in Washington, D.C.; the Lockwood Art Lessons in Kalamazoo, Michigan; the New York School of Design in New York City; Art Instruction, Inc., in Minneapolis, Minnesota; and the Frank Holme School of Illustration in Chicago, Illinois (which included Frederic Goudy, Oswald Cooper, and W. A. Dwiggins on both student and faculty rosters). But the biggest of all was the Federal School of Commercial Designing founded in 1919 in Minneapolis. It occupied a three-story-high, block-long headquarters, had branch offices in New York and Chicago, boasted over seventy-five advisors and full-time faculty members, claimed over three thousand home-study students annually enrolled, and offered "a well-rounded, practical preparation for a profession." Its lavish 1924 catalog asked the questions: "What would you give to be able to draw professionally? Do you long for the ability to make splendid pictures, such as you see daily in advertisements, attractive story illustrations, richly colored magazines covers?" Prospective students were invited to join "the newest art, the youngest great creative force, in the modern business world."

Hyperbole attracted students, yet there was some truth to the notion that commercial art was a creative (and financially viable) alternative to mundane jobs. While couched in vocational terms—commercial art might appear on a par with automotive or electrical repair services—the art correspondence schools were in the vanguard of progressive change. Women, who were not encouraged to enter college, were singled out as beneficiaries of a correspondence education. "Yes, you read it right," declared the Federal School's catalog. "It's true. Woman is [sic] constantly taking a larger place in the modern commercial world. . . . Buyers of commercial art just as readily buy from women as from men. . . ." And the Washington School of Art proudly supported intellectually challenged applicants as well, stating in its 1928 catalog, "We take great pains with backward students. . . . Don't hesitate to enroll because you lack an education. . . . Courses include punctuation, and a 25-cent pocket dictionary will give you the correct spelling of all words you will likely have occasion to letter."

Times have changed. Design pedagogy has measurably evolved since the heyday of the correspondence school. But the existence of these schools challenges the myth that in the nascent period of commercial art, all skills were learned on the job and a formal education was unnecessary. Despite exceptions to the rule, it was impossible to achieve proficiency without an iota of instruction. Although commercial art could be learned in one's spare time (according to the ads, remember, so could accountancy, dentistry, and, alas, brain surgery), the requisite skills were nevertheless learned through a course of study—they were not acquired by osmosis. Although the vast majority of commercial artists attained their true expertise on the job (which is still the case today), to become employable they were nonetheless required to have, if not certain aesthetic principles, at least a keen knowledge of their craft. Therefore, the education of a commercial artist in the early twentieth century is fundamentally the same as the education of a graphic designer today.

The average duration of a correspondence education, however, was months. Today, a total undergraduate design curriculum can span four years, and a graduate program ranges from two to three. The additional time spent in school is commensurate with the increased demands that business has made on the profession. Designers are currently employed as conceptualists, strategists, and aestheticists, as well as in management and consulting positions—a far cry from the piecework freelancer of yesteryear. Knowing the basic skills of design is no longer enough to ensure success as a graphic designer. An undergraduate education barely imparts enough practical instruction to keep up with an ever-widening practice that has grown to include multimedia as a major component of the design equation. Once in the field, of course, a talented practitioner can grow by leaps and bounds, but like other professions where technology, art, and science intersect, the complexities involved in graphic design today require foundations that can only come from intense study through school or apprenticeships (and the latter is much harder to find in this competitive environment).

What with various specialties (corporate, retail, editorial, etc.) and subspecialties (direct mail, website, packaging, environmental, etc.), the education of a graphic designer today is as complex as any technical profession—if not more confusing. For unlike degree programs aimed at those professions governed by established standards, graphic design, which does not demand certification, has few strict regulations and hardly any blanket requirements (other than "knowing" the computer). Most undergraduate design programs more or less offer the same basic courses, but standards vary among institutions.

Advanced courses differ even more widely depending on the specialties and expertise of the permanent or adjunct faculties. Despite the tremendous increase in college, university, and art school design programs over the past two decades, it has been difficult to impose a formula that ensures a well-rounded education. Consistent with this swelling of design programs, certain institutions experiment with new programmatic methods in order to compete. The variegated nature of graphic design education is the same as during the correspondence school days, only more so.

A general handbook for how graphic design should be taught (and learned) has eluded those who have attempted to define a standard curriculum. Which is not to say that such a goal is doomed, only difficult given the nature of the field. *The Education of a Graphic Designer* does not presume to be such a book, but it is a survey of how design educators think about the ways shifting professional, technological, and pedagogical paradigms might be (and in some cases already are being) addressed in undergraduate and graduate programs. This is a book of theories, proposals, and practices; it covers a wide range of educational concerns, from the dichotomies between theory versus practice to traditionalism versus postmodernism; it looks at the new definitions of graphic design, tracing the evolution from production artists to author/producers; and it considers such topics as ethnicity, eccentricity, and social consciousness within the academy.

The Education of a Graphic Designer is loosely based on a 1997 education conference, "How We Learn What We Learn," sponsored by the School of Visual Arts, which examined how the confluence of history, theory/practice, and new media might be balanced in the educational environment. Accordingly, the book is divided into three sections: "How We Learn What We Learn," which includes twenty-six critical essays on the essence of learning and teaching; "How I Learned What I Learned," comprising interviews with a range of design practitioners and educators on the ways in which they were educated; and "How We Teach What We Teach," a diverse and unique selection of syllabi that deal with the increasingly more specialized needs of students.

Taken as a whole, this book is both a white paper on the state of today's design pedagogy and a potential guide for student and teacher alike in the search for viable methods and progressive ideas. Read individually, each essay, interview, and syllabus provides possible models for individuals and institutions.

1. How We Learn What We Learn

Education in an Adolescent Profession

Katherine McCoy

A discussion of graphic design education necessarily expands to include professional practice and theoretical research. These three components—education, practice, and theory—are interactive and describe the scope of any profession.

But *is* graphic design a profession? The field did not exist at the beginning of this century, and still there is little agreement on the proper nomenclature. Are we graphic designers, graphic artists, commercial artists, visual communicators, communication designers, or simply layout men and pasteup artists? These are just some of the English-language possibilities, and every language shares a similar lack of agreement on terminology. Graphic designers themselves are not the only ones having difficulty defining their role. Graphic design's professional status is by no means universally accepted. For instance, the U.S. Immigration Service and Department of Labor remain uncertain if graphic design is a profession, although they clearly recognize the professional status of other design fields, including architecture and industrial design.

ADVERTISING AND THE INDUSTRIAL REVOLUTION

Graphic design was a spontaneous response to the communication needs of the industrial revolution in capitalist market-based economies, invented to sell the fruits of mass production in growing consumer societies. This has led to the unfortunate assumption that visual communications is a subset of advertising. Many schools in the United States persist in defining the whole field of activity as advertising design or commercial art. Yet, all societies have far broader communication needs than strictly commercial ones. Marxist and socialist political and economic systems have not labored under such a definition, as they have not had the same needs for market-based commercial messages. It seems that the more socialized a country, the more graphic design is associated with cultural and political roles on the side of either propaganda or resistance. In the past three decades, many free-market countries have gradually recognized that there are graphic needs beyond advertising, leading to a split between advertising art direction and "pure" graphic design.

EDUCATION THROUGH IMITATION

As the fledgling field of graphic communications developed, knowledge, mainly of graphic arts techniques, was assimilated on the job, through apprenticeships or trial and error. The new graphic artists used intuition and common sense to solve their communication problems for the first half of this century. Although art schools existed in this time period, the emphasis was on fine art with little interest in applied design. It was professional practice, not education, that developed spontaneously as the first phase of graphic design's professional development.

The early luminaries of graphic design that today's design history books venerate were nearly all self-taught visionaries who relied on their exceptional creative abilities to produce their design solutions—landmarks of originality, power, and inventiveness. In fact, this early reliance on the individual's brilliance remains a significant value among many designers today. Through the years, any education policy discussion at a graphic design professional organization board meeting usually includes forceful comments favoring the continuing tradition of the self-trained graphic designer as the best source of innovation and excellence. The concern seems to be that the establishment of educational standards would result in a bland homogeneity of practice—that, in raising the bottom levels of education, we might lose the peaks of brilliance.

This distrust of structured education seems anachronistic to many of us who have seen the substantial growth of design education since World War II, and particularly in the last twenty-five years. Although, until recently, education has lagged behind the development of professional practice, it has produced some excellent models for basic standards and methods for undergraduate education, and is now well into exploring the possibilities of postgraduate education. At least, this is true in our more distinguished schools.

Art schools and university art departments have been slow to realize that design is not simply a commercial application of fine arts ideas and processes. Acceptance of graphic design as a separate and distinct discipline—with significantly different intentions, history, theory, methods, and processes—has been quite slow. Compounding the problem has been growing eagerness among university art departments to compensate for shrinking fine arts enrollments with graphic design programs, whether prepared or not. Entrenched fine arts faculty are teaching graphic design and many start-up graphic design programs rely on just one inexperienced M.F.A. design graduate. As a result, the number of mediocre university-level graphic design programs has grown drastically in recent years, diluting significant progress in the graphic design education community.

APPRENTICESHIPS, ABSTRACTION, AND SIMULATED PROFESSIONAL PRACTICE

Graphic design education has had few models to follow. Before the twentieth century and the industrial revolution's division of labor, which separated conception from production, the European typefounder and printshop apprenticeship were our only precedents. Architecture, the only design field to predate the century, provides us with the French Beaux-Arts model of architectural education. Although the atelier was often formalized into something close to a small-scale "school" setting, students emulated the master and reiterated the classical orders. This could be interpreted as an imitation of the "professional practice" of the time. Students repeatedly practiced on increasingly complex projects until they acquired the skills of the master. In some smaller ateliers, the students acted much like apprentices, contributing to the more mechanical and elementary portions of the master's professional projects.

The Bauhaus, while it used the master/apprentice workshop method, was a revolutionary school model that contributed much to design education. The Bauhaus attempted to organize and codify the revolutionary ideas of the early twentieth-century "isms" and protomodern experiments into an educational method for the new industrial era. The modernist imperative for abstraction and experimentation was applied to a system of design education fundamentals. The Bauhaus Basic Course was the first in design education to declare that basic design principles underlie all design disciplines, that primary design education should begin with abstract problems to introduce these universal elements before students proceed to tackle programmatic design problems applied to specific scales, needs, and media. This emphasis on abstraction and experimentation, and the rejection of accepted traditional formulas, represented a radical new attitude in education.

After World War II, the Bauhaus idea had a major impact on design schools in the United States. Many adopted the model in its pure form, requiring design students in all disciplines to begin with the system. Today, if one peels away the layers in any design program, the persistent residue of this movement is evident.

Yet, the Bauhaus lessons of the 1920s took a surprisingly long time to be established in European and U.S. schools, largely due to the limited resources of the depression years, German politics of the 1930s, and World War II. Before the war, the United States benefitted from the arrival of a number of Bauhaus émigrés who introduced these revolutionary ideas to both established universities and new schools. Ludwig Mies van der Rohe, László Moholy-Nagy, and Herbert Bayer settled in Chicago, with Moholy-Nagy beginning his New Bauhaus. After World War II, Mies's Armour Institute and Moholy-Nagy's Institute of Design (as it was later called) were soon integrated into the new Illinois Institute of Technology, where much of Mies's influence remains in the architecture program, but little beyond Moholy-Nagy's memory remains at the Institute of Design. Walter Gropius and Marcel Breuer went to Harvard's school of architecture, and Josef Albers to Yale. Their influence today might come only from the momentum they gave to those institutions, enabling them to grow and prosper into the present.

Unfortunately, the Bauhaus idea that design fundamentals should precede applied design has been limited mainly to introductory art and design courses, after which design students rapidly move into their areas of specialization. Once in specialized graphic design courses, most schools immediately focus students on applied projects that simulate or imitate professional practice—a modern version of the apprentice system—rather than continuing an orderly sequence of fundamental design concepts and methods.

INTUITION AND INDIVIDUALISM

This lack of a formalized method has been almost universal in our art schools and university art departments until recently. The typical approach has placed a premium on creativity, a flash of intuition, the Big Idea, and educators have encouraged this, through exposure to "samples and examples," as one of our best U.S. educational thinkers has described it. Graphic design magazines and competition annuals have been most students' only resource. Emulating the work of renowned designers could be seen as a weak continuation of the master/apprentice system without the benefit of personal contact between student and master. The Big Idea's reliance on personal intuition and creativity makes it difficult to formalize a codified educational method; educational success is limited to the level of brilliance in both teacher and student.

Following the examples of the great pre- and postwar graphic art pioneers, the Big Idea approach relies primarily on image associations. Drawing on surrealism, it employs unexpected combinations of images and/or contexts to create ambiguity and surprise—the "picture is worth a thousand words." As this approach is essentially semantic, typographic expression becomes a consideration only when used semantically as an image element, with little attention to page structure or systematic message organization. This approach was brilliantly employed by the best of New York advertising in the 1950s and 1960s. But as advertising and "serious" graphic design diverged in the succeeding decades, this approach became associated with advertising's commercialism. (Polish, German, and Japanese poster designers are notable, however, for their continuing powerful use of this imagery—and perhaps it is time for a reappreciation of this rich form of imagery.)

THE NEW STRUCTURED EDUCATIONAL METHOD

Fortunately, the past twenty years have seen a number of American graphic design programs develop carefully structured curricula based on educational methods that go far beyond the superficial simulation of professional practice and the "aha" intuitive approach. This new development is another descendant of the Bauhaus as well, but by way of the "Swiss school" of graphic design. The great Swiss innovators of the 1950s and 1960s can be seen as representing the classic phase of modernism, the heirs to Bauhaus graphic design and other early modern European graphic designers. These Swiss innovators applied the Bauhaus functionalist ethic to a systematic graphic method that shared the Bauhaus values of minimalism, universality, rationality, abstraction, and structural expressionism.

This fresh and highly professional graphic design was first transmitted beyond Switzerland to the rest of Europe and the United States through Swiss design magazines and a few books, notably *Graphis* and the "Swiss" bibles by Müller-Brockmann, Gerstner, Hofmann, and Ruder. Then, in the late 1960s, several professional offices began to practice these ideas to solve the needs of large corporate clients in Holland, Great Britain, Canada, and the United States. The method, symbolized by the typeface Helvetica, was enthusiastically adopted by several corporate and institutional design groups, including

Container Corporation, Ciba-Geigy, Herman Miller, IBM, and Massachusetts Institute of Technology. Montreal's Expo '67 was a feast of Helvetica and systematic environmental signage, as well as advanced architecture. Eventually, American corporate culture embraced Swiss school graphic design as the ideal corporate style.

Although Swiss school graphic design was first adopted in the United States by professionals in their design practices, soon several leading U.S. graphic design schools followed suit, going directly to the source. A number of Swiss teachers and their graduates, from Armin Hofmann's Basel school in particular, put down roots in schools including Philadelphia College of Art, University of Cincinnati, and Yale. (The Swiss influence seems to have been particularly strong in U.S. and Canadian schools; Europeans have often expressed a certain mystification at this North American reverence for the Basel method.) Manfred Maier's book, *Basic Principles of Design*, on the Basel foundation program was finally available in the United States in 1977, spreading this method further. Under the influence of this highly structured educational method and its emphasis on the prolonged study of abstract design and typographic form, these American schools began to carefully structure their curricula. Based on objectivity and rationalism, this educational system produced a codified method that was easy to communicate to students, giving them a foundation for a visual design process and composition that went far beyond the superficial emulation of their heroes.

This classic modernist graphic aesthetic is distinctly different from the predominantly semantic imagery of the Big Idea. It stresses the grammar of design and is rather neutral to content. Regrettably, this language of structural geometry has often resulted in a sameness of form that is more the look of function than truly communicative function—an emphasis on formal purity rather than on content. As this aesthetic spread, however, a number of Europeans, particularly in conjunction with the Ulm school in West Germany, began to apply semiotics to visual communications problems. Related explorations in the science of signs were taking place in structuralist philosophy, linguistics, literature, and film theory. Other efforts to develop scientific design processes through communication theory and computer design method began in Great Britain and at the Illinois Institute of Technology during this period. Although the Swiss school never embraced these communication theories, some of the sounder graphic design schools outside Switzerland have gradually begun to incorporate theory into their curricula, providing some foundation for their syntactic formal experiments.

DESIGN HISTORY

Soon after the advent of more structured curricula, design history entered the scene, becoming another major new influence in graphic design education in the 1980s. Until the past few years, U.S. students received instruction only in the history of fine art—a few were lucky enough to study some architectural history. Although today a number of U.S. schools have design history courses, most of these have only one survey course. And it is likely that the vast majority of graphic design programs still have none. Although the

British seemed well into this new field when U.S. educators became aware of it, there were virtually no texts available until the publication of Philip Meggs's book *(A History of Graphic Design)* in 1983. The first graphic design history conference, held also in 1983 at Rochester Institute of Technology, drew attention to the idea that graphic design *had* a history—a revelation, and an unfortunate testimony to the adolescent state of our profession. A field without a formalized body of history and a community of academic historians could hardly be called a profession.

A concern is the impact that graphic history continues to have on graphic designers' formal vocabularies. From the outset of the discovery of our history, both students and professionals have avidly examined historical graphic styles. In fact, graphic design history too often seems like one big garden of juicy styles ripe for appropriation, resulting in a rather empty graphic eclecticism in the field. Too often, current history courses are taught as superficial surveys of graphic style with no examinations of social, cultural, and political contexts. This only furthers many graphic design students' tendency to stylistic imitation. On the other hand, the discovery of historical design forms was an important element in the development of a graphic postmodernism in which the field shed its preoccupation with modernism, an obsession with perpetual "newness," and expanded its vocabulary of forms beyond the strict minimalism of the Swiss school.

True academic graphic design historians in the United States today could probably be counted on one hand, perhaps two. For the first twenty years of graphic design history courses, the faculty, having never taken such a course themselves, had to become instant self-educated experts. Presently, most faculty teaching history have had only one undergraduate course during their own educations. Sadly, it is still nearly impossible to pursue a graduate degree in graphic design history in the United States—some Americans seek advanced degrees from British universities with well-developed design history programs.

GRADUATE STUDY

A major increase in graduate programs and their enrollments is a healthy indication of our growth. In the past twenty-five years, graduate study has become recognized both by young designers and their potential employers as a valuable asset for professional practice. But the greater significance of graduate schools is their contribution of research and theoretical exploration. Whereas undergraduate schools must necessarily concentrate on a broad spectrum of fundamentals, graduate programs provide specialized focus and faculty resources. These graduate programs are developing much-needed theory that will, in turn, advance the level of graphic design's professional practice and produce far better educators with advanced degrees.

A number of promising programs are now offering graduate students opportunities to pursue in-depth research and experimentation in design theory, methodology, philosophy, history, criticism, technology, and new design languages. Graduate study should never imitate professional practice; rather, it should challenge students to look deeply into the discipline and into themselves to connect design to its culture, its history, its users, its society, and its technology. A problem yet to be corrected is the persistence of many small mediocre graduate programs attached to large (and equally mediocre) undergraduate university programs, in which graduate study is largely a remedial extension of insufficient undergraduate work.

Ironically, the increasing quality of undergraduate education is proving to limit somewhat the number of prospective graduate students. Many students now leave undergraduate school with impressive portfolios that demonstrate well-developed formal sensibilities, particularly in typography and computer skills. The downside of this success is a tendency for these graduates to regard education as a passive process, spoon-fed from teacher to student and complete in four years, rather than lifelong self-initiated learning. This attitude can lead to a plateau of competence—resulting in the predictably slick work we see around the world—and discourages further growth in challenging graduate study.

ACADEMIC POSTMODERNISM

In the late 1970s, for the first time in the United States, education began to lead rather than to follow professional practice. No sooner had the rules of the Swiss method begun to be taught in the U.S. design programs than they began to be broken by a movement that has been described by many terms, but most often as "postmodernism" or "new wave." As professionals and their clients in the United States grew increasingly committed to the Swiss school, certain educators—often early proponents of the Swiss school themselves—began to experiment in their personal graphic design practices, questioning the rigidity and minimalism of graphic modernism.

Working from a modernist foundation, they began to dissect, to multiply, or to ignore the grid, and to explore new spatial sensibilities, introducing layered complexity, pattern, and, frankly, nonfunctional design elements with references to historical design forms. This postmodern (or "late modern" or "decadent modern") wave began outside the corporate and professional mainstream, causing a great deal of debate in the graphic design press for a time. These educator/designers had the independence and experimental attitude necessary to move into new realms, as well as a new awareness of design history and contact with Switzerland's enfant terrible, Wolfgang Weingart, also primarily an educator. They also benefited from their tolerant cultural and educational clients who were willing to take risks with topics appropriate for experimental solutions. The professional design community began to look to art school publications for new ideas, as educators' work appeared in national design exhibitions with increasing frequency.

These experimentally inclined educator/designers applied their discoveries to their teaching, and their teaching experiments to their personal design work. With liaisons made with a few notable young professionals engaged in similar experiments, their academic postmodernism provided a model for a new generation of design students who are now in the mainstream of professional practice in the United States, still filling the graphic design magazines and annuals with examples of what (for better or worse) has become another accepted graphic style.

New wave graphic design was an experiment in formal issues, often indulgent, frequently analogous to the postmodern movement in architecture, and equally controversial at its inception. Yet, even as postmodernism spread quickly throughout all the arts, including music, literature, fine arts, and theater, a new influence arrived in design education—poststructuralist critical theories, including deconstruction, began to find their way out of literary criticism and into several of the more theoretical and experimental of U.S. graphic design programs. Coming largely out of French literary theory, the emphasis here is not on the author/creator (as in new wave) or on the scientific construction of the design solution itself (as in functional modernism), but rather on the reader/viewer and the possibility of multiple interpretations. Applications of these theories offer the opportunity for other, more subjective and personal layers of meaning, in addition to the purely objective and the informational. These strategies encourage new wave graphic designers to work with layers of meaning and content, as well as layers of form. In addition, this new focus on audience interpretation challenges designers to tailor their visual messages to the special characteristics of each project's target audience.

The deconstruction of meaning holds important lessons about our audiences for visual communicators, but poses some problems as well. While these theories applaud the existence of unstable meaning because of audiences' varying cultural contexts and personal experiences, this can be at odds with the client's need for a single, clear interpretation of the message. Designers find themselves cast in an authoritarian role within this critique. And this focus on theoretical and critical language dynamics sometimes seems to diminish visual values in graphic design, leading to a predominantly verbal approach, as copywriting's dominance has done in advertising design.

Most importantly, we now have a community of educators who not only teach, but also practice experimentally and initiate original theory and research in graduate studies. We seem finally to have reached a fair consensus that graphic design is not commercial art but a true professional discipline encompassing practice, education, and theory. But we hear a continuing debate as to whether this profession should lean toward art or toward science. The most recent influences add a third contender to the art/science debate. Literary and critical theorists see design as a language to be read—that graphic design might be considered a form of visual literature.

Although all three orientations are preoccupied with communication and meaning, each stresses a different component of the sender-transmitter-receiver communication model. Design as art is concerned with personal content and expression; design as science is concerned with the systematic presentation of objective information; and design as language is concerned with the audience's reading or interpretation of text and content. It would seem that the answer to this debate is that all three components are valuable—that nearly every communication problem requires an understanding of all three. In a mature profession, there is both the room and the need for specialized inquiry, and our schools can offer intensive investigations of the entire spectrum, each choosing its orientation based on its resources and potential. Certainly, graphic design will be the richer for the exploration of all three directions.

THE TECHNOLOGICAL FUTURE

As for the future, we must first look back to the past. The division of labor that separated the specialized graphic designer from the technologies of reproduction may come to an abrupt end, thanks to the computer revolution's impact on design, reproduction processes, media, and distribution channels. Professional boundaries are blurring between client, author, designer, reproduction specialist, and audience. Writing, designing, and publishing are converging; many designers are publishing, many clients are relying on nonprofessional desktop publishing, and many audience members are building personal websites.

Just as graphic design has reached some consensus on the parameters of our profession, technology is transforming visual communications. A postindustrial information economy, the successor to the industrial revolution's belching smokestacks, has new enlarged design requirements that go far beyond the print-based commercial communications of manufacturing-based economies. Interactive information and communication technologies require substantial, new visual communication strategies and theory. The incredibly rapid technological advance in the past fifteen years of computer-related design is severely challenging educators to respond and to incorporate these new dimensions into graphic design curricula.

A profession specializing in visual communication would seem to be centrally located in this communications revolution. In the explosion of information breaking over us, there are tremendous quantities of data in need of processing. Computer technologies can fulfill the role of modernist Swiss school objective systems design, as we have seen in desktop publishing. The question posed is, How can all this data be turned into information, and the information into communication and meaningful messages? How can design assist our audiences to turn knowledge into wisdom? It may be that within an environment of abstracted technologically generated data, the designer's personal viewpoint and interpretive forms may be the humanizing element essential to make the vast quantities of abstract data meaningful, useful, comprehensible, and compelling to our audiences.

But we need highly trained designers to apply visual communications expertise to the entire range of communications technologies, especially in time-based interactive media, computer interfaces, and software that incorporate new dimensions of sound, motion, time, and virtual space. We need graphic designers who are literate in computer science; and we need far more designers literate in cognitive theory and perceptual processes who can give comprehensible form to electronic virtual environments. Design for interactive communications may not be a subset of graphic design, but may in fact be a sister discipline. While design for new media originates in many of the same visual communications history, theory, and method, it must also reach far beyond. This expanded knowledge base points to the possibility that four-year degree programs may not provide a sufficient grounding for this incredibly wide and complex field. Educators are beginning to consider a new model based on a four-year predesign program followed by a two- or three-year professional degree, similar to law or medicine.

Our schools must contribute the training, theory, and research required for this revolutionary dimension of design—and very quickly too, because a number of other fields are moving into this domain very aggressively, in a number of other university programs including computer science, journalism, communications, technical writing, film, and photography. As educators respond, we must retain and enhance graphic design's core value as a cultural activity. Designers can offer a compensating balance to the coolness and the abstractions of technology. Educators puzzle over the best relation of new media design curricula to current visual communications curricula.

Emotion, subjective interpretation, and hand gestures are what humans can contribute and computers' expert systems cannot. Highly technological societies will likely put a premium on subjective human values. This suggests the possibility of a renewed appreciation and new applications of our earlier, intuitive, image-oriented, hand-generated design approaches. Design as a cultural activity, including aesthetic and personal expression, may be the essential source of values, emotions, and play that we all need in the digital domain.

Graphic Design Education as a Liberal Art: Design and Knowledge in the University and the "Real World"

Gunnar Swanson

Although this essay concentrates on issues of graphic design education, my arguments also pertain to education in other areas of design; most apply to arts education and many are relevant to postsecondary education in general. I assume a university setting, although many of the ideas presented in this essay apply equally to art schools. Finally, just as the essay calls for a broad view of design education and a broad context for design, I hope it will be read in a broad context and the arguments applied wherever appropriate.

INTRODUCTION

With all the pressures on higher education and all the questions facing graphic designers and design educators, why reconsider the basic premise of graphic design education? Since inertia tends to discourage basic change, why not concentrate on excellence within the current system?

The answers to those questions center on both fairness and survival. Ask most graphic design teachers what happens to their students who do not become graphic designers and you will get the same silence or lecture you hear from basketball coaches when someone asks about players who don't go on to the NBA. Not just the reaction is comparable, the whole situation is. Measuring the success of college sports by the number of players that go on to play professionally often leads to players being cheated out of a real education and a chance for a satisfying life. We need to consider whether our attitudes toward "professionalism" in design education do the same.

GRAPHIC DESIGN EDUCATION

Though hardly homogeneous, the vast majority of graphic design programs, whether in vocational schools, art schools, or universities, are, at least in concept, vocational training programs.

The Bauhaus, which was grounded in craft ideology and stressed intuitive solutions to design problems, provided the model for much of modern design training.[1] Hannes Meyer, the architect who became director of the Bauhaus after Walter Gropius, brought in experts from other disciplines as speakers, but his tenure was too short to have established a design theory at the Bauhaus. When László Moholy-Nagy formed the New Bauhaus in Chicago in 1937 (which later became the Institute of Design at Illinois Institute of Technology), he included lectures by philosophers and scientists.[2] Since then, various other programs have introduced semiotics, literary theory, etc., to their curricula, and there is a growing recognition that a wide-ranging education is needed for a synthetic and integrative field such as design to progress.

By "synthetic" I mean that design does not have a subject matter of its own—it exists in practice only in relation to the requirements of given projects. The path of progress for the field is not defined by the next great unsolved design problem. Design is "integrative" in that, by its lack of specific subject matter, it has the potential to connect many disciplines.[3]

Even while some design programs are strengthening their liberal studies requirements, the tendency toward professional rather than general education at colleges and universities has been growing for the past two decades. Graphic design programs are, on the whole, doing well. Students and parents alike seem to be impressed with the idea that there will be a job waiting at the end of four years of study, and at many schools, graphic design has made up for declining enrollments in traditional fine arts programs.

As the estimated two thousand graphic design programs in the United States pump out more graduates than there are jobs in traditional graphic design firms and corporate design departments, the natural tendency may be toward entrenchment of professional training. Each school would reason that, in fairness to its students, it must do a better job of providing entry-level job skills so *its* graduates have a chance in this competitive job market.

In light of this tendency toward professionalism, it may seem counterintuitive that I suggest that we not only increase the augmentation of design training with more liberal studies, but also reconsider graphic design education—as a liberal arts subject.

THE HISTORICAL CONTEXT OF THE LIBERAL ARTS

The concept of liberal arts was first delineated by Aristotle. He characterized liberal studies as those studies fitting for the education of a freeman. He made "a distinction between liberal and illiberal subjects," the latter being those that would "make the learner mechanical . . . [and] make the body, soul, or intellect of freemen unserviceable for the external exercise of goodness."[4]

Aristotle defined the liberal arts as having four points. First, they are not mechanical. Second, they are not utilitarian, i.e., they have *intrinsic* value; even if extrinsically useful, their pursuit is useful in and of itself. Third, if an area of study is undertaken as a liberal study, there must be no specializing that would restrict the mind. Finally, liberal arts study must be undertaken for its intrinsic value, not merely to earn a living or to impress others. (Thus, intrinsically valuable studies undertaken for the wrong reasons would be disqualified as illiberal.)

It would be easy to dismiss this classical view of the liberal arts as a product of and for a society where routine work was left to slaves. Although the distinction of liberal versus illiberal studies came to light in that cultural context, the development of reason, moral grounding, and pursuit of truth was a prerequisite for citizenship in the fullest sense. Despite their primary interest being intrinsic, Aristotle recognized their utility in building a democratic society. Since our conception of democracy is broader based and more inclusive than that of the ancient Greeks, the current cultural context does not argue for the reduction of liberal studies, but rather for broadening their influence.

It is not clear what subjects Aristotle considered liberal, but the Greeks and, later, the Romans came to agree on seven liberal arts: the trivium of grammar, logic, and rhetoric and the quadrivium of arithmetic, geometry, music, and astronomy. In medieval times, reason was subordinated to revelation until St. Thomas Aquinas harmonized Christian doctrine and Aristotelian philosophy with the addition of theology—reason leading to the knowledge God had revealed. The humanism of the Renaissance rediscovered Aristotelian liberal education through the rediscovery of classical literature and came to equate liberal education with literary studies.

It was not until the nineteenth century that various concepts of liberal education akin to Aristotle's theories were reintroduced (reconsidered, of course, in the light of modern knowledge). Cardinal John Henry Newman's views are seen as more or less purely Aristotelian, but practical values played some part. In his lectures during his tenure as rector of the Catholic University of Ireland in the 1850s (published in 1873 as *The Idea of a University),* Newman claimed that "when the Church founds a university, she is not cherishing talent, genius, or knowledge for their own sake, but for the sake of her children . . . with the object of training them to fill their respective posts in life better, and of making them more intelligent, capable, active members of society,"[5] but his main emphasis was on purely intrinsic value. According to Newman, the University's "function is intellectual culture. . . . Intellect must have an excellence of its own . . . the word 'educate' would not be used of intellectual culture, as it is used, had not the intellect had an end of its own; that had it not such an end, there would be no meaning in calling certain intellectual exercises 'liberal,' in contrast with 'useful,' as is commonly done. . . ."[6]

The nineteenth-century English critic Matthew Arnold modified Aristotle's view that the pursuit of knowledge is intrinsically worthwhile and the fulfillment of man's rational nature. Arnold concentrated on *building* rationality—in his view, knowledge is important in that it allows one to develop abilities and live a harmonious natural life.[7]

The value of the liberal arts, however, was not universally assumed. Harvard instituted the elective system in 1883 with the purpose of allowing students to move in the direction of their future careers. Johns Hopkins University was founded in 1876 as the first research institute in the United States. In 1890, the Harvard Graduate School of Arts and Sciences was established in much the same mode. Its main purpose was, and still is, the production of college teachers with doctoral degrees, while producing scholarly research that is, at least in the ideal, not solely utilitarian.

A movement for "liberal culture" in opposition to both utilitarianism and research was significant enough that, in 1909, Charles William Eliot, who instituted both the elective system and the graduate school, was replaced as Harvard president. Within a few years the debates over educational philosophy died down. Most universities soon accommodated utilitarianism of one sort or another and the liberal arts.[8] The notion that professional training, general education, and research were incompatible lost most of its voice in the early part of the twentieth century. This accommodation of multiple approaches continued, expanding the nature(s) of the university. By the mid-1960s, Clark Kerr, then president of the University of California, coined the term "multiversity," comparing the "idea of a university" to a village with its priests, the idea of a modern university to a one-industry town with its intellectual oligarchy, and the idea of a multiversity to a city of infinite variety.[9]

In such a "city of infinite variety," which provides the football team for local and national entertainment, the hospital where babies are born, as well as scholarship, professional training, continuing education, and a multitude of other services to diverse publics, Kerr recognized that "There is less sense of purpose than within the town but there are more ways to excel."[10] The clarity of Cardinal Newman's goals may be lost, but the opportunities are more numerous and varied.

COLLEGE EDUCATION TODAY

It may be that universities have survived by being, to a great extent, all things to all people. Higher education has largely escaped serious damage from parallel charges of elitism and abandonment of traditional standards, eggheadedness and mundaneness, or impracticality and bourgeois debasement by maintaining a wide variety of virtues, thus maintaining support of an eclectic plurality.

However, attempting to be all things to all people has produced some paradoxes. For example, the same psychology course may be a start toward the understanding of human behavior for one student, a "breadth" requirement for another, and an introduction to what will be a specialized field of study and research for a third. An art history course might add spiritual enlightenment to the psychology class's list of aspects; an English class might also provide remedial communication for native speakers and, increasingly, language training for foreign students.

Largely because standards of excellence and paths of career progress are more clear within the research/publishing/specialization path than they are in a teaching/personal enlightenment/broad education one, the liberal arts have become less an approach to integrated learning and more of a list of fields defining "broad education." Even though the vast majority of students have no intention of specializing in a given academic subject, classes tend to be preparatory for graduate study and, thus, preprofessional education.

Although there may be careerist tendencies, the system of students with traditional subject majors assumes preparation for life as well as vocation. Philosophy teachers, for example, do not measure their success based on whether the majority of their students become philosophers. Likewise, the goal in literature is not only to create producers of literature or literary critics, but to create literate people. By contrast, ask teachers of graphic design about students who don't make careers in design or a related field. Most often, those students are seen as failures. There is little feeling that graphic design education has prepared the student for life or a career other than design.

On the whole, design schooling has not helped students become broader-thinking people who can help shape a democratic society. The tools for analysis and insight of many disciplines have broad extra-disciplinary application for understanding the world. The tools of graphic design do not seem to serve much purpose beyond a graphic design career. Graphic design education is not, for the most part, education. It is vocational training, and rather narrow specialized training at that.

VOCATIONAL TRAINING FOR A CHANGING VOCATION

It has become a cliché of career counseling to point out that most of today's jobs won't exist in fifteen years and most jobs that will exist in fifteen years don't exist now. Certainly the changing names of programs—commercial art to advertising design to graphic design to visual communication and sometimes back to graphic design—testify to the fact that, although there may be graphic designers in fifteen years, graphic designers will likely be doing something very different from the present vocation of graphic design.

Most four-year graphic design programs try to teach something beyond "entry-level skills," but preparing students for their first job is often seen as practical education. It is questionable whether such job training could rightly be called education or even if it is rightly deemed practical. If simulating a "real-world" environment is the best preparation for a designer, design training should take the form of apprenticeships—what could be more real than the real world itself?

The entry-level jobs of the past were largely in production. Since pasteup artists are mostly a thing of the past, courtesy of small computers, many programs now struggle to produce computer operators. It is only faith that makes us assume that upward mobility will be available to the contemporary version of the often-trapped (and now largely unemployed) pasteup artists. The QuarkXPress®, Adobe Illustrator®, and Photoshop® jockeys, today's electronic pasteup artists, may soon find their skills obsolete in the next technological revolution.

Design teachers should teach basic principles of form and communication, but are, by teaching what *they* were taught, teaching the graphic designers of the twenty-first century how to be mid-twentieth-century graphic designers. Educators can and should examine trends (we know, for instance, that electronic communication will increase and become more flexible than it is currently) and try to prepare themselves and their students for the future. There is only one thing, however, that we really know with precision about the future—it will be different from today. Therefore, the best thing we can do for design students is to make them adaptable.

GENERAL EDUCATION AND ADAPTABILITY

The correlation between general education and adaptability makes a belief in general education for designers widespread, although hardly ubiquitous. This belief is often tempered by a distinctly anti-intellectual streak in design teachers. In the mid-1970s, an industrial design teacher of mine told me I was "too articulate" and that great design happens when designers have no other way of expressing themselves than with form. Paul Rand, perhaps the best-known living graphic designer and design educator, recently wrote that a "student whose mind is cluttered with matters that have nothing directly to do with design . . . is a bewildered student."[11] Clearly, many design teachers and many design students see "academic" classes as time stolen from their true purpose—the design studio.

Rand's denial of "matters that have nothing directly to do with design" places design education clearly in the realm of vocational training. In addition to his questionable assumptions about the separability of form from meaning, Rand's statement assumes that any current list of subjects that "have nothing directly to do with design" will apply in the future.

Sharon Poggenpohl, a professor at the Institute of Design at IIT, argued well for the opposite stance.[12] She adopted the term "contrarian" from Wall Street where long-term players, recognizing the cyclical nature of the stock market, determine what everyone else is doing and then do the opposite. I believe design educators must be contrarians and look at the fact that "practical education" is neither practical nor education and move beyond, as Charles Bailey puts it, the present and particular.

GRAPHIC DESIGN AS A LIBERAL ART

What would graphic design as a liberal art entail? It would no doubt take a variety of forms. Certainly, the current trend toward history and theory would be an element, but the switch to "liberal" design will require a change in outlook. We must begin to believe our own rhetoric and see design as an integrative field that bridges many subjects that deal with communication, expression, interaction, and cognition.

Design should be about meaning and how meaning can be created. Design should be about the relationship of form and communication. It is one of the fields where science and literature meet. It can shine a light on hidden corners of sociology and history. Design's position as conduit for and shaper of popular values can be a path between anthropology and political science. Art and education can both benefit through the perspective of a field that is about expression *and* the mass dissemination of information. Designers, design educators, and design students are in a more important and interesting field than we seem to recognize.

DESIGN AND SCHOLARSHIP

What form the new liberal field of design would take is unclear. Currently, there is no clear role for design scholarship. Unlike most traditional fields of scholarship, design has no subject matter of its own, so it is hard to find models for this new approach. Design, in practice, exists primarily in response to an externally generated need or situation. Richard Buchanan, chair of the Department of Design at Carnegie Mellon University, pointed out that the "subject matter for the designer is an indeterminate problem, made only partly determinate by the interests and needs of clients, managers, and the designer."[13] This contrasts with the more clearly defined subject matter found in other academic fields.

At present, design scholarship largely takes the form of historical analysis or criticism. Although there is a place for the history of design in and of itself (just as in the histories of science and many other academic fields), it would be absurd to suggest that *any* field abandon itself wholly to the contemplation of its own past. Design in any full sense will, of course, involve methodology and the creation of designed objects.

Clearly, most design programs would include a significant concentration on skills. This would hardly be unique to academia—language programs do not hesitate to have students conjugate verbs, chemistry students learn laboratory procedures, and there are professional aspects to social science classes. Technique will probably be a large part of any design program, but the meaning of techniques will take on more importance.

Buchanan has suggested rhetoric as the closest available model for design.[14] Rhetoric, as a field of study, is both the practice of verbal persuasion and the formal study of persuasive verbal communication. Design may be seen as the visual counterpart to rhetoric. Buchanan is quite persuasive in his argument that through designed objects, "designers have directly influenced the actions of individuals and communities, changed attitudes and values, and shaped society in surprisingly fundamental ways."[15] Buchanan writes primarily of what is usually called product design or industrial design, but the case for graphic design as a parallel to rhetoric is more obvious.

Graphic design, more than other design areas, is usually directly about persuasion—intellectual, logical, aesthetic, and emotional. Thus, the balance of practice and analysis of rhetoricians clearly makes sense for graphic design. This is not to say, however, that the formal procedures of rhetorical study should be applied to graphic design to the exclusion of all others. Grammatical, semiotic, theatrical, anthropological, psychological, physiological, philosophical, and political perspectives also need to be considered.

DESIGN AS A LIBERAL ART VERSUS DESIGN PLUS LIBERAL ARTS

Mark Salmon and Glenn Gritzer argue for integration of liberal arts, in general, and social sciences, in particular, into the professional design curriculum.[16] They reject the strategy of art faculty introducing social science material because of lack of academic preparation on the part of faculty, and that of team teaching with social scientists because of assumed lack of willingness on the part of faculty. Salmon and Gritzer advocate parallel content, where social science courses that correspond to the design curriculum are offered. For instance, interior design students would study courses on marriage and family, sociology, and occupations, while their design courses would cover domestic design, office design, etc.

Such courses are to be encouraged, but while parallel disciplines are the basis for understanding the context of design, we can hardly expect a real examination of design issues by nondesigners. Research into issues of typography and understanding, for instance, generally misses the questions a designer would ask. (Broad categories, such as sans serif typefaces, are often assumed to be homogeneous, alternative design solutions are rarely considered, etc.) Other fields can provide a framework for basic consideration of some design issues, but we cannot rely on them to advance design any more than medicine can rely solely on the work of biologists. The concerns of design will not be directly addressed by academia until it *becomes* an academic subject.

BALANCING SKILLS AND UNDERSTANDING

A primary task of design education is to find the balance between skills training and a general understanding that will benefit students, the field of graphic design, and working professionals. Bailey charts his ideal balance of skills and knowledge in British elementary and secondary education. Under his scheme, students in the earlier grades will be primarily involved in learning "serving competencies" or skills. Later, social sciences and other "inquiries into goings-on themselves manifestations of intelligence," will share the stage with, and ultimately take over from natural science and the like, or "inquiries into goings-on *not* themselves manifestations of intelligence." Bailey acknowledges that his allocation applies only to "a liberal and general education. Nothing is said . . . [about] specialist training."[17] If for no other reason, Bailey's particular division cannot be applied directly to graphic design education because it ends at an age before most design training begins. It does, however, offer an analytical framework for considering components of an education.

It is too early to assign the activities of students in the hypothetical liberal field of design, but it is interesting to observe that the present pattern of education is often the opposite of the most common forms of professional training. At the risk of overcategorizing, most professional education begins with general knowledge, moves on to an overview of the profession's underpinnings, and concludes with specialized activity.

As a general pattern, design training runs in the opposite direction. Although usually preceded by a "core" class, common to many of the arts, undergraduate training tends to be specialized design skills. It is only in the upper division, if at all, that undergraduates are introduced to history, theory, or a broader perspective on design. Early postgraduate work is often remedial skill enhancement, and it is only at the level of M.F.A. study that many design programs introduce what resembles the abstract overview provided a freshman in an introductory social science course.

IS DESIGN IMPORTANT?

Designers and design educators spend much time and energy talking about developing public awareness of design and how to gain recognition for design. Victor

Margolin points out that arguments over legal theory and even literary theory appear in popular magazines because people can see their importance to their lives, but design remains unnoticed.[18] Can studying design be of general, not just professional, interest? Can the study of design inform other areas of study? We assume that a design student would benefit from studying anthropology; we need to consider whether an anthropology student would benefit from the study of graphic design. Do we really have anything to offer outside of the sometimes questionable promise of a job?

Even a field as abstract, specialized, and self-referential as cosmology recognizes that its activity, in addition to its intrinsic value, ultimately matters because of its relation to general knowledge. In *A Brief History of Time*, Stephen Hawking writes:

> What would it mean if we actually did discover the ultimate theory of the universe? . . . In Newton's time it was possible for an educated person to have a grasp of the whole of human knowledge, at least in outline. But since then, the pace of the development of science has made this impossible. . . . Seventy years ago, if Eddington is to be believed, only two people understood the general theory of relativity.[19]

Hawking noted that relativity is now widely understood, at least in outline, and an ultimate theory of the universe could be absorbed by nonphysicists. The real importance of the goal of cosmology for the world's best-known cosmologist seems to be that philosophers could understand science as they did in the eighteenth century. Hawking bemoans the fact that science has become so technical and mathematical that only specialists can understand, and the scope of philosophy has been reduced from the great tradition of Aristotle and Kant to Wittgenstein's statement that "The sole remaining task for philosophy is the analysis of language."[20] If a unified theory of the universe could be understood by everyone, Hawking suggests:

> Then we shall all, philosophers, scientists, and just ordinary people, be able to take part in the discussion of the question of why it is that we and the universe exist. If we find the answer to that, it would be the ultimate triumph of human reason—for then we would know the mind of God.[21]

The point is that, although each branch of study may be an end in itself, the progress of each field is doubly validated as it contributes to general knowledge. The revolutions in physics that Hawking seeks to surpass would not have come about without previous breakthroughs in mathematics. The revolution in literary criticism of the 1970s and 1980s would not have come about were it not for previous breakthroughs in linguistic theory.

In light of those linguistic and literary revolutions, I should point out that I don't share Dr. Hawking's disdain for Wittgenstein's goal of language analysis, although I do agree that a single task for any field might represent a too-narrow viewpoint. If the word "language" is used in the broadest sense, then language analysis is at the core of much of the humanities and social sciences. Design, and graphic design in particular, is in the position to be at the center of this study.[22]

Design's past failure to have carved a proper academic niche for itself may, in the end, be one of its saving graces. Design as a professional practice has often bridged fields as diverse as engineering, marketing, education, and psychology. Design as an academic study can do no less.

NOTES

1. For a discussion of the development of modern design education, see Victor Margolin, "Design Studies and the Graphic Designer," *Proceedings of the Graphic Design Education Association 1990 Symposium,* 58–62.

2. Margolin, 60.

3. For an expanded discussion, see Richard Buchanan, "Design as a New Liberal Art," *Papers: The 1990 Conference on Design Education,* Industrial Designers Society of America, 15–16.

4. Aristotle, "Politics," in *Aristotle on Education,* trans. John Burnet (London: Cambridge University Press, 1903), 107–9.

5. Cardinal John Henry Newman, *The Idea of a University* (Garden City, N.Y.: Doubleday and Co., Image Books, 1959), 9.

6. Newman, 149.

7. Paul Hirst, "Liberal Education," in *The Encyclopedia of Education,* vol. 5, ed. Lee C. Deighton (New York: Macmillan Company & Free Press, 1971), 505–9.

8. Louis Menand, "What Are Universities For?" *Harper's* 283: 1699 (December 1991).

9. Clark Kerr, *The Uses of the University* (New York: Harper & Row, 1966), 39–40.

10. Kerr, 41.

11. Paul Rand, *Design, Form, and Chaos* (New Haven and London: Yale University Press, 1993), 217.

12. Sharon Poggenpohl, "A Contrarian Approach to Graphic Design Education," *GDEA Proceedings 1990,* Graphic Design Education Association.

13. Buchanan, 15–16.

14. Richard Buchanan, "Declaration by Design: Rhetoric, Argument, and Demonstration in Design Practice," *Design Discourse, History, Theory, Criticism,* ed. Victor Margolin (Chicago: University of Chicago Press, 1989), 91–109.

15. Buchanan, 1989, 93.

16. Mark Salmon and Glenn Gritzer, "Parallel Content: Social Sciences and the Design Curriculum," *Design Issues* (fall 1992).

17. Charles Bailey, *Beyond the Present and Particular: A Theory of Liberal Education,* (London: Routledge & Kegan Paul, 1984), 114.

18. Margolin, 73.

19. It is said that, shortly after Einstein published his theory, Sir Arthur Stanley Eddington was

asked if it were true that only three people really understood relativity and that he was one of them, he replied that he couldn't think who the third person might be. See Stephen Hawking, *A Brief History of Time* (New York: Bantam Books, 1988), 167–68.

20. Hawking, 174–75.

21. Hawking, 175.

22. The choice for design is not as simple as "do we want to become the center of the new academy or do we want to continue as we have?" Universities of all sizes are cutting budgets. Support staff reductions and across-the-board cuts can only go so far before the pain of cutbacks will be greater than the pain of making basic decisions. Universities looking at departments to eliminate will naturally choose the "lesser" professional programs. Design and nursing have been the first targets at more than one school.

How High Do We Set the Bar for Design Education?

Meredith Davis

Until recently, there were fairly clear expectations of design education programs. Designers were secure in the scope of their business; the body of knowledge necessary to practice graphic design was known. College and university graphic design programs expected to be judged on their ability to prepare graduates who could quickly enter the practice as inventive form makers and billable employees. Always subject to the successes or failures of the economy, designers took comfort in knowing their primary competition resided among other designers and that young professionals would work their way up through the ranks as had their predecessors. While all of us could point to "stars" who did not attend college, no one believed self-education to be a workable national strategy for educating young designers. During the last decade or two, however, these conditions have changed.

BACKGROUND

Several years ago, it was estimated by a well-known design employment agency in New York City that there were roughly 350,000 practicing graphic designers in the United States. This estimate is probably low and does not account for the cottage industry in graphic design made possible by easy access to computer hardware and design software. Because there is no licensing or certification in graphic design (as there is in architecture), these 350,000 practitioners may or may not hold degrees in design. It is very unlikely that many of them hold graduate degrees in their discipline. Anyone can call him- or herself a graphic designer, regardless of academic preparation for professional practice. In fact, the U.S. Department of Labor, in its *Index of Occupational Titles*, classifies graphic design as a "trade" that does not require college study.

On the other hand, graphic design has been firmly established as a discipline on college campuses since the 1950s and accounts for increasingly high proportions of student enrollment in art schools and universities. In the best graphic design departments in the country, selective admissions practices turn away as many as ten students for each freshman admitted to degree programs. The introduction of computers and design software in high schools and the workplace, as well as high visibility for new media, are likely to produce burgeoning interest in college and university graphic design programs well beyond the next decade and well in excess of growth in the field.

It used to be that colleges served the profession by educating intuitive problem solvers in the principles of visual composition, technical understanding of typesetting and printing, and presentation skills. The dilemma for contemporary graphic design educators is the expanding and shifting definitions of the profession for which it prepares young designers. Rapidly changing technological, economic, and social forces demand different design responses than those society expected decades ago. Entirely new areas of practice emerged in the past five years, some of them not well served by the traditional art-based education of most designers. At the same time, many employers lament the poor quality of students' general education and problem solving in other academic areas (such as writing, history, computer science, and the social sciences), which suffer as schools sacrifice one set of skills and knowledge in favor of another. What should constitute the content of a first professional degree in design is now very much the subject of debate.

If one were to believe college catalogs, however, the mission of the nearly two thousand undergraduate design programs around the country[1] are roughly the same: to produce a fully prepared, entry-level design professional. Whether a two- or four-year program, art school or university, schools claim to provide a comprehensive design education matched to almost any area of graphic design practice. Most two-year programs have abandoned their original technical/vocational missions and purport to substitute for two to four years of education in a bachelor's degree program. Despite the fact that the number and background of faculty, curricular offerings, facilities, and resources greatly influence the quality of educational experiences in these two thousand two- and four-year programs, college catalogs present convincing arguments that there are no professional limits on what their graduates know and can do in design. Only the most design-savvy prospective student, parent, guidance counselor, or employer can cut through the rhetoric of admissions offices to assess the appropriateness of one program over another.

At the graduate level, where the number of programs is growing, the same confusion about mission occurs. Students enroll in these programs to compensate for poor undergraduate preparation, to specialize or refine skills, to change careers after baccalaure-ate study in another discipline, to upgrade methods and knowledge that did not exist during their time in undergraduate school, to focus on theory and research, and/or to qualify for university teaching careers. The pedagogy in these programs varies from independent study in which students meet only periodically with individual faculty, to piggybacked undergraduate and graduate registration in the same courses, to fully devel-oped graduate-level curricula that speculate on the future of practice and attempt to build a research culture in the field. There is one Ph.D. program in visual communications in the United States (at the Institute of Design) and several in development at other universities. Clearly, schools are struggling to determine the appropriate models for graduate education and to address the growing need for research and advanced study in the field.

In most professional fields, accreditation standards address the difficult problems of defining appropriate minimum criteria for the evaluation of educational programs and providing some level of evaluation understood by the public. The National Association of Schools of Art and Design (NASAD)[2] is the government-authorized body for the accreditation of graphic design programs in U.S. colleges and universities. NASAD's overly general, fine arts–based criteria have handicapped efforts to improve the overall quality of design programs through rigorous assessment of success. Many of the best programs in the country forego NASAD accreditation in the belief that its standards bear little resemblance to the professional practice of graphic design and out of frustration that accreditation teams rarely even include designers. The American Institute of Graphic Arts (AIGA) recently worked with NASAD to revise guidelines and criteria for the accreditation of graphic design programs in hope that more comprehensive definitions of standards and review processes for professional design curricula will improve the overall quality of academic offerings.

FINDING THE "BIG IDEA"

When I attend meetings of designers, I hear the same complaints. "My client now has his secretary designing the newsletter." "I can't outbid those twentysomethings with Macs in their apartments." "My client wants a website but can't tell me why." The phrases are not-so-subtle indications of shifts in the profession and the expectations of clients. Computers and design software provide public access to the means of design and production, at whatever levels people deem satisfactory. And while designers lament significant losses of quality in many instances, the bottom line is that some clients can't see the difference, don't care, or are not willing to pay for it. It makes little sense, therefore, to continue to educate tens of thousands of students each year solely in the design and production of beautiful form. This is not to say that the need for inventive form will go away or that educational institutions should completely abandon this as an objective of their programs. But it does signal that the survival of the profession may depend less on its traditional education in art-based concepts and more on responding strategically to changes in the business, social, and communication environments. While many schools claim their graduates can handle the analysis and solution of large-scale or complex communication problems, rarely are their college experiences grounded in study that supports designer development of successful strategy at the levels demanded by today's design problems.

Design methodologist J. Christopher Jones describes a hierarchy of design problems. At the lowest levels are components and products. These represent the types of design problems that exist in simple societies like those in the early history of this country. At the upper levels of Jones's hierarchy are system-level problems (demanding related products or activities) and community-level problems (involving related systems). Design problems at these higher levels are characteristic of complex postindustrial societies like the one in which we live.

While our design problems usually exist at the system and community levels, our design responses are not always congruent. The automobile, for example, was designed as a "product" for getting us from one place to another whenever we want to go. Because it was not conceived as a product nested within several related systems, it also created traffic jams, neighborhoods divided by interstates, and unprecedented levels of air pollution. Unfortunately, much of our graphic design activity (and design education) also approaches design problems at the product and component levels. We frequently define our task as simply designing a brochure or Web page. Even corporate identity, the classic "systems" problem in graphic design, is reduced to a product by most graphic designers, beginning with the components of logos and typefaces and expanding as a graphic standards manual. Rarely are these identities envisioned as part of a communication system that includes how salespeople work with customers, branding of products sold by the company, where design activity is located within the corporate hierarchy, and technology used for communicating among employees.

The teaching strategies in most design schools discourage systems-level thinking by asking students to design products (a book, brochure, multimedia presentation, etc.), usually outside the context of the systems to which they belong and even, in some instances, outside the context of use. Project briefs are written by faculty, not students, and the criteria for success (legibility, good composition, original idea, etc.) are usually known before the student begins work. The outcome is usually critiqued by faculty and students or other designers (rarely by clients or audiences), using the language of the fine arts or the technology with which the design was produced. Students rarely ask whether the problem is worth solving, move beyond simple demographics in defining audience, or explore how the product fits into the larger context of the client's organization—let alone the audience's culture and everyday lives.

Innovative curricula, like the one at the Institute of Design, are beginning to tackle these issues. Coursework focuses on design planning and the development of large- and small-scale strategies that address complex communication and business problems. These are not classes about running design offices, like those one might find in the business components of many design curricula. Instead, this instruction prepares students to function at the highest levels of corporate decision making and in the solution of complex problems in the workplace and education. Practical methods for defining and assessing design problems and the audiences they serve are at the core of these curricula. New technology is not seen as a means for replicating traditional design processes (such as pasteup and photo retouching), but as a means for addressing audience needs and business processes.

WHO'S OUT THERE?

It is difficult to practice design today without confronting marketing data as the mantra for successful communication solutions. Focus groups, usually defined in broad demographic terms, dominate our lives, expressing their preferences in response to questions most designers find confining. If you are not convinced that the age of the mass audience is dead, visit your local newsstand to see magazines targeted so narrowly that teenage boys who surf in southern California now have several reading choices. Ironically, at a time when technology makes it possible to reach unprecedented numbers of people with massive amounts of information at exactly the same time, we recognize the need to tailor communication for increasingly specific definitions of audience.

If, as designers, we're not thrilled with the work of marketing specialists who poll audience opinion in terms of what already exists, what can we offer as an alternative? Where is the compelling research that supports our intuition that there are better ways to describe how people are different than by their past buying habits?

There is no deficit of theory or research about how audiences perceive and process information. Yet, these are rarely the content of a designer's education. Folklore and intuition dominate most designers' rationales and are poor ammunition in the face of marketing's numbers. Fields such as linguistics, cognitive psychology, anthropology, sociology, and other social science disciplines hold enormous insight for the work of graphic designers, yet most college graphic design curricula indirectly discourage enrollment in such classes by the few credits they make available for nondesign study. Furthermore, design schools do little to integrate social science issues into project briefs when students do engage in appropriate coursework. And issues of audience generally take second place to issues of aesthetics in most design critiques. It is little wonder that employers find young designers self-absorbed with making personal statements in client-based work and incapable of presenting convincing arguments for their design solutions to nondesigners.

At the same time, existing theories about how audiences interpret visual and verbal messages have rarely been evaluated within the context of design in ways that derive transferable principles. There is a need for considerable research to develop practical strategies for reaching conclusions about the design of information. In a handful of graduate programs, students and faculty work to move theory into practice. North Carolina State University, for example, divides its two-year master's curriculum into three critical content frameworks built around the issues of audience: cognition, culture, and new information environments. The first framework applies research from cognitive science, linguistics, and learning theory to practical communications solutions that address differences in audiences' cognitive styles. It examines how recurring schemas and stereotypes exert powerful influences on social cognition. The second framework looks at how culture shapes and is reflected in communication artifacts, drawing heavily from social theory, anthropology, criticism, and art and design history. The third framework explores the implications of study in cognition and culture for the design of human interaction with new technology and the building of communication communities. North Carolina State University will allow its students to extend such research through a Ph.D. program in design that makes parallel coursework available in a variety of nondesign disciplines.

While the students who graduate from these advanced programs function well in contemporary design practice, the objective of their studies is speculative and focused on the future, not on staffing mainstream offices or redressing past deficiencies in the student's design education. The model for these programs is not the atelier or graduate study in painting or sculpture, it is the complex interdisciplinary environment in which design is likely to be practiced in the future and in which designers will play a formative role.

Clearly, the criteria against which the effectiveness of design education should be measured have changed. The diversity of these criteria signals the need for radically different programs from which students and employers may choose. It may no longer be possible to provide a "general" education in design and expect graduates of these programs to excel in practice. New standards of excellence encourage new methods of instruction and curricular innovation that are responsive to shifting definitions of professional practice. In other cases, schools push the profession to seize emerging areas of practice that are likely to dominate the future and that could be lost to less-creative problem solvers. Finally, schools recognize the need to study the discipline of graphic design as well as the practice, to add to the body of knowledge for which there may be no current practical use. As the profession prepares for practice in the next millennium, it must partner with schools and set high standards for both the field and education.

NOTES

1. There are only 110 architecture programs in the United States and 47 in industrial design. The ratio of students to professionals in graphic design far exceeds that of other design disciplines.
2. The word "Design" was added in the 1970s when graphic design enrollments began to skyrocket.

Future Te\<a\>ch

Moira Cullen

Any attempt to map design education, much less divine its future, is as elusive as answering that eternal question: What is design? There is no one elemental reply.

But scanning the horizon for landmarks, one trend tracks clear—a meteoric rise in the number of design programs and students, beginning around the time the word "Macintosh" flashed across millions of television screens on Super Bowl Sunday in 1984.

> A new technology does not add or subtract something. It changes everything.
> —Neil Postman, *Technopoly,* 1992

The twentieth century draws to a close, accelerating a communications evolution that began when centuries of spoken patterns were rerouted by Gutenberg and his revolutionary machine of mass production. Print became the standard and books the new medium. Momentum surged with the quick capture of images, a decidedly faster read, as first photographs and then television raced over language, ethnic, and cultural barriers to reach even wider audiences.

Today, a dizzying array of electronic media hypersensed by sound, motion, and interactivity promises to revolutionize the way we shop, read, meet, and learn. We have come to understand that computers are more than tools, they are media; location is more than physical space, it can be virtual; and literacy can be measured not only in text, but by image. More and more, it appears, we are what we see.

> Mastery of the image may be the instrument and symbol of leadership in the new world order.
>
> —Daniel Singer, *The Nation,* 1994

As in the past, those who command the new media will hold the power to signify its use and meaning. Today's technologies further collapse hierarchy, exposing issues of influence and control that turn more on content than on distribution. We have conceded that the computer has democratized the design process, rendering the roles of author, designer, and producer accessible and often interchangeable. We have yet to comprehend the full significance of broad-based interactivity, as communications shift from mass market to one-to-one. For as products and systems are strategically branded to drive user response, design becomes more concerned with persuasion than with decoration; less about style than about emotion; more about clarity, understanding, and context.

> Design plays a central, not merely ornamental, part in the creation of meaning.
> —Derrick de Kerchhove, McLuhan Program in Culture and Technology

Ironically, technology has affected far more than the process of design. Indeed, the advent of digital media may have activated design's inherent purpose by hot-wiring design's integrating principles broadly and deeply into the backbone of cultural expression. For in a new economy that is knowledge- rather than product-based, symbolic thinking—the designer's ability to give visual form to ideas and draw clarity from chaos—is highly prized by a society awash in infinite choice and perpetual change.

Is this the future? If so, it points to an expanded role for design. But the promise rightly raises doubt: Will designers be prepared to meet the brave, bewildering communications challenges of an increasingly complex world?

> Design education must undergo a radical awakening. Educators need to realize they are educating students who will be spending fifty years of their professional lives in the new millennium.
> —Meredith Davis, North Carolina State University

Typically, speculation on design, education, and the future leads with technology questions: New media? What are the new applications? How and by whom are they taught? Software, hardware? What is needed? And what can schools afford?

> In today's environment there are so many kinds of active delivery systems, we seem to be headed towards a kind of media-independent education—the 'versioning' of ideas. How do you want to save this image?
> —Chris Pullman, WGBH Boston

Often overlooked are pivotal social concerns. What are the cultural and cognitive implications of technology? The impact of demographic repatterning? What of the quality of life in an environment linked globally by communications yet cleaved by special interests—national, economic, individual, even operational?

> It is left for designers to champion meaning over function; people above technology.
> —Gillian Crampton Smith, Royal College of Art

Not surprisingly, design may emerge as the quintessential twenty-first-century profession, a vital form-giving, wayfinding, meaning-making synthesis of art, technology, and social science. Expansion of the profession's size and of the possibilities for practice comes in the midst of confusion as educators scramble to revamp curricula, define new degrees, establish new programs, and defend the existence of others.

The situation is further complicated by calls for accreditation and curricular standards, clarification of graduate and undergraduate goals, and demands for increased professional involvement in education and greater academic contact with the profession.

> Experience in the workplace, and a thorough knowledge of the history of one's specialization is indispensable. . . . But such experience . . . is rare among students as well as among faculty.
>
> —Paul Rand, *From Cassandre to Chaos*, 1992

Should schools turn out generalists or groom specialists? Can they honor diversity of experience and culture and integrate foreign students speaking multiple languages, whose populations often exceed 30 percent of a department's total enrollment? What of concerns raised over discerning parameters between industry internships and programmatic sponsorship, heightened competition, increased tuition, faculty funding—the list goes on. And then there's the price of technology.

> Schools are fooling themselves if they think they can keep up with the technology investment. The big issue in the future will be accountability, the cost of education: Where is the money going?
>
> —Tom Wedell, SkolosWedell

The sheer number of students merely amplifies concerns, threatening to rock the sense of collegiality the profession has known. Who could have imagined that forty years after Yale University introduced the first postsecondary program in graphic design, there would be some 800–1,500 degree-granting, award-giving, one-, two-, three-, and four-year graduate and undergraduate colleges and universities, and private art and technical schools engaged in various forms of design education?

> As many as 350,000 individuals currently practicing think of themselves as graphic designers; schools graduate as many as 10,000 students each year.
>
> —RitaSue Siegel, RitaSue Siegel Resources

At these annual rates, there will be 70,000 new designers (compared to a total of 50,000 lawyers) practicing in the year 2000.

The notion of educational training for designers has come far since the turn of the last century, when the Bauhaus curriculum first united arts and crafts. The experimental community lasted just fourteen years, yet the ideology remains at the core of modernist and postmodernist design teaching. But as an educational model, the Bauhaus, along with Ulm and other dominant influences, was framed by the values of an explicit culture and formed in decidedly different times.

> Many educators complain that students aren't the same as they used to be: shorter attention spans, few risk-takers, more passive in their expectations. This group comes out of a fundamentally different culture. They have been totally conditioned by communications. Our models don't fit—they need to be rethought.
> —Meredith Davis, North Carolina State University

The nineteenth century cast a model of the designer as artist—a heroic craftsman, most likely Caucasian, European, and male, whose talent was measured in intuition and skill. The influence of this ideal persists, even though it excludes at least half the designers in practice today.

> The designer is the facilitator; if the designer is the hero, there is something completely wrong.
> —Dietmar Winkler, University of Massachusetts

Moreover, the complexity of new communications problems coupled with the diversity of contemporary culture requires a broader knowledge base and more sophisticated skill set than intuition alone. The profession needs to advance an understanding of design that integrates the digital dimension, values collaboration over isolation, and promotes conceptual and technical competence—defining an evolving, versatile professional who is by turns a strategic communicator, a visual thinker, and an informed, responsible citizen.

> Designers have an especially powerful combination of skills, but they become useful only if we have the methods to understand complex problems.
> —Patrick Whitney, Institute of Design, IIT

But is the goal learning or earning? Historically, divergent approaches to design education have always sparked controversy. Today's debates on theory versus practice, experimentation versus application, and education versus vocation are no exception. Is it a school's responsibility to train designers for short-term employment or to educate them for life?

> School is for the long term. You choose to learn because it nourishes you for your whole life, not just for your next job.
> —Sheila Levrant de Bretteville, Yale University

What, then, are the subjects, concepts, and skill sets required of a twenty-first-century graphic design education?

Just as the first wave of the computer revolution in graphic design subsided, the World Wide Web hit the shore with its shock-waved swells. Still, the undertow of new technology will continue to ebb and flow, as affections alternate between the intimacy of the hand and the intrigue of the machine. Students, educators, and professionals need to actively engage a more holistic sense of "design" as a strategic discipline, mindful of its meaning as both noun and verb, as a physical act of making and a cognitive process for creating.

> We need to teach that the important intimate relationship is not between the designer and the board/screen/image, but between the presentation of the information and the users of that information.
>
> —Patrick Whitney, Institute of Design, IIT

Experimentation and bold ideas are the lifeblood of liberal education. But along with providing core foundations and theory, can educators enrich design studies by crossing departmental divides to include subjects from other disciplines—humanities, history, business, psychology, semiotics, a second language, dance, music, physics, and film—and still keep pace with technology's relentless pace? Newer software, faster hardware, sound, motion, narrative sequence. So much more to know, teach, and learn—all in too little time.

> We must abandon the notion that undergraduate education can do it all.
>
> —Dietmar Winkler, University of Massachusetts

What about process?

> We have to educate a new kind of professional, one who has broad knowledge of a variety of things and knows how to put those things together—to parallel-process several things at the same time.
>
> —Red Burns, Tisch School of the Arts, NYU

And media?

> Multimedia? Graphic design has to decide: Are we going to get involved in this, or not? If schools ignore it, graphic design will be disconnected from it.
>
> —Mr. Keedy, CalArts

Culture?

The biggest challenge facing design and design education is internationalism—an understanding of different cultures and how to work with others.

—James Miho, Art Center College of Design

And values?

We must stop inadvertently training our students to ignore their convictions and be passive economic servants. What I have in mind is nurturing a crop of active citizens, informed, concerned participants in society who happen to be graphic designers.

—Katherine McCoy, Cranbrook Academy of Art

As design evolves as a profession, it mirrors the practice of medicine, itself a human-centered meld of art and science whose growth has been both challenged and advanced by technology. As a community, the medical arts include a broad range of professionals, from RNs to GPs, podiatrists to plastic surgeons, neurologists to analysts, from hands-on, healing house calls to high-tech surgeons operating in virtual reality. At the higher levels, the educational track is legendary for its rigor—a generalist knowledge base and an overview of practices upon which to build specialist skills. Still, Hippocrates encouraged learning outside the box, advising that "the physician who seeks wisdom is equal to a god."

Art is long, but time is fleeting.

—Hippocrates, *Aphorisms*

The millennium approaches, placing design at a crossroads in a time of transition. Doubtless, there will be a shakedown among the profusion of schools. And as the profession assumes a new order, individuals and institutions increasingly will be called to articulate their strengths and demonstrate value. Nevertheless, design educators and professionals alike must seize leadership of the moment, for if they do not, those who bypass the professional track but share the software and have access to the hardware will.

I think this is the best of all possible times to be a designer. Design is continually expanding. We can pick where we want to go. There are not as many formal rules.

—Graduate student

Design education occupies a central but by no means solitary place in the profession; no single location, no isolated ideology, no dominant pedagogy, but rather a network of learning in an extended web of varied and multiple contacts that decentralizes the process of learning and strengthens the social contract between schooling, the profession, and the community. Technology as provocateur becomes both metaphor and a means for interaction and collaboration. Learning to design gives way to the notion of designing to learn, as boundaries are crossed, partnerships formed, and resources shared.

Links, human and electronic, are made between design schools and other institutions, organizations, industries, and enterprises. Local resources and technology centers share in the burden of technical training in the latest software, freeing schools to concentrate on theoretical, conceptual, and cultural studies. Students reinforce their personal commitment to education by bringing their own computers—BYOC—bearing all or part of the cost with schools providing basic applications and output devices. Professional organizations assume more active and visible roles: initiating forums that challenge the education and professional communities, surveying programs and curricula to uncover new educational models, and encouraging experimentation that promotes open, vigorous debate—just as the media and the profession redouble efforts to cultivate and demonstrate broader understanding of design's strategic commercial, cultural, and aesthetic relevance.

> The future needs the whole man. I shall keep on considering the process of education more important than the finished product.
> —László Moholy-Nagy, *The New Bauhaus*

Meanwhile, the profession grows in stature, competence, and compassion as students of many ages and beliefs define themselves as designers—as generalists and specialists conversant in myriad media—moving widely, eagerly in the world.

That Was Then: Corrections and Amplifications

Lorraine Wild

Two hundred years ago, a woman had to be able to start with grain to make bread, and a man making a wagon had to start with a tree . . . too much of that has been lost. . . . Density and complexity of a vision come from a single person making a single thing. . . . In our time, people are infatuated with thinking . . . but this notion that the idea is adequate all by itself is just absolutely wrong . . . an idea has no meaning until it finds physical form. . . .

—Calvin Tomkins, "A Single Person Making a Single Thing"

About eighteen months ago, I gave a talk in Holland that was turned into an essay published last summer by *Emigre*. The essay is titled "That Was Then, and This Is Now: But What Is Next?"[1] That essay really attempted to do two things: first, to describe the conditions that we all face in the post-Macintosh, Macromind Director environment of graphic design today; second, to map the trajectory of design pedagogy and show that much of it is actually at odds with the massive shifts in design practice wrought by new technology.

THE STATE OF THE PROFESSION

A few months before I wrote "That Was Then," I attended the 1995 American Institute of Graphic Arts National Conference in Seattle, and many presentations that I saw there influenced my observations on the state of the design profession. The theme of the conference was "change," which was generally translated to be about the shifts in design practice brought on by digital technology. I summarized the main issues that many speakers in Seattle described as follows:

- the increase in media "options" beyond print makes all communication problems more complex
- given the media options, each designer has less command of all of them, and knows less about the medium and the audience
- those increased options for receiving information have splintered audiences into many, many more "micromarkets"

- this results in "micromarketing," yet, ironically, no one is quite sure who the audience is, especially on the Net
- at the same time, everyone is supposed to be thinking and acting globally

What results from this tension between micro- and macro-audiences and multiplying media formats is that the demand for more conceptual, research-driven solutions increases with the shift away from print; but, simultaneously, design practices are now saddled with print production duties, which, while billable, can become threatening if they aren't managed with great efficiency through constant technological investment in upgrades and retraining.

Not that this mess has necessarily been bad for graphic design business or education. In the past few years, we have seen a mushroomlike growth of firms servicing new media and new academic programs dedicated to graphic design and new media. Still, the climate we practice in is different. Unless you are a graphic designer, it is not at all clear that anything resembling the traditional role of the graphic designer is really necessary and/or needed in the new media. Lots of new, interesting, visual things created in new media turn out to have been produced without the participation of someone the profession itself would even call a graphic designer. This raises the question of how the visual side of new media is produced and what, if any, role the graphic designer plays in its production.

Authors versus Teams

Successful design consultancies have had to develop "divisions" within their own offices to handle the very different types of time and effort required by these more complicated scenarios. Large-scale design projects often require multidisciplinary teams because they span the broad range of media options just described. In either situation, it is much, much harder for designers to retain control over the projects and their clients the way they used to. And while graphic design education has sporadically paid attention to the need to train designers to work collaboratively, their training is typically based on designers maintaining their specific identity as the originators, "authors," or controllers of visual ideas. (Graphic designers have often looked toward architecture as a model, where authorial control is maintained by the architect even in the largest of collaborative projects. For a good example of this desire to emulate architects, see Massimo Vignelli's recent declaration that he no longer refers to himself as a graphic designer—because they are only concerned with the superficialities of style—but instead as an "information architect."[2])

But what is often experienced by designers who get new media commissions—for instance, website design—is in many cases a team-production model based less on maintaining the integrity of the "author" and more on the entertainment industry paradigm where authorship is granted to the director, the producers, maybe the screenwriters, but typically not the people who create the visual nature of the product. In the movies and TV, a final project is only as good as the director or producers will allow it to be. They, not the artisans, have the power to "green light" ideas. They are the "authors." Those who want to operate outside of these conventions ("independents") generally do so at their own expense.

The structure of finance in complex, high-production-value multimedia projects may be similar to that of movie production (i.e., it takes a lot of money to pay for the time to do all that programming and production), and that has led to the assumption that the team model of the film industry, which differentiates authors from artisans, may be the appropriate process paradigm. But the logic of the new media does not necessarily support a hierarchical division of creative roles. What is demonstrated by software programs like Director is a new situation where the conceptual phase (or authorship) of design development in new media is hardly separated from final design or production. The line that divides design from both editorial development in print and directing or screenwriting in film, and the final production of either media, is blurred in multimedia and up for grabs.

There are a lot of graphic designers who will admit (after a few stiff drinks, maybe) that this blurring of the role of the designer comes with mixed blessings, and that the techno-optimism of outlets such as *Wired* masks a crisis of identity for design. No one wants to get caught saying "this will kill that," but there is a real sense that the game has changed. This is complicated by the irony that the practice of design was, until recently, supposed to be an invisible force. In the post–World War II optimism of the fifties and sixties, graphic designers championed a hidden process that was supposed to deliver a visually potent product—communication enhanced by visuality—orchestrated by the designer/author. While new media may demand an author or a team, it is not clear that it needs or desires an invisible (or omnipotent) design hand.

By its most mainstream definition, graphic design does not initiate its problems or projects: it is assignment based. It provides a service, and, ideally, it is supposed to mediate seamlessly between the sender (i.e., the client) and the receiver (i.e., the audience). Now, no one in academia has bought this line for a while. The collusion and culpability of the designer have been fodder for much discussion in design theory for many years now, but this theoretical challenge has never quite translated to the larger world. One could argue that our culture has gotten hooked on a high level of visuality without even knowing, more or less, where it comes from. Relatively high (but constantly pressured) fees have assuaged the bruised egos of the legions of creative people who have both benefited by, and been resentful of, the invisible role that they have played in this major realm of our larger culture.

Some of graphic design's elders spotted the tendency of technology to devalue the work of the graphic designer earlier than the younger generation did—mostly because the younger generation of designers were too busy trying to master the new technologies, and, perhaps, were so enthralled with the illusion of control that they did not see the subtle changes that were taking place in the issues of authorship and authority. In his essay "The War Is Over," Milton Glaser observed that business had proclaimed the value of design precisely because it had figured out how to exercise control more thoroughly than ever, and that this constituted a triumph of bad values over the humanistic intentions of designers. He maintained that graphic designers had lost ground on many different aspects of practice, and that this could be blamed on digital technology: that it had actually made it easier to produce design and had therefore contributed to an overpopulation of designers (which put fees and value under pressure). He also noted that the computer had given clients greater control over designers' efforts: for instance, the client can possess and manipulate a digital document (which has eliminated the need for "the original") without consulting the "originator."

Glaser also cited what he referred to as the "punitive" tone of contracts that ask the designer to sell rights to their work for "all purposes throughout the universe, in perpetuity" (a clause that is, in part, a defensive reaction on the part of corporations to their own inability to predict media and formats), and the inequity of work-for-hire contracts that "presume that the client initiates and conceptualizes the work in question and that the designer merely acts as a supplier to execute it." Not surprisingly, he sees these statements and others like them as a sign that designers are losers. Of course, lots of younger designers have never known anything different, but he ends his powerful statement with the idea that designers literally have to start from scratch to create "a new narrative" for our work.[3]

Recommendations for the Future

Whether one agrees with Glaser's scenario or not, the new sociocultural environment of design challenges each person working within it. In this context, two very different responses to the challenge illuminate the state of graphic design discourse: the first demands that the designer become a marketer; the second, an anthropologist.

The first view says we should adjust all of our work to the demands of technology, business, and marketing. This view is expounded in some detail in the first three issues of *Critique,* a San Francisco–based graphic design magazine. *Critique* often champions the notion that designers are public communicators who should scrupulously avoid personal artistic expression. Its point of view accepts the inevitability of the leaner-and-meaner business arrangements described by Glaser and the old paradigm of the invisibility of the designer.

In a recent issue, editor Marty Neumeirer states:

> Increasingly, the haves and the have-nots of graphic design are separating along conceptual lines. The designer who demonstrates an ability to think independently and strategically will attract the patronage of serious clients. The designer who follows the line of least resistance, or who indulges in purely artistic pursuits, will find that . . . wealth and power are elusive indeed. . . . [quoting another designer] "Sometimes we . . . Quark and Quark and Quark . . . this all takes time, and there's a limit to what clients will pay for these production-oriented tasks. With conceptual work, you can get your idea in two minutes and charge for two days. And it will be worth every penny, because it will be stronger than a design based only on looks."[4]

In contrast to the literal marketplace of design concepts expounded by Neumeirer, the second "anthropological" viewpoint challenges the designer to be an interpreter rather than conceptualizer of context. At a more sophisticated level aimed primarily at design educators, Michael and Katherine McCoy, in "Design: Interpreter of the Millennium," maintain that an important job for designers of the near future is the interpretation of technology for the audience, and they advocate that education should prepare students for that specific role.

The McCoys do not choose to focus on the aesthetic and syntactic static created in the act of interpretation; rather, they emphasize a "cleaned-up" version of a reception theory–based model to describe communication transactions, particularly for multimedia. They state:

> Design for interpretation involves the audience in the creative process . . . graphic communication does not truly exist until each receiver decodes or interprets the message. Interpretive design challenges the viewer to participate and affect the outcome. . . . Designers will be . . . more involved in the design of experience . . . creating potential and open-ended situations for users to explore. Audiences will "finish" designs as they negotiate nonlinear and malleable situations. . . .

They go on to recommend the addition of research techniques that straddle the fields of anthropology and marketing—such as "video-ethnography"—to give the young designer insights into patterns of use.

The McCoys quite rightly note that the end of broadcasting as a modernist paradigm creates opportunities for more-focused graphic communication dedicated to narrow audience groups. As I noted at the beginning of this piece, this is no small shift and must be seen as a new condition of culture that demands a response on the part of design. The McCoys address this condition by asserting that "When the designer does not have to speak to the broadest common denominator of a mass audience, a richer conversation among peers emerges." Yet, since the invention of form is never mentioned in their description of design at the end of the millennium, it seems as if communication will be more about strategy and less about the visual.

Like Milton Glaser, the McCoys also refer to the Darwinian economics of digital technology:

> Sophisticated desktop publishing and multimedia software allow virtually anyone to do everyday design work; designers can no longer rely on their traditional skills alone. Designers must deliver conceptual innovations and new insights, the things that computers cannot do. This challenge will lift design beyond a service trade into the role of interpreter for culture.[5]

Will designers "from subcultures" design for their own subcultures, or is there something almost too prescriptive or paternalistic in that equation? Isn't what unites the designer with his or her audience something more subtle: the fact that the designers are users as well? As individuals, designers are related to the larger social context more intimately than the typical interpreter/interpreted relationship implies.

TEACHING DESIGN

The Conceptual Curricula

At CalArts, my colleagues and I, during recent years, have watched increasing numbers of our graduates get snapped up by multimedia firms. Given the context just described, this has made us increasingly nervous that the curriculum we've provided somehow hasn't prepared the students for the conditions they would find upon graduation. For the second part of the *Emigre* essay, I tried to describe how to make graphic design studies a more viable training for future designers. At that time, I wrote that design would have to be redefined as a conceptual practice, while graphic design would have to be more clearly identified as a specialty within it.

I suggested that in addition to teaching basic visual syntax, composition, typography, and the other skills usually associated with graphic design education, the following issues had to be added to the education of young designers to strengthen their conceptual skills:

- more attention on "learning how to learn"
- attention to writing to facilitate conceptual and expressive communication
- study of the operations of verbal expression, rhetoric, semantics, and narrative and storytelling as part of the basic structure of communication
- the grammar of film and film editing as part of the basic communication structure
- the structures and narratives in games
- critiques of communicative systems as artificial constructs
- an understanding of the social, cultural, and functional possibilities of real and simulated public and private spaces
- techniques of collaboration, teams, negotiation, and consensus building
- the history of design expanded to include the social and cultural development of media
- and, finally, a study of fantasy, surrealism, pranks, simulation, bricolage, and other forms of subversion as a stimulant to the possibility of a more entrepreneurial approach to design.

I presented this laundry list as the framework of a new and idealized design curriculum. Life is not ideal, and curriculum plans are just starting places, but it seemed important at that time to articulate the missing elements of design education, especially since what seemed to be lacking was related to the uses and theories of language. This bias against language in graphic design teaching is part of our DNA that we still carry from the invention of basic design courses at the Bauhaus. Teaching based on modernism looked for universal images to substitute or supersede verbal communication. In arguing for these new design "basics" in the *Emigre* article, I claimed that educators should acknowledge the weakness in graphic design's tendency to focus on the visual translation of a concept, in isolation, as a framework for understanding the potential communicative powers of new media. In "That Was Then," I did qualify that my assault on the visual did not deny the critical presence of the visual, but I then went on to say that the concentration on craft attached to visuality was, perhaps, what needed to be altered. Both as a designer and an educator, this conclusion—the basis of my article—is what I now think needs challenging itself.

Searching for Paradigms?

The current prescriptions for what education needs to cope with the new technologies (mine included) define the conceptual work of graphic design as being largely verbal—which falls in line with most of the language-based, rationalist, linear, scientific biases of the rest of both academic and business culture. The visual, to many design educators, is a remnant of the "old" graphic design—before we got postmodernism, structuralism, poststructuralism, politics, and became seemingly sophisticated about theory and criticism.

Disdain for the visual also falls in line with what has to now be seen as a persistent thread in modernist art education, post-Duchamp and post–Moholy-Nagy (who, of course, said that any designer's idea that could not be described over the telephone was not an idea at all).[6] This thread denies the power of visual craft. It diminishes what happens in the process of subjecting oneself to the rigors of learning a tradition, or working a medium over and over until one can invent with it, in favor of the freedom of operating in a purely conceptual mode without the alleged restrictions of tradition, which is seen to hinder the creativity of the artist/designer. It is a common attitude in contemporary art education that meaning is privileged over the technique used to convey meaning; or as they used to say at CalArts, "No technique before need."[7]

But another phenomena of recent years, despite the academies' seeming disdain for pure form, has been a huge interest in form-making that reflects the expanded capabilities of the digital technology. The renaissance in typography and typeface design of the last few years is the strongest example of this.[8]

The attention paid through award shows, annuals, and endless compilations of "cutting-edge" design on the surface appears to be an old, familiar celebration of novelty that mirrors the way the profession has always explained itself, even in the days when it was just plain old commercial art. But is it not ironic that all this is going on while so many designers are expressing their doubts that visual talent is even needed when it comes to new media (again, because of the question about authorship and who will really get to drive projects)?

But the questions are, What constitutes graphic design craft, and why should we care about this? Can graphic design now be defined only as a conceptual process? Can we ignore the form-making aspect of it, which is, in fact, the only way it is ever seen? And where are all these conceptualists of the future going to find the "commercial artists" of the future to translate their big ideas into beautiful or seductive or remotely interesting forms that anyone else will want to look at?

If you only judge design by its conceptual content, there is a tremendous amount of strong work from the history of design that is quite meaningless in terms of subject matter: posters by A. M. Cassandre for liquor and cosmetics, posters by one constructivist or another extolling the Bolsheviks' next five-year plan, etc., etc. Years ago, during what might be called the "heroic" phase of graphic design history, it was assumed by many writers that all the great artifacts of graphic design had actually been effective. As design writing, theory, and criticism have become more sophisticated, much more complex narratives have been attached to these objects, and not every story ends in success. Still, we look at these things because their forms have made a contribution to our culture, and we wish to understand what that means and how that works. We are compelled by the look of these things.

What is obvious is that, whether looking at design or the contemporary design scene, the work that affects the community of design, and the public perception of it, is visual. It does not matter if you are looking at the high or the low, professional or vernacular: if you are looking at all, it is because of the way it looks.

I know that it is somewhat politically incorrect to say what I just said, but I am beginning to think that the only way to salvage graphic design, and enable it to grow in the face of both of the juggernaut of technology and the demands of the market, is to allow for the real development of the individual voice in graphic design and to recognize that the individual voice manifests itself in the forms that it makes—independent of the needs of the project or the marketing analyses.

Of course, the phrase the "designer's voice" is not foreign to designers' and design educators' ears. It has been used to signal a variety of things. It could mean the simple acknowledgment of the role of the designer in communication, or it could mean the designer taking a more active role in generating content. It is probably true that the design community (or the design education community) had to go through the issue of the designer's voice first as a philosophy, because it was so at odds with the definition "design = problem solving" derived from modernism. But now, as they say, the rubber hits the road: philosophy must be put into practice.

Back to the Visual

If, in old or new media, design is still, in the end, a visual practice, then the quality of this visuality must be nurtured. And that is problematic given the simultaneous challenge to design from both the producers of the medium who demand that we be specialists and the software interface that insists we be generalists. Any look at the magazines or the annuals will show that we are going through a period of visual disunity. It has been a while since there was a dominant idea about correct process or form; if anything, the correct notion, in academia as elsewhere, is that form should be reflective of its context and time. So, without repeating history, given how different times and problems are, how do we nurture form in a way that doesn't close off the future for the young designer?

In many ways, the answer seems to be in a revitalized discussion of technique, but in this there are at least two cautions. The last time technique was stressed really strongly was in the context of Swiss-influenced processes and projects, which invariably ended up leading students to essentialistic stylistic conclusions frequently based upon abstraction. The resulting style was so co-opted over time that it eventually lost its communicative power. This raises the second caution regarding technique: that it is hard to conceive of it not resulting in style, and style has a life cycle that makes designers uncomfortable. It' starts out as originality; it's adapted widely; it becomes a cliché; it slips down-market; it becomes an embarrassment; it becomes a fetish; and then it's ready for revival (or so we are led to believe).

CRAFT

Rather than talk about technique, perhaps it is useful to talk about craft. A contemporary mistake (one that I am guilty of myself) is to define craft in terms of digital technology. It is true that the more deft one is with understanding and using the hardware and software, the more flexible one can be in devising solutions to problems and getting them to the production phase. Nevertheless, to define craft only in terms of the use of a given technological skill does not adequately address the way that knowledge is developed through the skill as opposed to just being overlaid as a concept over technique.

Another common mistake is to define graphic design craft as that which only has to do with the materials and processes of printing. For instance, in another essay in *Critique,* "The Genius Matrix," craft is defined as the choices a designer makes using paper and color and dimensions, which might be part of what we would call craft, but doesn't begin to include everything that constitutes craft.[9]

My personal interest in the idea of craft stems partially from my own experience as a student at the Cranbrook Academy of Art, where "the crafts," such as weaving, ceramics, and metalsmithing, were taught with great vigor. As a young designer, I was always slightly confused and more than intrigued by the apartheid that had set in between what was understood as design and what was understood as craft: we all made things for use, but an unarticulated real split somehow reflected the idea that some things were being "designed" for mass production and other objects were "crafted," or one-of-a-kind.

In my ongoing research to try to understand the whole issue of craft, I encountered *The Art of the Maker,* a book by British design-theorist Peter Dormer. He discusses craft in the context of two different types of knowledge (which I will try my best to paraphrase). The first is theoretical knowledge: the concepts behind things and the language we use to describe and understand those concepts. The second is tacit knowledge: knowledge gained through experience, or know-how.

The tacit knowledge required to make something work is not the same as a theoretical understanding of the principles behind it. Theory might help you understand how to make something better, but craft knowledge (sometimes also referred to as "local" knowledge) is necessary to know how to begin in the first place. For Dormer, these two types of knowledge are completely intertwined, because if we rely only on theory, we never get things made (as any graduate studio faculty can attest), but if we only rely on experience, it takes too long.[10]

Tacit or craft knowledge is hard to teach because a lot of it cannot even be described, but has to be experienced. Some of it can be described in a sort of step-by-step way, but teaching this way leads to ossification when the same steps are assumed to be adequate in any situation (as the example of the Swiss school of graphic design recalls). To continue to paraphrase Dormer, the more sophisticated a craft becomes, the less you can explain its actual process. Craft knowledge is acquired through doing or making, and as you master a craft, you think less about the conceptual basis of process, even as you address more complicated conceptual issues. Craft knowledge, though hard to get, achieves the status of a skill once it is taken for granted and not considered every time it has to be put into use. It is a knowledge of familiarity, and breeds confidence.[11]

Knowledge gained through familiarity also includes that which we know through the senses, connoisseurship: recognition not only based on attribution or classification, but also just knowing what is good (having an eye) based on experience. This allows problems to be recognized almost instinctually. If you've ever listened to *Car Talk* on NPR, you hear those two mechanics solve car problems over the phone, not based on overall ideologies of automotive function, but based on years of tinkering—taking things apart and putting them back together.

Craft knowledge stands up to scrutiny (measured by the question, Does it work?) but on the flip side, craft knowledge is very personal because it has been gained through intimate experience.

A critical part of the private aspect of craft knowledge is the dialogue that goes on between the practitioner, his or her expertise, and the goal that the practitioner is trying to make or find. This, again, may constitute what is meant in graphic design when we speak of the "designer's voice" as that part of a design which is not industriously addressing the ulterior motives of a project, but instead follows the inner agenda of the designer's style. This would be what guides the "body of work" of a designer over and beyond the particular goal of each project. In this way, craft is tactical rather than conceptual, seeking opportunities in the gaps of what is known, rather than trying to organize everything in the matrix of a universal framework.

Dormer expands his idea of craft knowledge beyond the fields that we conventionally call the crafts. In *The Art of the Maker*, he states, "in a general sense, tacit knowledge is an aspect of all thinking, including conceptual thinking in such disciplines as mathematics, theoretical physics, or philosophy. There is a craft to such thinking and one learns it, becomes expert and applies it to solve problems. . . . But I want to claim for practical work a special sense of tacit knowledge, which is that the core . . . is unrecoverable by words. The thinking in the crafts of (the visual arts and crafts) resides not in language, but in the physical processes involving the physical handling of the medium."[12]

Dormer goes on to describe how the craft process creates knowledge. The activity of craft is seen, in great detail, to be essential to human activity and transcends the narrow confines of functionality that is often attributed to what might be described demeaningly as vocational skill. An active world of making and creativity opens up for the practitioner who defines craft in this manner. Again, from Dormer:

> The purpose of skills is to put them to use; unless one's aim is limited to repeating the designs of other people, then one of the skills one needs is the ability to experiment. Experimenting, which is often described as playing around, itself demands judgment—it involves improving one's sense of discrimination. It may well be that one produces designs that are only "good for me" (and no one else) but it still matters that one has an understanding of why it is good. . . .[13]

Interestingly, utilizing this richer definition of craft, which equates making with meaning, it becomes possible to better account for the individual visions of many figures of graphic design history who are "marginal," i.e., not producers of huge bodies of client-based work and for that reason not necessarily well compensated or, in some cases, not even well recognized because the work is seen as too personal or eccentric. But they created bodies of work that resonate, look better and better over time, and, at the least, make more sense. A consideration of craft allows understanding of the development and value of the individual designer's voice within the well worn and too facilely understood construct of visual communication, both high and low. Rather than applying a universal standard for material production to become the measure of quality or importance in graphic design, we can begin to see a wider range of possibilities for cultural production. All the elements of the design process—the client, the problem, the context, are in constant flux, but the designer's voice remains constant, a signature, an ethos built out of conceptual and personal and practical accretion of experience.

I look at my own list of guilty pleasures, designers whose work I love above all else because of its integrity to itself:

W. A. Dwiggins, who, working out of his garage in Boston during the depression, reinvented American typography by bringing arts and crafts values to design for machine production, all while running his completely handcrafted puppet theater.

Alvin Lustig, trained as an architect, worked as a printer and then a designer, who insisted on the personal mark as the talisman of modernism, refusing to specialize by designing interiors, signage, and the first cheap paperback publications of high-modernist literature. (He is the author of one of my favorite definitions of design: "I propose solutions that nobody wants, to problems that don't exist."[14])

Imre Reiner, an eccentric antimodernist typographer in Switzerland, who after World War II, when "objectivity" was the goal of graphic design, rebelled by promoting an even more subtle subjectivity by lending the inflection of the scrawl and the hand to the public language of classical typography.

Sister Corita Kent, southern California nun and printmaker who, in the 1960s, seized upon the idea of using the language of pop culture to speak to her local audience about spirituality, which she did by cutting and mixing historic and contemporary advertising headlines, copy, and logos, and writing poetry (her own and others) over and under them. She subverted and appropriated the public discourse before those words were even in our critical vocabularies.

Big Daddy Roth. Why? I really can't explain, except that I think it has something to do with consistency of vision inventing a new language.

And finally, that other big daddy, Edward Fella, artist of design here in Los Angeles, who mutated himself from a "commercial artist" to a designer of the highest caliber by working on problems only as he defines them and sets them up. His explorations of antimastery (exemplified by his dictum, "Keep the irregularities inconsistent"[15]) liberate design from the surface of perfection associated with digital competence, simultaneously getting down and dirty with the vernacular while attaching it to the free play of language and form associated with art and poetry of the highest order.

Each of these designers invents (or invented) in ways that transcend the frameworks of conceptualization and theory that mark present design, particularly current academic design, discourse. Their work suggests an alternate path of craft and making as knowledge production, which I feel now needs to assume a critical place in design education and design production. With regard to my essay of eighteen months ago, while I would not back away from the prescriptions that embrace the rigors of conceptualism, generalist and specialized, I would now add to it the central role of craft knowledge and the use of the tacit and tactical in everyday design processes.

I am highly self-conscious of the weirdness, in 1997, of arguing for a reenergized and reinvented teaching of basic color theory or basic typography—including scribes, classicists, modernists, and on to the digital—as well as drawing and composition. But as Edward Fella has said, "Rules are meant to be broken, only exceptionally,"[16] and the wonderful ambiguity of that sentence points to the ultimate goal of craft: not to produce uniformity, but to produce the exceptions.

The discussion of graphic designers working in an open way through their craft, from the edge toward the center, tacitly, parallels the interest in some architecture circles with the "everyday." These architects reject strategic overviews in favor of more localized tactics that grow out of an appreciation and immersion in the forms, forces, and functions of the street and the city. In their readings of critics such as Michel de Certeau, understanding how mundane and ordinary tasks of everyday life are practiced leads to ways of observation and working that connect architect's, designer's, or artists' experimentation and expression with daily reality. This daily reality is seen to be below and beyond the market, tied but resistant to the technological format within which we exist. De Certeau describes this condition as follows:

> Beneath the fabricating and universal writing of technology, opaque and stubborn places remain. The revolutions . . . lie in layers within it, and remain there

hidden in customs . . . and spatial practices . . . the place on its surface seems to be a collage . . . in reality, it is ubiquitous. A piling up of heterogeneous places.[17]

In *The Practice of Everyday Life* (note: not the "Theory" of everyday life), de Certeau also describes the idea of "casual time" as the gap where creativity occurs in contrast to "the empire of the . . . functionalist technocracy."[18] This gap in time suggests a space where individuals improvise and make do with what exists and create their own reality. Like craft, this creation is tactical and not strategic. Like design practice, casual time works with what is at hand and makes do within the constraints of the moment.

Contrasting the theory of language with the practice of speaking, de Certeau describes "everyday creativity" as the difference between knowing a language ("competence") and being able to use it expressively ("performance").[19] Echoing this definition, Fella, Lustig, Sister Corita, and even Big Daddy Roth perform within the constraints of their craft to create public communication with an intensely personal voice.

Combining these brief notes from de Certeau and Dormer allows one to develop a simplified series of complements that describe the basis for a pedagogy based on craft knowledge and conceptualism. The dualities are as follows:

tacit and tactical	and	the strategic
craft process	and	formalism
doing and making	and	theory and interpretation

In essence, I am advocating that a practice of craft can supplement design theory and reposition the activity of design as central to knowledge produced by design. For me, this is what is missing from all the descriptions of the future of design as a purely conceptual activity.

For the past five years, I have found myself increasingly frustrated with the conceptualization of design into a theoretical and interpretive knowledge system, which has relativized and devalued the types of knowledge and pleasure gained by engaging with passion in the craft itself. I have come to realize that the knowledge gained through activities, that can be described as tacit, tactical, everyday, or, simply, craft, are equally powerful and important. I believe that these activities must form the foundation of a designer's education and work. Without this second type of knowledge and commitment to work within the framework of craft activity as knowledge, design withers. Craft is a window into what designers do and a difference that marks our activity as valuable both in the making and production of ideas. By emphasizing and strengthening the understanding of how the difference of craft contributes to the message of the medium—of new media or any other media, past or present—the contribution of craft knowledge as design knowledge will define a more complex and interesting path for graphic design.

NOTES

1. "Graphic Design and the Next Big Thing" in *Emigre,* no. 39: 18–33.

2. Andrew Blauvelt, "The Info Perplex," *Emigre,* no. 40: 6

3. Milton Glaser, "The War Is Over," *AIGA Journal of Graphic Design* 13, no. 2 (1995): 48–50.

4. Marty Neumeirer, "Secrets of Rebellion," *Critique* (autumn 1996): 36.

5. Katherine McCoy and Michael McCoy, "Design: Interpreter of the Millennium," *U&lc* 22, no. 4 (spring 1996): 4–5.

6. Sibyl Moholy-Nagy, *Experiment in Totality* (Cambridge: MIT Press, 1969), 92. Taken from "Pens and Needles: Robert Brownjohn, Conceptual Design" by Katy Homans (thesis, Yale University, 1982).

7. "No technique before need" is an abstraction of an explanation of conceptually based art education. For a program description that reflects this idea, see Catherine Lord, "School of Art—Dean's Statement," *California Institute of the Arts Bulletin* (1989–90/1990–91): 15–16.

8. For examples, see Rick Poynor, *Typography Now: The Next Wave* (London: Booth-Clibborn Editions, 1991) or Rick Poynor, *The Graphic Edge* (London: Booth-Clibborn Editions, 1993) or any number of AIGA or ACD 100 annuals since 1990.

9. Nancy Bernard, "The Genius Matrix," *Critique* (winter 1997): 39–48.

10. Peter Dormer, *The Art of the Maker: Skill and its Meaning in Art, Craft and Design* (London: Thames & Hudson, 1994), 11–13.

11. Dormer, 21.

12. Dormer, 23–24.

13. Dormer, 50.

14. R. Roger Reminton and Barbara J. Hodik, "Alvin Lustig Remembered," *Communication Arts* (May/June 1983): 94.

15. Edward Fella, unpublished comment, 1997.

16. Edward Fella, unpublished comment, 1997.

17. Michel de Certeau, *The Practice of Everyday Life.*

18. de Certeau.

19. de Certeau.

The Big Squeeze

Lorraine Justice

In the mid-eighties, design educators said, "The computer is just another tool." We have come a long way from those initial ideas about design education and technology, and are now at the point where technology is so enmeshed within the core design curriculum that there is no turning back. Technology is currently used in every phase of the design process in most every design class and has left no design project untouched. Technology has allowed designers to do more and be more, resulting in expanded job opportunities and tasks, which are reflected in current design curriculums.

So, what is happening to the traditional design curriculum in light of the infusion of computers and other technologies? It is being squeezed. The traditional content of the curriculum is being added to by the new technologies that students learn during their design education. Students typically learn about computing hardware, software, and other technologies such as the CD-ROM and the Internet, in addition to specialized technologies in the printing and manufacturing industries. Teaching technology in design programs has an immediate impact on the student and potential employer: when the student is technologically literate, the employer doesn't have to train them.

What has this done to the design studios and design curriculum as a whole? They are being squeezed. At one point, the design educators said, "We will incorporate the learning of computing skills into the studio courses." Print projects are now set, laid out, and separated on the computer before going to press—which is also computerized. We can easily make changes to our design work and provide visual effects that were not possible a decade ago. As the technological options for print media change, so does the content of design classes in order to respond to industry needs without losing sight of the traditional design curriculum.

What is happening to the rapidly growing area of interactive media design now taught in most design departments? It is being squeezed. The design faculty said, "We will add this new area into our curriculum because designers are needed for these products." Interactive design has moved the computer, formerly a tool, to the level of medium. This distinction has initiated the creation of new design content, which has been added to the traditional curriculum. The area of interactive design has grown beyond the boundaries of the design department. Students are finding they need courses in computer-human interface design, video, sound, filmmaking, and more to adequately understand the possibilities of interactive media. The number and kinds of electives that students were once able to take are now more tightly focused on the area of interactive media.

What has happened to the choices of electives and alternative studies for design students in universities? They are being squeezed. The design faculty said, "The students could use courses in human factors and film studies." Learning how to use the new technologies, the latest software and hardware, is so time intensive, for both faculty and student, that it requires a continual relationship with "third-party help books," and an experienced network of users and software helpline technicians. This increased time usage can hardly be compared with that involved in past practices, such as learning to ink the perfect circle or using the latest marker-rendering techniques. Those words have an old and hollow ring to those who are mired in the latest software-imaging packages. Keeping pennies taped under plastic triangles is a distant memory as the tight wrapper is ripped from the box of a new Zip drive. Even though educators suffer under the weighty demands of time and technology, they see it as a chance to make new things in new ways and to share those visions with the students.

What has happened to the amount of time available in each design course? It is being squeezed. The design faculty said, "We will have to fit everything in." Before computers, faculty may have had a full semester to teach a beginning typography course. Now, they have a full semester to teach typography and the several software packages the students will use to complete the typography projects.

Faculty tasks greatly expand when they teach technologies in their classrooms. Not only must they learn the new software and hardware, but they must provide a different studio setup, interact with technology personnel, and maintain computer setups at school as well as at home. In addition to all this are the daily classroom details that arise in relation to technology. Did everybody learn the new release? Will the version the students are using on their new home computers work on the school computers? Should we evaluate the students' work in the same way? How do we keep the students in the classroom when they want to work on computers elsewhere? The days of the traditional design studio are gone.

What is happening to the time students spend on design? It is being squeezed. Students must keep up with the new technologies as much as the faculty have to. They are responsible for purchasing and maintaining a system, for finding a way to evaluate their work with their faculty instructors, and, above all, for having a portfolio that reflects their technological expertise.

It is time to unsqueeze. Some schools are leaping to the forefront by making interactive media a separate educational area. There is great overlap between what is being offered in the print media area and the interactive area, and much of this content can be covered in new or revised core courses. Students in traditional and new areas of design still need typography, layout, color, photography, and other general visual-communication skills, but the similarity ends there.

Interactive media education requires content of its own for students' understanding of timing, editing, narration, navigation, pacing, information layering, and more. The area of interactive media has stretched from animated and passive viewing of media that is self-expressive to the more scientific, methodically produced and tested medical software interface. Designing for these different types of software requires different types of knowledge than what was typically available in the traditional curriculum before computers. A proliferation of books relating to interactive media design is starting to eclipse the corpus of traditional design content that students and faculty have needed to study to stay up-to-date.

The faculty need time to learn the new software well enough to get the students started in their own design directions. The days of the design instructor knowing every software and hardware function are over. The new design studio has turned into more of a team effort for learning all the various parts of software, as well as for critiquing each other's work.

The faculty need time to discuss the technology with colleagues and students, and to consider purchases that need to be made. They need, with the help of others, to set up and maintain computer labs. They need to redo their syllabi to reflect the new tasks required in class. They need to keep current with what other schools are offering so their students can compete.

These changes have started on a small scale in some design departments across the country and will continue to evolve. A slow evolution is not a bad thing, as it gives us time to assess and evaluate technology and the design field. Not all departments will do things in the same way. Some design departments will focus on more self-expressive types of work and others will focus on more research-oriented work, as they do now. We need all these types of design departments to accommodate the varied and increasing demand for designers as we squeeze in these next few years before the new millennium.

Design Interactive Education

Max Bruinsma

THE MERGING OF CONTEXTS

Some time back I began a lecture for postgraduate students of art and graphic design by stating that they had probably all learned the wrong trade. Most of them had an educational background in disciplines that today could be best described as "old crafts." Now it was not my intention to demoralize them, but I wanted to confront them with a problem that is at the heart of being a designer or an artist or a writer or an editor these days. Of course, as a writer, critic, and editor, I was talking about my own problems too. To an ever-expanding extent, the work of artists and designers overlaps the work of other specialists in the field of cultural communication. And this is not only the case in complex applied multimedia environments—it holds true even for the autonomous or fine arts.

For what is the context of art and design today? How do they function in our culture and society? What is the role of artists and designers in what is called the information age?

It is obvious that understanding the idea of "information" is a most important key to these questions. More than ever, the bulk of cultural production files under "info." We need to be updated every second on any topic to be able to exist as cultural beings. Information—from the hard facts of economy and the news to the seemingly trivial data transmitted by advertising and the entertainment industry—is at the core of our existence. But such "information" is not the stuff that evokes what the great eighteenth-century German philosopher Immanuel Kant called *Interesseloses Wohlgefühlen,* the kind of thing that is in itself valuable, without any connection to practical use or economic gain. That is where the great idea of autonomous art comes from: the creation of a thing of beauty as a value in itself, as a purely spiritual thing that has no use but being precisely that, a thing of the disinterested mind. These days it is hard to be disinterested. We are bombarded by information and we are compelled to do something with that information, to act on it, to deal with it.

In this cultural panorama, both artists and designers are, in a very practical sense, "information agents"—that is to say, they traffic meaning; they transport ideas, concepts, and opinions; they visualize structures and contexts. In short, they condense information into cultural content. By calling both artists and designers information agents, I want to stress two aspects of visual culture today. First, the visual production of artists and designers functions in a framework that embraces such diverse media as paintings, books, catalogs, magazines, computer terminals, television screens, films, installations, exhibitions, and performances. These same media are employed by other information agents too: writers, directors, producers, advertisers, politicians, salespeople, musicians, actors, supermodels, TV-makers—all of these, and more, make use of the same media, the same formats, the same information, the same concepts as those used by artists and designers. Of course, each of them works differently and from another background, another bias, a different idea of what to accomplish through these media. But they all are, so to speak, in the same room. In fact, they work together in constructing our visual culture, a realm where visual information flows freely from one context to another, constantly shifting form, changing content, but, at the same time, adding up to this all-embracing fabric called "late-twentieth-century Western visual culture."

The second aspect is the viewer of all this visual productivity. The eye of the postmodern viewer has acquired a great proficiency in "reading" information—be it verbal or visual, an artistic or a consumer product. Designers and their clients, the providers of information products, should be well aware of the growing visual literacy of their audiences. Whatever they design, the viewer will read it into his or her own context. No artwork or design is an isolated or autonomous object anymore.

Of course, to some extent this has always been the case—any cultural production relates to culture as a whole. But there are some interesting historical differences. A century or more ago, no sane and civilized person would have thought of putting a painting next to a vacuum cleaner in a museum and saying, "Behold, our culture!" This person would be well aware that both products were, in a very general sense, cultural products and, as such, things of their time, but they would never be put on the same level, let alone be confused. Nowadays, we're quite used to seeing paintings and industrial products on the same level as cultural products, each with its own context, but not necessarily of a fundamentally different nature and sometimes quite easy to confuse. When Jeff Koons puts a vacuum cleaner in a glass box, it's art. When Sears puts a vacuum cleaner in a cardboard box, it's a product. So nowadays it's the box that makes the difference, not the product itself! And there are a lot of artists who not only use, but themselves make, perfectly functional products and present them as artworks, and many designers who make perfectly viable artworks that are sold as products.

There are strong reasons to argue that the practices of art and design are slowly but surely merging, and that for both designers and artists it's more a question of context and concept than of principle that decides whether they're making art or design. They work in the same room, and they can choose the box in which they want to present their output.

TALKING ABOUT BOXES

I've avoided mentioning computers for some time, because what I am saying here is applicable to cultural production at large, not only to computer-based art and design.

But, of course, the computer environment is the best example of a context in which traditionally different disciplines merge.

It is no coincidence that the computer is the epitome of the information age. For a computer, any input is information—it's all the same: artwork or design, photo or video, image or text or sound, moving or still—it's all bytes and pieces. One of the interesting things about computers is that their architecture compels their users to adjust to a certain practical routine in handling that digital information, which is technically the same for everyone, whether they are working on a hypertext or an architectural construction or a graphic design or an interactive artwork. Behind the computer, they all go through the same moves. These moves are fundamentally different from the moves students have learned to be the traditional skills of an artist or a designer. They can't sketch on a computer the way they used to do with a pencil on paper, and they don't build their designs on the screen the way they used to build them on their drawing boards. On a computer, the basic thing you do is to order information. And the next thing you do is to edit that information. Practically, you do these two things regardless of whether you are an artist, a designer, an architect, or a writer. When using a computer, you order and edit.

Now imagine that in the very broad field of what I call the production of visual culture—of visual art, graphic design, television, advertising, film, journalism, photography, performance, and theater—a growing number of professionals start using the computer as their main tool to conceptualize and design their visual statements. If this were the case, regardless of the materialization of a project or the box in which it is presented, all these disciplines would necessarily share a way of conceptual thinking. On a conceptual level, all these disciplines would work the same way; all would have to address the same practical questions of ordering and editing information.

And this is what is happening now. I don't say that working with computers is the only way to make art or design these days, but I do say that when the computer becomes a very important tool in the creative processes of our culture, which it already is, this will affect culture at large. In many manifestations of today's visual culture, you don't have to see the computer to know it has been there. And if artists or designers want to be culturally effective, if they want to reflect meaningfully on what makes the society in which they work tick, then they have to be aware of these things. A designer can make beautiful and valuable books and posters or even websites, and not be part of what these books and posters and sites are about; an artist can make beautiful and valuable paintings or sculptures or even CD-ROMs, and not be part of the contexts in which the work is shown.

CHANGING EDUCATION

What does all this mean for graphic design education, apart from the obvious fact that design education can't be isolated anymore from education in other fields of cultural production?

How do the effects of the computer, new media, and the changes in our communication environment reflect on today's design education? Did these technical and cultural innovations change education, and have educators adjusted themselves appropriately?

Not completely. Insofar as graphic designers are communications generalists par excellence, they are supposed to be capable of managing any formal aspect of communication processes, regardless of the medium for which it is produced and through which it is presented. But they should become more conscious of the fact that they're not the only ones who communicate. Designers have to rethink their role in multimedia communication. The traditional role of a designer as a rather autonomous professional who gives form to work that other professionals have finished earlier has become unproductive—or even counterproductive—in a lot of communication processes. In the new electronic media, any formal decision has a direct effect on the contents that are being communicated. Thus the designer has, in effect, become coauthor and coeditor of the message.

This new, extended role of the designer has already been compared with "collective enterprises" like television, film, and theater. In these media, form and content are formulated jointly by a range of specialists in areas such as scenario, direction, set design, camera, dramaturgy, and acting. More and more, graphic designers are becoming members of similar teams of form-and-content givers. Their role as sole-responsibles for the formal end product is strongly challenged. Thus, graphic designers have to reconsider their place in the new hierarchy of design teams in a computer-based environment. Graphic designers' main contribution to the effectivity of communication products is today more a matter of "conceptual functionalism" than of formal virtuosity. Now that they can do virtually anything they want, the main question for designers ought not to be what or how, but why. Why would you want to use any of these new and sophisticated technologies? Too often the answer is, Just because they're there. Designers should be able to argue their choice of means on the basis of the content they want to communicate *and* formulate it consistently with the technical, social, and cultural characteristics of the media they use. In the end, designers should be trusted to say to their clients, after careful analysis of the brief, "You don't need the fancy website you ordered—you need a few good people at the phone."

For design education, these visions of the extended role of designers point back to a functional archetype we know from architecture: the designer as *homo universalis*. For, to encompass all the aspects that touch on the design process—to weigh all of these against their influence on form and content of the design—the designer has to have knowledge of an incredibly broad array of social, creative, communicative, and technical processes. He's back again: the designer as *demiurge*, the quasi-omnipotent creator of worlds! The problem facing the Leonardos of our times, however, is that all these aspects are infinitely more difficult to knit together than they were in the Renaissance. A corporate graphic design manager at a large industrial firm seemed to point to this problem when, during a discussion, he related an image of vast project teams in which the graphic designer is just one of the specialists. But the same individual was driven to near despair when confronted with the question of who should bind together all these specialist efforts? Who should have an overview and direct the concept? "That is a problem," the corporate design manager said.

For design education, specialism versus generalism is the implicit problem beneath the debate on the consequences of working with new media. Of course, one needs specialists—operators, programmers, HTML editors, illustrators, image manipulators—just as one needs photographers, typographers, and printers. But maybe there's an even greater need for designers who are capable of seeing the whole picture before it's made. People who know enough of each specialism to direct the totality of the ever-more-complex design process. These are not necessarily the same people who execute the visual end product. In multimedia communication, the role of the designer is shifting from visualizing to conceptualizing.

This implies, in effect, a division into two aspects of graphic designers' activities. On the one hand, there are the specialists, the conceivers and (technical) realizers of presentations, the "imagers"; on the other hand, there are the generalists, the conceivers and managers of conceptual consistency. Of course, these two extremes are not divided in the absolute sense, and it will be up to personal interests and individual talents of designers to decide which direction they will want to explore. It's a difference of scale *and* of content. Both generalist and specialist are creative "conceptualizers" in the sense that they have to think up something that isn't exactly there, be it image or concept. Traditionally, graphic designers have always had a strong conceptual side to their work, and they have always worked in an argumentative way. Actually, they've always tended more toward generalism than specialism. And you *can* be a specialized generalist, as long as your trade is consistent and not too complex. Now it is exactly *here* that things have changed a lot in recent years. The "trade" has subdivided into very diverse and technologically complex specialisms, and what is probably even more important: the divisions between design and other fields of cultural production have, as I have pointed out, been blurred to a rather dramatic extent.

TEACHING TO COMMUNICATE

So, in a world of "desktoppers" and savant typographers, what is the role of the professional graphic designer? And how can they be best educated? It is here that the "division" takes place: alongside the people who can deal with technologically complex details—the "digital artisans," as they are beginning to be called—we need designers who can deal with organizing highly complex clusters of communication tools. They're the ones who can bind together, in meaningful and enticing ways, the different contextual and technological levels of the product. They have to be able to judge content in terms of the organization of very diverse forms and means and media. Thus, they have to have a thorough basic knowledge of *all* the forms and means and media. Their main asset is the argumented vision, not so much the actual visualization. They formulate the concepts and map the contexts.

When such is the state of the profession, it becomes clear where lies the problem or, better, the challenge of current design education. The way it is organized, certainly in Europe, design education delivers neither specialists nor generalists. Design academy alumni know the basics of their trade, but they are not seasoned typographers, book or exhibition designers, nor Web whiz kids. On the other hand, the art and design schools are too much geared toward the mediation of more or less specialized knowledge to deliver real generalists—designers who have developed the broad general knowledge and the trained academic thinking that will enable them to cope with complex conceptual problems.

In this diffuse situation, an "interactive" supply of knowledge seems to be the best that design education can offer. In order to cater to the realities of the work, which asks for very diverse professionals, we need to diversify design education—not by installing ever more specialized but autonomous schools and courses, but by structurally uniting the contexts within which young people learn whatever they want, and have, to learn about communication. Customization would be, in my opinion, the best way to link the disparate demands of the "market" to the diversity of interests among students. They should be able to make their own courses—an argumented choice from a broad range of specialized and general subjects on different levels—obviously within predetermined criteria. This not only means that the "walls" between the design disciplines and the ways in which they are taught should be opened, it also—and primarily—implies a much easier communication between art, design, and scientific education.

The term "communication" is used here in the sense of "communicating vessels"; students in any institution—university, art, or design schools—who qualify and are interested should be stimulated to follow courses in the other institutions. Theory, criticism, and practice should be linked in a more meaningful way than they are now. For a certain type of designer/generalist, we need to strengthen the academic level of thought, for which an overlap between art schools and universities would be helpful. For others, there should be more ways to acquire practical experience in the fields that they cover as theoreticians and/or organizers. The educational institutions should think about what they can mean for each other in terms of preparing their students for a world in which any one thing has to do with everything else. And most of all: they should teach their students—be they academics, designers, or artists—to work together, to understand the complexities and challenges of each other's projects, and to realize that these projects are different faces of the same dice.

So don't just teach interactive design; design an interactive education!

2001: A Design Odyssey

Steven Skaggs

When my buddy Manny called me, there seemed to be a strange urgency in his voice. He wouldn't tell me what was going on, so I caught the IRT over to his shop. I climbed the stairs to his third-floor studio and poked my head in the door. His Mac's flying-toaster screen saver provided the only light in the room. Manny sat at his drawing table, hunched over a pile of green goo. The stuff trickled from his fingers, and he seemed to be deep in meditation as he repeatedly tightened his grip, allowing the jellylike substance to drool between his fingers, dripping on the table.

"What's up, Manny?"

"Just waitin'."

"Sarah ain't gonna be callin' ya, man, she's been seeing Tito."

"Waitin' for Agatha. And for Bob to tell me what more he wants me to do with this stuff." He raised a slick, green hand.

"Hey, you're the boss of this place . . . who's Bob?"

Without lifting his head, Manny gestured across the room.

Filling the space between floor and twelve-foot ceiling stood a black plinth. Its surface was smooth, but not reflective. A low humming sound emanated from somewhere in or around it, I couldn't be sure which. If I listened attentively, I could hear the twittering of thousands of birds, voices of people, wind—I blinked and then realized that, no, it had shifted into a song. "Material Girl," Madonna, 1982, I thought. I'd always been good with songs.

"Umm, Manny?"

Manny still didn't look up. "That's Bob. Been here since last night. Says we're waiting for Agatha." The gel was dripping from his fingers onto his keyboard.

I knew Manny to be an industrious guy, someone who'd always worked in the trenches, you might say, yet justifiably the proud owner of Manny Sepulveda Designs. He was not someone who sat idle.

Then I heard distinctly another song. It was an old Bruce Cockburn number: "How come the future has to take such a long, long time when you're waiting for a miracle."

Manny had heard it too, which was a relief. "You can hear it in your head even over here," he said.

Then, a voice, "Agatha will be here soon."

I backed away from the plinth. "Manny, do you think you could fill me in on what's going on here?"

There was a pause. Manny's lips curled into a tight smile. "Uh, well . . . Bob's a muse." Manny looked up to register my take, which remained dumbfounded, so he continued. "The deadline for that calendar project was on top of me. I was totally blocked out on what to do. By last night, I'd gone through every single issue of *Graphis* from the past five years, ripped off maybe twelve different looks, knocked out a Greiman thing, a Carson thing, a Manwaring thing. But nothing seemed right. I didn't know where to go."

I nodded my head, so he continued.

"About nine o'clock, I heard something that sounded like a long sigh. At first, I thought it was me 'cause I'd been doin' my share of exhalations. But this was like the mother of all sighs, man—long, and like a chorus of many voices trailing into the deepening night. When I looked up, there was Bob. Introducing himself, he began to mess with my head. I mean, I began to hear the thoughts just like you're doin' now, but he's idlin' now—last night he was running like a hundred. Ideas like never before. And here in my hands was this goo. Watch this."

He shook the handful of material in the manner of someone extinguishing a match. The green gel morphed into a white sheet, which rattled crisply in the air. He began to crumple the page. As he did so, it changed back into green gel. He rolled the glob between his two flattened hands, then tossed it onto his desktop. Striking the surface, it bounced—a multicolored rubber ball. Catching the ball, he began to stretch the spheroid into a chrome disk. It reminded me of watching someone forming pizza dough, except I could see my open-mawed reflection on its surface. Picking up a pen from his desk, he rapped it against the disk, making a metallic clang.

"Between this stuff and the ideas Bob started pumping into me, I could have gone on all night without running out of steam. Well, see for yourself, there's the calendar." Manny gestured to a structure standing beside his desk.

I saw what could have been a coil of plumbing snake, except that it was big: the girth of the coils was as large as a beach ball and the entire coiled structure stood some eight feet tall. Looking closer, I noticed that the coils were made of smaller coils. It reminded me of the way rope is made of strands of smaller cords that are themselves made of strands of yet smaller threads.

Manny explained. "Bob suggested that the pace of the work week sets up this kind of—uh, how did he put it—a fundamental rhythm. Conventional calendars stack all the Mondays, Tuesdays, and other days of the week because they are days of the same category. Making a Monday-to-Sunday strip, I circled it around so that a succeeding Monday falls just above the first Monday. Bob pointed out that this maintains a consistent direction for time—no jumps backward, just a continuous flow forward. He called this the 'arrow of time.'

"I saw it making a spiral shape that could continue onward forever, making a kind of tube. I colored the months so that they related to the seasons. By the time I completed fifty-two of these spirals, I'd moved from January through December and it looked like a large spring. I stepped back to look at the entire spiraling cylinder and then Bob provided me with the insight that this path could coil also, so that January 1, 2001, lay atop January 1, 2000. And that's just like a year—you know, the whole spring thing goes around in its own circle. The seasonal colors clearly define the solstices and the equinoxes. You can imagine the sun in the center. Well, that yearly course made a larger spiral, which can be continued for as many years as you want. I decided to do a century version: one hundred years laid out so that 2100 is placed just over 2000. Of course, this meant yet another coil. So that's what you're looking at there. If you look real close, you can see that the one large spiral is made of one hundred coils, which are comprised of fifty-two coils each, and these fifty-two coils are divided into little seven-segment coils. You could carry the concept down to the level of hours and up to the level of millennia, but I stopped here for lack of space.

"You know, man, with these ideas and this morphing material, I'm going to be bigger than Glaser."

I was pondering the disquieting consequences of my buddy Manny becoming the next Milton Glaser when we heard Bob.

"Agatha is here."

We heard a low rumbling sound, felt a vibration. Soon, a second plinth materialized, standing shoulder-to-shoulder with Bob. Agatha was identical in size and just as featureless as Bob, but pearl white, and she droned with a hum that was a fifth of an octave higher in pitch. Together they made a pleasant harmony.

Bob's voice tended to be deep and resonant; Agatha's was cool liquid that rolled over its sibilants like a brook over weathered pebbles.

"Hello, my name is Agatha. I'm the muse traffic manager. Some of us call folks like Manny constipators, but let's just call him idea-needy, and we understand that everyone gets that way from time to time. We try to provide assistance in such dire cases by sending an available muse, such as Bob. One of my jobs is to answer any questions you might have concerning the nature of our visit. There are usually a few."

Manny sat still, his creative euphoria somewhat interrupted by the term "constipator." He seemed to be pondering its implications and not coming around to asking a question, so I seized the moment. "Look, Manny Sepulveda is a good friend and an excellent production artist, but now he's thinking he's going to be the next Milton Glaser. What in the heck has happened to give him that kind of creative leverage?"

Agatha's reply began as a humming sound that reminded me, for the briefest instant, of the air rushing toward an old attic ceiling fan. I could sense a soft breeze as her voice settled into her mellifluous speaking tone. "You ask about the seven ingredients," she started. "You see, what you think of as graphic design has seven distinct parts. These parts are really quite different in nature. A person who has strengths in one or two may be weak in others. It is not always easy to find one individual who possesses all seven."

"You mean by 'ingredients' the process of meeting the client, making the image, getting it mass-produced—that sort of thing?"

"Well, these are certainly part of the process of design, but there is an even more fundamental level to design. It is really so basic that it is easy to overlook.

"The thing that you are making, the thing you sometimes call a 'design,' is just one of these seven parts. And they are all intermingled. In fact, the designed thing is really dependent on the six other factors. For instance, do you think you could produce a successful design product if you had no objective—no problem—toward which to work?"

"I see what you mean, you certainly need to know what it is you're trying to do: a problem to be solved."

"Precisely. So, the designed product is always made in response to some objective. You can say that the objective helps to shape the design."

"Yeah, that makes sense. Right, Manny?"

Manny was beginning to look concerned. "What difference does it make what the parts are and how they come together? The ingredients I care about are to get the project completed on time, make the client happy, and, if I'm lucky, show other designers that I am hip to what's happening in the design world."

You could hear two or three seconds of humming as Agatha booted up for another statement. She revved up softly like the purring of an electric cat before she spoke. "Manny, your statement has raised many questions. But I am addressing the issue of how it is that we work as muses—what we have that is so rare among you humans. And that story begins with the seven ingredients. I've mentioned two of them, the design product and the project objective. A third is very basic, but is extremely important: the material from which the design product will be made. Bob will help us demonstrate."

The green morph ball levitated off Manny's desk and hovered in the air in the middle of the room. "There's some material," we heard Agatha's voice say. "And here's your objective."

At that moment, I had a sense of being aware of the concept of "calendar," but it was not clearly focused, was neither visual nor verbal; it was just a sensation of the idea of calendar. At the same time, Manny and I became aware of a glowing, hazy light some seven or eight feet from the hovering green morph ball. It was as if the hazy glow was a representation of my thoughts. Between them stood the calendar sculpture that Manny had made with Bob's help.

We heard Agatha continue, "See, Manny's calendar sculpture is a pleasant fit between the objectives and the material from which it is fashioned. One can say that the designed product is crafted not only from the material but also from the objective. A different material or a different objective would cause a different product to be made."

This sounded simple enough, though I'd never thought about it in exactly that way, especially that the design could be thought of as "crafted from" the project objective. But, at the moment, what I wanted to know was how my thoughts were projected into the room and how the morph ball levitated.

"There are two more pairs of ingredients," she continued, "and they are perhaps more important than the three ingredients we have mentioned so far. The material must be shaped with tools. Your fingers are tools, a computer is a tool, knives, pencils, markers, and erasers are tools. You must understand the tools if they are to have any value."

I thought of the time I'd first encountered a computer. Promising the art director that I knew how to use a Mac, he hired me to help on a rush project and directed me to a Mac II in a back cubicle. I guessed I'd be able to figure it out pretty quick. But there I was, unsure how to turn it on. There was no on-off switch. Who ever heard of a machine with no on-off switch. I pressed every button I could find: still, the screen stayed dark. Eventually, it occurred to me that perhaps the machine turns on through pressure on the screen itself. The art director happened by at that moment, finding me caressing the dark screen with my fingertips! It seemed a self-evident thing, but Agatha was certainly right in saying that understanding how to use a tool was vital.

Agatha seemed to pause while I reflected on the embarrassing memory, then continued. "But the tool does not work in a completely independent way. Something else also influences the journey from material to product. Form. In theory, every possible form is equally likely to be employed, but form cannot 'take shape' until it is created with a tool. And each tool, when used on a material, is able to execute only a small percentage of all possible forms."

Manny spoke up. "Yeah," he said, "remember the time I tried to make that thin ring out of wood? The pine wood kept splitting, and the carpenter said that the grain of the wood was preventing a ring of that size from being possible."

"That's right, every combination of material and tool has a certain set of forms that are possible and others that are set aside once that tool is picked up. From a limitless reservoir of potential forms, the selection of material and tools constrains the designer to a smaller subset. Which is lucky because the possibility of using an infinite number of forms would take a limitless amount of time to decide. Of course, a tiny fraction of infinity is still large; indeed, it's still infinite—as a philosopher named Zeno once realized long ago. It is amazing that any deadlines are ever met." There was a strange segmented humming and buzzing that I suddenly realized to be the laughter of a muse.

Manny's eyes were starting to glaze. Fortunately, Agatha brought the discussion back to something more concrete. "Look, when you have to do something, thank goodness for constraints of material and tools, because it allows the sampling of a few forms, and when you understand the tools and materials, those forms will be, once again, a nice, comfortable, fit.

"But beware. The understanding of a tool must be more than an intellectual exercise, it must be an intuitive understanding. That requires a lot of time playing with the tools, in combination with various materials, to gain an instinctive sense of how to handle them."

Manny asked, "Can you muses really visualize all possible forms?"

"That's what Bob gets paid, so to speak, to do. He dreams forms: all the forms that can be dreamt, and more, because muses are not limited to the dreams of humans.

"But there are two more ingredients, and they are also, in a sense, varieties of tools and forms. Just as tools and forms are needed to shape material, so are conceptual tools and conceptual forms needed to move from the project objective to the designed product. The conceptual tools are language, metaphor, similarities, codes, rhetoric—in short, all the devices of communication. The conceptual forms are all things that can be thought. Bob and I will spare you that vision.

"It will come as no surprise to you that the adept handling of the conceptual tools and forms can come only after a great deal of play. Ideas and concepts must be juggled awhile before the juggler gets a sense for their balance and spin. Designers are concept jugglers."

It had begun to rain. Rivulets of water dribbled hurky-jerky down the window-panes behind Manny's desk. A red car veered rather carelessly through the street.

"That 1968 Pontiac GTO was designed by Bill Porter's GM styling studio. Porter understood the nature of metaphor. The open grill is an athlete's mouth sucking in more air. The wheel-well flarings become biceps and quadriceps. Enter the muscle car. The car sets up a certain kind of attitude. It speaks of power, sex, masculinity, pure testosterone. Today, it also carries a wistful nostalgia to people who were young in 1968. In 1968, nostalgia wasn't a part of the picture. And to people in some parts of the world, the car stood then, and stands now, for Western excess. So, the message of the car is dependent on many conditions of time and space. The concept juggler understands this dependency."

Manny looked concerned. "I don't care what the car means to whom, it's going to wreck if that guy keeps driving it like that on these slick streets."

Agatha started her meditative boot-it-up purr before speaking, "You're right, Manny, the utility of the car as a conveyance is not affected by its style. That's why designers must keep in mind the distinction between utility function, the car as convey-ance, and meaning function, its ability to be a message.

The morph ball and glowing light had disappeared. Manny's hundred-year calendar still sat in place. On the floor was a piece of paper with a diagram on it showing the relationship of the seven ingredients to each other:

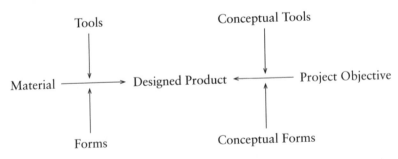

"Bob and I hope that you have enjoyed our visit. We leave this diagram as a souvenir."

"Hey," Manny blurted out, "how will I be able to do this creative stuff without you?"

I followed up, "Yeah, can he develop some of this ability without needing to call on you guys?"

Agatha hummed awhile before replying. "Your institutions are aimed at one side of the equation or the other. Your industry and some of your technical schools concentrate on the movement of material to designed product. Your universities that offer challenging humanities and liberal arts educations provide a fine insight into culture and the conceptual tools required to move from project objective to designed product. Even allowing that some of these institutions are more successful than others in doing either of these tasks, Bob and I have made clear that both sides are crucial in graphic design. Not many of your institutions excel at both.

"It is very difficult to become fluent in both material and conceptual sides," she continued. "The task is all the more difficult when young people try to manage this in four years of formal education. Even if they attend the most competent schools and work with the best equipment, they have two things going against them. The first is that they are young, the second is that skill in both material and conceptual tools requires time and patience.

"Being young means that they have not had much experience absorbing the culture around them, and even less experience with cultures that are, in time or space, distant from their own. Simply living can lead you to such an understanding, at least at the intuitive level. That was the beauty of the old way of design—the vernacular way. People simply worked for the local subculture to which they already belonged. They absorbed that single isolated scheme and continuously rolled its own symbol-set back into the mix. Commercial artists could concentrate on picking up technique, because by simply existing in the environment for which they produced, they were bound to become skillful with the limited array of conceptual tools that were needed.

"The situation has changed, and don't think for a moment that what Chuck Anderson and those guys do is vernacular. They roll the symbol-set of an extinguished past back into the present: a Jurassic Park of cloned extinct symbol creatures roaming about a postmodern landscape. It is not an unself-conscious vernacular, but a highly studied and self-conscious appurtenance of style. Chuck Anderson has the breadth to step outside his culture and borrow from another one next door. If he can go to more than one neighbor, he may keep himself from becoming bored.

"Today's designer needs that kind of breadth. To get it without a formal education, you have to live very long or very hard. Unfortunately, no one manages to live very hard for very long."

The muses began to vibrate. They were growing dim. Manny was staring at his calendar.

Agatha's voice was further away, "We have another call. We must go."

"Any last suggestions before you leave?" I pleaded.

"Only this: have your institutions, educational and professional, look at ways of working together more actively. Find a way to base graphic design upon a full liberal arts and humanities foundation. Increase cooperative education programs with private industry. Allow a longer gestation period for both technical training and conceptual growth. Look at going to a minimum of five or six years for a degree. Call the degree anything you wish, but remember: it must be an alternative for a long and hard life or it is worthless."

As they began to dematerialize, I caught the merest essence of a remark between the two of them. Bob asked for the address of the next constipator, Agatha answered 232 East Thirty-second Street. The last thing I could make out was Bob's droning response: "Milton again, huh?"

Remaking Theory, Rethinking Practice

Andrew Blauvelt

BEYOND THE GREAT DIVIDE: PRACTICE VERSUS THEORY

Unlike the recent skirmishes around issues of aesthetics and legibility in contemporary graphic design practice, the adverse reaction to theory crosses the generational divide, drawing dismissal and condemnation from likely and not-so-likely suspects.

This condition is not surprising. First and foremost, graphic design is a practice, as such it seems destined to oppose theory. This schism is rooted in the division of human labor that separates thinking from doing, head from hand, the means of reflection from the means of production. Second, in the prevailing anti-intellectual social climate affecting all claims to knowledge these days, we should not be surprised at the level of skepticism directed toward anyone proclaiming a theory of anything.

The arguments made against theory in graphic design can be sorted out in two basic reactions. On the one hand, there is a fear of overintellectualizing the practice of a profession whose relative "simplicity" is often expressed with disclaimers such as, "Well, it's not brain surgery." Perhaps graphic design isn't a physically invasive procedure, but certainly there's the same potential danger of mind-numbing results. Even J. Abbott Miller, a designer who writes about the history and theory of graphic design, recently asked, "One always hears complaints about the 'dumbing-down' of design in journalism, but shouldn't we be equally critical of the 'smarting-up' of design for academic audiences?"[1] This comment represents something of a milestone insofar as it even acknowledges that theory is being used, if only to claim its use has gone too far. Another variant of the anti-intellectual reaction to theory is harbored in the deepest depths of design mythology. Theory, precisely because it is characterized as external to the design process, is seen as disruptive to a designer's "intuition," dousing the flames of the designer's proverbial creative imagination.

On the other hand, there is a concern that theory is simply too vague and abstract to be useful for graphic designers. In this line of reasoning, theory (always described monolithically and without specificity or definition) does not and cannot respond to the particularities of graphic design practice, rooted as it is in the materiality of the so-called real world. Apparently, theory is ever only about abstractions on the ephemeral and immaterial. Conversely, graphic design is seen as irreducibly complex, grounded in the messy realities of ink and paper, too constrained by industrialization and capitalism to ever rise to the lofty heights of theory.

TOWARD A THEORY OF PRACTICE

This impasse between theory and practice in graphic design must be bridged, not for the sake of theory, but for the sake of practice. However, the challenge is to both theory and practice. For theory, it means engaging in the making of graphic design, not simply as a means for critical reflection *about* work, but a critical intervention *in* work. For practice, it means rethinking the very definitions and limitations of graphic design, not simply to add a little intellectual glamour to an everyday practice nor as a rallying cry to colonize other areas of creative endeavor, but to finally understand graphic design as a form of social practice.

Thus, the title of this essay is "Remaking Theory, Rethinking Practice," not "Rethinking Theory, Remaking Practice." As such, it is my attempt to question why thinking automatically aligns itself with theory and how making positions itself almost exclusively in terms of practice. Rarely do we consider that theory is something that is made—let alone something that is *creatively* fashioned. Theory is seen as something "out there," like storm clouds on the horizon or, perhaps more fittingly, a fog bank, slowly and completely enveloping our minds. In this scenario, theory is preexistent, waiting to be discovered, waiting to happen. By understanding that theory is fashioned, refashioned, and self-fashioned—not merely fashionable, preordained, or predestined—we can begin the process of putting theory to work.

It is also important to recognize that graphic design, no matter how it is practiced, fashions its own theories about making that help give it meaning, significance, and legitimacy. Just as it is impossible to honestly entertain the notion of being outside of politics, it is equally impossible to imagine any practice of design that is somehow independent of, or beyond, a theory of practice. Just as sociologists are able to formulate theories about social practices, it is possible to construct a theory—or theories—about the practice of graphic design. However, unlike social scientists who are often left on the sidelines to describe, graphic designers can actively redefine their practice from within.

THE TURN TOWARD THEORY

The very fact that we can have a design conference in 1997 with the word "theory" in the title—well, the subtitle at least—demonstrates that something is afoot. As the literary critic Terry Eagleton relates:

> Theory on a dramatic scale happens when it is both possible and necessary for it
> to do so—when the traditional rationales which have silently underpinned our
> daily practices stand in danger of being discredited, and need either to be revised
> or discarded. This may come about for reasons internal to those practices, or

because of certain external pressures, or more typically because of a combination of both. Theory is just a practice forced into a new form of self-reflectiveness on account of certain grievous problems it has encountered. Like small lumps on the neck, it is a symptom that all is not well.[2]

Indeed, all has not been well recently for graphic design. And both internal and external forces have acted in concert to disrupt the practice of graphic design, forcing it to a new level of self-consciousness and self-reflexivity. The most obvious factors have been the technological challenges and opportunities imposed by the introduction of the personal computer, which transformed the way graphic design is produced and distributed. With the threat of every personal computer owner becoming a desktop publisher, graphic design was in danger of demystifying its professional practice and abdicating its perceived role as a "gatekeeper" to mass communications. Simultaneously, the personal computer expanded the range of media and skills needed by graphic designers in the areas of motion, sound, and interactivity, for example, which threatened the very definition of graphic design rooted in the world of print. Unfortunately, both conditions only serve to emphasize the dependency of a definition of graphic design predicated on a set of (ever-expanding) technical skills. Faced with the prospect of massive mechanical de-skilling and pervasive digital re-skilling, it is no wonder that graphic designers seek their social legitimacy less in terms of what skills separate "amateurs" from "professionals," but in the "value-added" notion of design as a potent social and cultural force.

Coinciding with these technological challenges is a more widespread public consciousness of design itself. If the 1980s initiated the age of designer "things" (e.g., jeans, water, and furniture), those discrete objects have coalesced in the 1990s around a constellation of various marketable lifestyles. The advent of niche marketing effectively disrupted the notion of mass markets and, with it, the idea of mass communication. The idea of "audience" itself has changed as the cultural geography of society has changed, altering the demographic composition of not only potential audiences, but also graphic design students and practitioners.

The introduction of theory into the design curriculum is the logical consequence of such challenges, as teachers, students, and practitioners attempt to come to terms with these internal and external changes. Rarely does one encounter any course called "design theory." Rather, the introduction of theory into the curriculum has been through the back door—so to speak—of history classes, seminars on design issues, and, occasionally, in studio-based projects and assignments. If the 1980s saw the drive toward design history, then the 1990s have witnessed the move toward theory. Of course, the introduction of history into design curricula elicited less negative reaction than the move toward theory, in part, I think, because history was seen as a confirmation of the logical evolution of a craft into a profession. Plus, it certainly didn't hurt to have wonderful images of old, but recognizable, things: after all, a poster is a poster is a poster. History gave life to graphic design by giving it a past and, by implication, a future. Theory, like history, serves to contextualize the practice of design in any number of ways, not the least of which is to position it in relationship to other areas of intellectual inquiry. While a history of a discipline by its very nature defines limits and thereby creates autonomy, any multi-disciplinary theory of graphic design by its nature robs the discipline of some of its autonomy by questioning its limits.

In a recently published interview with Ellen Lupton, Lorraine Wild—one of those pioneering souls in the American design history movement in the 1980s—comments on the role of theory in relationship to practice:

> Theory has opened up a multitude of ways that we can understand our work, but it will not tell anyone how to produce a better or more interesting design. Graphic design will continue to be measured—or seen—through its visual manifestations, in all their variety.[3]

While this comment may be somewhat surprising, coming as it does from some-one closely identified with contributions to graphic design history, theory, and criticism, Wild's comments express a more widespread ambivalence about how theory might be useful to designers. While theory is given the possibility of informing our *understanding* of work, it is denied any possibility of contributing to the *making* of such work. This tidy division of labor, splitting the theoretical from the practical, only serves to reinforce the very difference—indeed, the very distance—between theory and practice, which is at the heart of the problem.

RETHINKING PRACTICE

Theory provides the basis with which to ask questions not only about work, but also through work. And if nothing else, what design lacks in terms of interesting work these days is not necessarily more visual variety, but rather more provocative questions and polemical answers.

But it would be misleading to suggest that theory is something that is only added to the design process or curriculum when, in actuality, it is something that is already there and is made visible, and once discovered, makes visible certain assumptions and problems. We can and do import theories and ideas from other disciplines in order to understand our work, but it is only through the integration and synthesis of these ideas into the very materiality and particularity of graphic design that we can begin to determine the rel-evance of such an operation.

Not surprisingly, I see the role of theory in design not as a set of outside influences, assorted bibliographies, academic electives, or ex post facto critiques, but rather as integral to the process of making graphic design. In this way, I concur with Jan van Toorn when he describes the role of the contemporary graphic designer as a "practical intellectual," someone who is actively engaged in critical reflection about the designer's process of making.[4] By recognizing that the theoretical is not simply something that is done either before or after work has been made, but rather is crucial to the very process of making, graphic designers can actively contribute to the (re)definition of their roles in the communicative process.

It has become a cliché to say that the role of the graphic designer is undergoing significant change. The danger of repeating this truism too many times is that it will be considered inevitable. An expanded role for the designer in the communicative process is by no means guaranteed. Rather than submitting passively to the vicissitudes of change, graphic designers must actively reconstruct their roles. This is, of course, happening on a small scale, as designers entertain broader notions of graphic design, engage in entrepreneurial actions that challenge the ideology of the marketplace, or broaden their own creative roles in the formulation of projects and problems.

That is why I believe the role of graduate education today must be research oriented if any constructive redefinition of design practice is to be entertained. While professional practice increasingly accommodates the kind of "visual variety" Lorraine Wild referred to previously, it has not had to confront, in any large, systematic way, the challenge of not simply having to solve communication problems, but to pose them. A truly radical design practice, in my book, will be one that actively disrupts the conventions of the design process and transgresses the professional boundaries and limitations of graphic design, and not one that merely bears the visual signs of radicalism as a kind of calling card.

But what is research in the context of graphic design? Typically, research is understood as "getting to know your problem or subject." While this is not necessarily problematic—in fact, we might say that it is essential—we should not let this be the only function of research. Research in graphic design, much like theory and criticism, asks some much larger questions than can be asked by any one design problem or solution. These questions, while specific, are also open-ended in the sense that they can be made manifest in any number of ways. So, while there is a tendency in both research and theory toward the abstract and general, there is also the necessity of grounding any answers or solutions in a particular context, in a specific material reality, and a concrete historical moment. And it is this balance of the general and the specific, the abstract and the particular, which will help keep the answers asked by research and theory from becoming universal claims to Truth. Modernist design theory and research tended to ask questions removed from any particular cultural context and any specific historical moment. By doing so, their answers were often presented as universal and ahistorical—placeless and timeless. A critical, theoretical disposition helps frame and limit the answers found in research by making them contingent—specific to the historical moment and the particular context from which they emerge; in effect, situated knowledge and timeliness replace objectivity and timelessness.

TEACHING THEORY IN GRAPHIC DESIGN PRACTICE

The central questions remain: What is the role of theory in the design curriculum? And what do we mean by "theory"? I can only answer these questions, which have been central to my own concerns, by relating specific examples in the formulation of a new graduate program at North Carolina State University.

We began by acknowledging that the graphic design faculty shared at least one common view: graphic design does not begin nor end in the objects it makes. While hardly an epiphany, it is a sentiment that is broadly acknowledged yet undertheorized. In order to more fully contextualize the practice of graphic design, it was necessary to adopt and adapt a model of cultural production and consumption from research done in cultural studies. This model recognizes that there are important stages or moments in the life of designed artifacts, from their production through their distribution and eventual consumption. It is important to note that this model is dynamic and cyclical, meaning that any stage can and does influence other stages.

We began by moving outward from the designed product, looking at the cognitive interaction between designed artifacts and those who use them—as viewers, readers, audiences, receivers, browsers, or consumers. It was also necessary to place the entire realm of design—designers, design artifacts, institutions, and audiences—within a larger framework of society and culture, which ultimately "authorizes" its making. Influence is reciprocal, so we examine how society and culture shape graphic design as well as how graphic design shapes society and culture. We also felt obliged to consider the impact of digital media on both graphic design practice and society from a position that is critical of the kind of technological determinism so rampant in the society and profession today. These three areas of cognitive interaction, cultural reflexivity, and technological innovation form a set of interrelated discourses about graphic design practice.

Various theories are introduced in topical seminars that cover these frameworks or topics. For example, in addressing problems of cognitive interaction, students are introduced to material from cognitive psychology, perceptual studies, and learning theory; or when confronting the social and cultural implications of graphic design, students are introduced to theories of representation drawn from anthropology, ethnography, and sociology; or when assessing the influence of digital technologies on practice and society, students study theories of other media forms such as television, film, video, and literature in order to grapple with a convergence of media in electronic environments.

Importantly, these seminars are connected to studio courses, which require the synthesis of ideas in the form of design projects that address, confirm, or challenge the ideas presented. The focus of such studios is the creative application of theoretical ideas in design projects, which are constructed by the students in such a way as to ask pertinent questions. Unlike the objectives of undergraduate education, students are not asked to solve problems, but are encouraged to pose questions. This represents a fundamental challenge to traditional forms of design education, which exist to replicate the status quo through problem-solving projects that confirm what we, the profession, already know. By contrast, problem-posing education centralizes the student as an active agent in the formulation of projects that question what we, as a profession, already know as well as things that we might never had considered.

In a problem-posing education, students must be able to critically examine their world and their role within it.[5] This means that a critical disposition on the part of the student and teacher is necessary to fully capture the radicalism of the proposition. Critical thinking and making skills are crucial for success. Students must be able to formulate questions that are not simply reducible to yes or no answers, because this is the prevailing logic that must be overcome. Questions that cannot be answered with a simple yes or no are, in fact, research questions. And if the practice of graphic design is more than an unending series of solutions to never-ending problems, then we might begin to understand graphic design as a researchable activity, subject to both the limits of theory and the limitations of practice.

NOTES

1. J. Abbott Miller, "What Did You Do in the Design Studio, Daddy?" *Eye* 6, no. 22 (autumn 1996), 6.

2. Terry Eagleton, *The Significance of Theory* (Oxford, England, and Cambridge, Mass.: Blackwell, 1990), 26.

3. Ellen Lupton, *Mixing Messages: Graphic Design and Contemporary Culture* (New York: Princeton Architectural Press, 1996), 173.

4. For a more complete explanation of van Toorn's position, see his essay, "Thinking the Visual: Essayistic Fragments on Communicative Action," in *"And Justice For All . . . ,"* ed. Ole Bouman (Maastricht, the Netherlands: Jan van Eyck Akademie Editions, 1994), 141–152.

5. For an account of problem-posing strategies in educational theory, see especially chapter 2 of Paulo Freire, *Pedagogy of the Oppressed,* rev. ed. (New York: Continuum, 1993).

Talking Theory/Teaching Practice

Johanna Drucker

Fourteen years ago, when I was a graduate student at U.C. Berkeley in the visual studies program in the College of Environmental Design, I had the rare opportunity (rare for a grad student) of designing my own course. It was titled Image/Structure/Culture—and was meant to introduce students in the college—future architects, environmental designers, and city planners as well as a handful of graphic designers—to the fundamentals of critical theory applied to visual images.

Now, of course, that's back when dinosaurs roamed the landscape and the ancient seas still covered much of North America; primordial chaos had not yet divided into the heavens and the earth.

At that time, *The History of Graphic Design* was just a sparkle in Philip Meggs's eye, and the beacons we held aloft to light the way were works like Estelle Jussim's pioneering books on technology and graphic art, which felt dramatically modern by contrast to the classics—Daniel Updike's *History of Typography* or William Ivins's *Prints and Visual Communication*. But I was consuming a diet heavy in French theory from structuralism to deconstruction in all their "post" and "neo" forms.

Zuzanna Licko, my classmate, was sneaking me contraband copies of industry reports on ductal (stroke based), pixel, and bit-mapped concepts applied to type design—as she was on the verge of buying one of the first of the first generation of Mac personal computers.

Rudy VanderLans, our other classmate, still freshly arrived from Holland, was thinking of starting a magazine, *Emigre* (in which he reproduced a page of one of my letterpress books), and I tried to discourage him from doing a journal since I thought it was so impractical. (I'd been around a lot of small-press publishing and didn't want to see him lose all his money.)

At that point in time, I had the enthusiasm of a convert for the subtle complexities of theory. I had the semiotic disease—breaking out in signs the way practitioners of formalism had broken out in spots and dots a few decades earlier—was steeped in the mysteries of psychoanalysis, discovering the fundamental mechanisms of "condensation" and "displacement" with the excitement of a young physicist introduced to Newton's laws.

My poster advertising the class proclaimed that it would examine materials from

"*Pogo* to Plato's Cave," according to some perverse reverse logic of chronology. I had set out to maximize the ten-week course (Berkeley was still on the quarter system) by including in the syllabus everything I had read, learned, or could imagine could be brought to bear from "theory" upon the visual image in all its infinite variety. My topics ranged eclectically from the esoteric to the banal and topics as diverse as camouflage in the natural environment (or, how a fish can aspire to be a tablecloth) to camouflage in the built environment (how the military makes a building look less like a building). I had no hesitation about linking the most improbable images—suggesting that a posed publicity photo of Marlon Brando as Marc Antony had a precedent in the gesture of an elegant skeleton from Vesalius.

I will probably never again approach a class with quite the same enthusiasm or sense of vertigo—relying as I did on pure adrenaline to motormouth my way through sessions in which I projected Rorschach inkblots or eighteenth-century silhouettes on the screen and babbled in free association in a verbal leapfrog from Jean Piaget to Roman Jakobson touching down briefly on Hubert Damisch—while I tried to formulate concepts such as "the process of closure, towards a theory of the picture" on the fly. It was fun to teach the writings of the strange, self-promoting, and dubiously gifted Italian connoisseur Morelli right alongside the work of Andy Warhol and the big-eyed children of Walter Keane while asking questions about the nature of authenticity, forgery, and fakes. But there was a fundamental dehistoricization in all of this. As if the principles of analysis could be lifted, like a perfect skeleton of ideal thought, out of the tissue and fabric of their own historical moment in order to function like a clean, ideal armature for understanding any image at any time. What are the visual features that make an image kitsch? I would ask. Or what characterizes a dramatic moment in a still image? Or how do we read complex narratives that interconnect a series of images as a "pictorial text"?

If I go back through the list of topics in that syllabus and, one after another, read down the list of references, I'm not so much shocked by its ambitious naïveté with regard to scope—"The Structure of Static Images" starring Charles Peirce, Ferdinand de Saussure, John Locke, Charles Morris, and a few Prague school semioticians thrown in for good measure, or "Representation and Illusion" according to the texts of Alfred Bazin, William Ivins, Madeleine Bunim, John White, Erwin Panofsky, and René Descartes, and so forth—I'm not, as I said, so shocked by its ambitions as by its major blind spot in ignoring historicity in all its many ramifications.

That blind spot is the blind spot of one's own historicity. As an artist friend has said to me, "We all enter theory at a particular historical moment." That moment, so naturalized, so familiar, blinds us to its specificity: That this was the early eighties in American academia; that I had a French professor for whom this theoretical material defined his role within an embattled department; that the first-world, white academic culture in which I was operating held out to me, as a young woman scholar, a belief that conquering "theoretical" concepts, acquiring theoryspeak, would let me "play with the boys" or, at least, play like them. All that was invisible to me at that moment. Divorced from any self-consciousness about my own history, it's not surprising that the one thing so conspicuously missing from my course was any sense of the way historical and cultural specificity informs every human expression.

My sense of representation, at that point, was roughly contained within this structural formation: an individual subjectivity intersecting with ideological codes and conventions of production, or the artist in front of the easel on which a painted landscape figures the image of the supposedly real world beyond its frame.

In representation now, the ante has been upped on attention to the technological aspects of mediation, but the essential structure is still the same. A recent liquor ad features an artist/designer (a man, since all real artists are still male, remember) transforming the "raw materials of nature" (here in the dashing human analogue of the supposedly sentient dolphin diving into a Johnny Walker Red sea) into the refined product of culture while the caption reads: "Imagination cannot be confined." Switching into a techno-key gives the motif new style, but the structure of "real" to "represented" remains the same.

So, jokes and flippancy and self-congratulatory remarks aside, here I am creating yet another syllabus through which to attempt this task again. And what is that task?

Well, on the one hand, it's somewhat the same: to provide critical skills for the understanding of the daily encounter with visual, verbal, and graphic images across a wide spectrum, from the most familiar to the most arcane, esoteric, refined, and banal. But now the task is reframed. It is not that all the theory talk or concepts are gone, but that they have to reflect the distance we have come since that time, the more synthetic digestion of theoretical texts and ideas. And, above all, from my point of view, it's a matter of reorienting priorities.

Within the title of that first syllabus lurked the term "culture," a concept that got seriously short-shrifted in the actual material covered by the course. But, like all truly Freudian slips of the typewriter, it was potently waiting to become the major term. Now, it's that term that interests me most, seems most significant, most compelling as an essential point of departure. I haven't given up on some of the old questions, or answers. How is it that these two images—one a painting, one a photograph staged to look exactly like it—are so fundamentally *not* the same image? How would a concept like "distinguishing the plane of discourse from the plane of reference" help us distinguish between the ways in which a viewer produces meaning?

But I am keenly aware that what I most want to communicate at this point is not a set of abstractions or models for analysis of "representational strategies," but something at once more urgent and more elusive. In constructing the new syllabus—which introduces critical concepts through a historical framework—my central concern is the communication of fundamental tools of analysis that can be applied to the ongoing lived condition of experience.

Why? On some level, I once believed, during those heady days of my fresh indoctrination into the jargoned wonders of poststructuralist vocabulary, that those many texts were a source for unlocking the secrets of representational structures. But, just as we can't any longer expect art exhibitions to attract an audience with titles like *Deconstructing the Phallic Mastery of Representational Strategies: A Study in the Implications of Lacan's*

Lack for the (M)other, so we can't, I think, expect that anyone will continue to be excited, or convinced, studying the lessons of Roland Barthes's in the analysis of "Italianicity." The learning of theory can be all too conspicuously akin to the activity observed by Le Petit Prince at the beginning of his story when a snake swallows an animal and is distorted to assume its contours. How many times have we watched someone swallowing Foucault or Freud or Kristeva and seen their sense of self and language distort into a frenzy of "discursive strategies," "drives and cathexes," or "abjection and desire"?

But now, as I consider the problem of framing this teaching task, asking how to formulate an intersection among the terms "teaching," "talking," "theory," and "practice" into a configuration that has some kind of effective meaning or real value, I find that I have to return the theoretical constructs to very specific relations with history and culture. It seems essential to lift the historical amnesia that theory can introduce (although it is no more inherent in theoretical texts to be ahistorical than it is in anything else) and to think about graphic form, cultural expression, designed objects, and even ideas in terms of the social institutions from which they emerge.

I've come to this conviction not only through my own work and projects, but, even more immediately, through the contact I've had with various students in the field of graphic design. I thought I would describe a few of these specific cases in terms of the generic issues they raise, and then finish with a quick description of the syllabus I have been working on for the following year.

It has been useful, and important, to me to consider the questions/concerns brought to my attention by the students.

One of the most striking moments in my recent teaching experience was when a graduating senior came to see me about her final project. She had been working on Komar and Melamid, was herself a Soviet émigré—a not insignificant point—and she had even invited the pair to campus to give a presentation. Afterward, she came to see me and we talked about how they had asserted that in the West, particularly America, there was "no ideology." It struck me that this assertion met with no resistance or surprise on her part. It was simply a fact. I was horrified. In part, the issue of cultural displacement has to be taken into account: that she had moved across the Iron Curtain late in the Cold War, and that Western-style consumerism made a stark, striking contrast to Soviet-style graphics, social agendas, and their communication in the public sphere. The ideology that structures and "naturalizes" every aspect of daily experience had rendered itself so successfully invisible to her that it disappeared. So, I showed her a couple of images, the cover of *I.D.* magazine, for instance. "Whose idea of identity is that?" I asked her. And then an ad. "Since when is it 'natural' for women to call attention to the virtues of office supplies by wearing a checklist of attributes on their chests?" I wondered.

But how does this happen? And how can it be undone? What is the basic Ideology 101 reading list that can provide an unmasking, a defamiliarization, of the lived condition? And how to do this so that it's not showing simply that one image, one issue, or one idea is ideologically charged, but that the whole total daily experience of living is "naturalized" through its ideological condition. That this *is* ideology. There is a wonderful passage in some critical theory book I read once (which? where?) that takes the description of a sunset—glowing, beautiful, the quintessential "natural" event—and systematically demonstrates the way every aspect of that "event," and one's observation of it, are embedded in cultural conceptions.

Another student comes to me. This time a grad student in design working on a project about books and the future of the book. Everybody says the book is over, finished. She wants to do a project on its future. Having read a few hyper-extreme works, she now wants to make a project taking off from them. What does she know about the history of the book? Nothing. Its physical origin and development? Its cultural role and history? How do you deal with such students? What I want to do isn't just to give them a dose of "the cultural status of the book in historical perspective," but to get them to understand once and for all time for themselves that all objects/discourses/discussions have a history to them, that you can't just pick up on a few contemporary popular references and "get" the current condition of the book—or anything else.

A third student arrives. This one is working on a project that will be in a "public space"—bus stop, street corner, an urban environment. But what is the public space as she assumes it? What is the nature of that urban environment? How do I get her to go from Habermas's tracing of the historical conception of the public sphere within eighteenth-century notions of the social to the current disintegrated condition of urban New Haven? This is a persistent dilemma—this linkage between critical theory and any kind of practice—design practice, research, writing, or whatever.

Finally, another student is working on a typographic design project and is reading various philosophical texts. One of these is by Heidegger and puts forth a theory of culture that taps into the "roots" of authentic underpinnings. But Heidegger has been taken completely out of context. There is no way the student can recover from that single reading a sense of how that particular concept of "authenticity" carried a political value in its context of postwar Germany and was severely and pointedly critiqued by Theodor Adorno. Not, that is, unless I say something. Is it too much to ask of the student to consider this enthusiastic use of Heidegger's concept in relation to a critical discussion of its assumptions? To see the other side of its supposed humanism? Will it have any effect on the outcome of the typographic design?

The answer to the second question is easy: not likely. The answer to the first question, like that posed by the needs of the other students, is more complicated. The problem is not to show that one image/text/bit of writing or type is ideological, historical, and subject to investigation through critical tools, but to try to provide a framework of metacritical tools that becomes intuitive. Instinctive. To nurture responses that can reply to the hyped and seamless face of contemporary style and culture with critical distance.

This brings me back to the syllabus for the new course—not that it is a be-all-and-end-all solution. It isn't. It's one attempt to present fundamental concepts that will be useful for students of art, art history, and design. Titled "Critical Intersections: Modern Art and Design: History and Theory," the course examines some of the many moments in the history of modernity when fine art and design were in dialogue.

The course is focused around a series of issues and a series of historical moments. It begins with the concept of the public sphere and development of the autonomous art object as key aspects of the advent of modernity. What is modernity? How is it defined critically? What are the problems of demarcating periods of history, and how do questions of stylistic transformation relate to these larger questions? How do we read Baskerville's and other modern type designs in relation to these issues? Is there any connection?

The course keeps several themes alive throughout: technological changes, cultural changes in the institutions in which both fine art and graphic design function, stylistic innovations, and an examination of both visual and verbal forms of language. Historically, the course moves forward through the invention and proliferation of industrial and mass production, to the utopian arts and crafts movements with their retro/historical styles, to the advent of the avant-garde and the major changes brought about through electrification, to the change from the industrial capitalism of the nineteenth century to the consumer capitalism of the twentieth century, to the development of the concept of the "spectacle" and the "simulacrum," and ends with a discussion of the hype of cyberculture and the appropriation of old counterculture sensibilities as a style motif of new electronic media in the service of transnational capital.

The idea is to interweave the critical with the historical, to try to make clear that theory, like practice, is linked to specific individuals and moments in time. For instance, to get them to understand the lineage of formalist modernism in terms of the Soviet avant-garde and its links to a language of militantism—to understand that the rhetoric of the "Left Front of Culture" bore within it certain features of the same repressive dogmatism by which it was ultimately destroyed, on the one hand, while, on the other, its stylistic innovations, so dramatic in their original moment, were absorbed into—even served as the basis of—the language of an international "modern"—that is, corporate—design that would have been anathema to the original designers.

Is it necessary for designers to know this stuff? In "talking theory" within the context of "teaching practice," history and theory offer a base within which to locate cultural references, thus contributing to the knowledge and vocabulary from which we make choices about the forms used in design. Theoretical tools also contribute to an understanding of what the design is doing and how it is doing it—through an analytic frame for meaning and communication.

But there is a certain caveat emptor aspect to promoting critical theory within a design context. I find myself particularly wary these days of the ways in which the acquisition of the vocabulary of theory becomes a part of the designer's portfolio in response to a change in the academic life of design, or the life of design within academic departments, journals, and conferences. Beyond a certain cleverness, there is the insidious stratification that starts to occur. Theory = dense/difficult vocabulary = what distinguishes the "smarties" from the "dummies" and then the "tenurable" from the "discards"—and before you know it, this field will just repeat the same old transformations that accompany the colonization of academic domains by critical jargon into a false hierarchy of the critspeak aficionados bent on the careeristic self-promotion of a theory class within the discipline.

This inevitably results in an ever greater distance between the real goals of theory—analysis of culture, power, and one's place within it—from the day-to-day activity of the practitioner; that is, dealing with clients in a highly capitalized and competitive field and producing graphic, visual forms.

So, what do designers need to know? What is the link between teaching theory and talking practice? Not old semiotics, but kind of living cultural criticism through which they/we can try and understand the fundamentals: the relations of money, power, and our own situation, particularly the position of the individual in terms of the nexus of corporate power and the implications of our complicity, dependence, and potential agency. What's at stake isn't so much the look or form of design practice, but the life and consciousness of the designer.

There is no mystery in unlocking the ideological bases of the cultural agenda. One has only to ask one simple question. Really, just one question unleashes the critical process: In whose interest? That's it. In whose interest and to what ends? Who gains by this construction of reality, by this representation of this condition as "natural"?

If there's any urgent, compelling mission in all of this, it isn't because thinking about communication and signs, "discursive strategies" and the "historical nature of design," and power and money will just get you more, it's because we have to face the very real challenges of helping give shape to a public imagination in which it will become possible, acceptable, and desirable to manage the diminishing resources of a small planet with diverse populations in a manner that is equitable and self-sustaining rather than to greedily participate in the Disney/Fox/Turner fast-food monoculturalization of the universe. Is that possible? That's not a question I can answer, but I think it is the question we have to keep asking.

Experience versus Education

Jeffery Keedy

So, you want to be a successful graphic designer with big clients and lots of design awards? Well, why waste time and money in design school when you can easily gain credibility within the field by networking at design functions and entering design shows? Use the money that you would have blown on tuition for something useful like office space, entry fees, and computers. Then, all you have to do is hire a few young people straight out of design school who—thanks to a good education, are proficient in the latest technologies and up on the latest styles. Young designers don't cost much because they are struggling to pay for student loans and new computers. And after they've been around long enough to qualify for a raise, you can get rid of them, because there are plenty more where they came from. After all, you are doing them a favor, you are giving them a "real" education.

Not long ago, all designers were self-taught or learned their craft as apprentices on the job. But today you would have to live under a rock to be unaware of contemporary design. Unlike designers of the past, today's self-taughts are functioning in a professionalized field that has established a loose framework of options for practice, as well as a plethora of information covering all aspects of design—the numerous books, trade magazines, organizations, and conferences. However, because self-taughts usually do not feel indebted to anyone, they think what they are doing is new and "original"—ignorance is bliss. As "outsiders," they feel no kinship or responsibility to other designers, leaving the rest of us with nothing but the privilege to admire their chutzpah.

Ironically, self-taught designers must establish themselves as "professional" to be competitive. This is accomplished by entering numerous design competitions and joining professional organizations—all the while reminding their peers in lectures and in magazines that they are, like commercial artists of the past, unencumbered by a formal education. But in our postmodern information age, what does it really mean to proclaim that one is self-taught? Should self-taught graphic designers be referred to as naive or folk designers? For some, it is simply a means of removing themselves from a practice while simultaneously co-opting all of its advantages. So why is the design community so complicit in celebrating the outsider's ability to exploit the rest of us?

Part of the answer may lie in the celebration of the self-taught as a particularly

American phenomena. Although there are successful and celebrated self-taught designers around the world, only in America do they wear their lack of formal education like a badge of honor. There is nothing Americans like better than the self-made man—it speaks to our pioneer heritage, blazing a trail over the meek and inferior, and staking our claim to whatever we can take. Anyone familiar with our popular culture knows that Americans think there is something inherently honest in ignorance. We celebrate heroes that are kindhearted idiots (Forrest Gump), self-exploiting sluts (Madonna), tacky performers of bad sportsmanship (Dennis Rodman), and adolescent taste (Howard Stern). Conversely, there is something cold, calculating, and devious about the educated and intellectual. When was the last time you saw an American movie or TV show in which the bad guy wasn't characterized as "real smart"? And it was our news media that described the Unabomber as a highly educated "genius." How fortunate for Americans that naïveté is more socially acceptable than the corrupting influence of education.

Of course, it is impressive to see someone enjoying success in spite of his or her lack of a formal education. But in design practice, is it really that surprising? Given the largely service-oriented role that design plays, one could only expect that the closer you are to mainstream thinking, the more likely you are to enjoy popular acclaim. Conversely, the more specialized one's knowledge and skills, the more difficult it is to achieve mainstream success. Uncritically celebrating the success of the self-taught designer, without qualifying such success, only serves to undermine our own credibility and history.

It is not my intention to single out self-taughts as parasites on an accommodating host, as the majority of them are ethical and responsible people. But a few high-profile self-taught designers exemplify an anti-intellectual undercurrent that has been grumbling away in the design community for some time. The proliferation of design schools, particularly the ones with graduate programs, have engendered a reactionary backlash. When was the last time you ever heard a design star talk about the importance of design education to practice? In contrast to the precocious vocabulary-abusing graduate student, the plain-talking self-taught designer represents a reassuring alternative to constant change and increasing complexity. Perhaps this is why some of the harshest criticism in design today is no longer directed at the undereducated, but at the supposedly overeducated.

The self-taught designers are not a big problem because there are not many of them, and most self-taughts are quick to exploit relationships with well-educated partners or employees. Our more serious problem is the fact that there are so many educated designers who view design education as a necessary evil instead of a lifelong commitment. As the saying goes, "A little bit of knowledge is a dangerous thing." Unfortunately, too many designers are content to depend on just a little bit of knowledge. They are confident that they can learn most of what they need to know on the job. They fail to understand that design education today is much more than vocational training, it is a process of discovery and renewal.

Anti-intellectual designers are critical of design education, even though they have absolutely no idea what goes on there, except in the design programs that have not changed in twenty years. Before new ideas and explorations are even developed and fully articulated within design education, they have often been dismissed as ill-conceived or just plain wrong by uninformed critics who are insufficiently prepared to understand what they are discounting. The true source of their anxiety is not the new ideas themselves (which they usually misunderstand), but the fact that they represent a change in design thinking.

Even though design education still has a long way to go in establishing parameters and standards, this certainly does not justify the lack of credibility it often seems to have. Designers who have been out of school for a while have no way of finding out what is going on in schools today unless they spend time in a classroom, attend an education conference, or read about it in design magazines. Unfortunately, most professional organizations dealing with education do so with segregated events that are primarily attended by educators and students. Or they hold a portfolio review in which practicing designers review student portfolios without the slightest idea of the students' curriculum, and then pronounce their approval or disapproval of the outcome. Design magazines are mostly uninterested in educational issues, except for reproducing snazzy-looking undergraduate work with little more than captions for explanation. They rarely publish graduate-level projects, fearing they are too complex or in-depth for their readership (*Emigre* magazine excepted).

The climate of anti-intellectualism in design is often bolstered by a false sense of professionalism based on real-world experience. Typically, this type of "professionalism" amounts to little more than platitudes and bromides—problem solving to get the ultimate correct solution, and the pursuit of timelessness that supposedly transcends its own era. These entrenched clichés are responsible for the banality of the cornball visual puns and pedestrian aesthetics that constitutes the majority of graphic design. As long as such simplistic thinking is tolerated in design, what little meaningful dialogue there is will be drowned in a morass of mediocrity. As you may have noticed, the harping and posturing by anti-intellectual professionals is not moving the discipline closer to becoming a real profession or increasing its recognition as being an important part of culture. Nor is it helping the next generation of designers to find their way.

To be professional is to be impartial and objective, guided by established precedence in your field. Although the word "professional" is used freely in design practice, graphic design is not a profession. Designers have no obligatory regulating body that oversees and safeguards standards of practice. Today, anyone can be a member in most graphic design professional organizations for the price of admission, and can print "graphic designer" on their business cards. The true professionals in graphic design are in design education. They are certified professionals whose credentials and practices are monitored by organizations like the National Association of Schools of Art and Design (NASAD) and the Western Association of Schools and Colleges (WASC). However, design educators are only professionals as educators, not designers. It is one of the ironies of the pseudoprofession of graphic design that the only true professionals in the field are frequently criticized by design practitioners for not teaching students to be more professional.

Many graphic designers do not understand that academia is not just a hothouse of wanton self-expression, but is actually the bastion of tradition. Design practice relies on design education to train people in the latest technology and to develop basic skills and literacy. But what many designers fail to recognize is that academia's most important role is in establishing continuity from the past to the future. It is the place where the canon is constantly being elaborated and reformulated. If certain values are deemed important to design, such values will most likely be articulated and perpetuated through education, not practice.

Graphic design will not grow up into a profession or fine art until it can view itself in a larger historical and cultural paradigm. And this is where design education comes in. One of its most important functions is exploring and defining the context of design and establishing a shared core of ideas, issues, and values that define practice. Personal experience teaches how to repeat the successes and avoid the failures of the past. Education teaches the value of past successes and failures, but in an unbiased, professional fashion. A personal experience is only one person's experience and never exceeds his or her limitations and biases, but education is based on a shared cultural past that includes many viewpoints and possibilities.

Design education is not just for training designers how to use tools, it is a process for developing and refining our understanding of ourselves as designers. Regardless of whether you believe design is a problem-solving profession of information architects or a socially responsible art form, education will broaden your understanding and strengthen your convictions. The more articulate we are in describing the issues and ideas that concern us, the better we will understand each other and others will come to understand what we do. Education and experience are the foundation of our future. If they remain at odds with each other, we will be building on shaky ground, and whatever we make will not stand for long.

If this sounds like more "preaching to the choir," then you have missed my point. Although it is important for designers to reach out and educate the public about design, actually, the ones who need to be educated are the designers themselves. The majority of practicing graphic designers are ignorant about the history, theory, and ethics of their discipline. They know how to use the tools, make out invoices and entry forms for competitions, but are at a loss when it comes to placing their work in a critical, historical, or cultural context. Graphic designers have to get a lot smarter about who they are and what they are doing before they will be able to convince others what they do is important. You may admire the moxie and talent of a self-taught designer, but the fame of an individual is limited and fleeting in comparison to the respect accorded a profession or cultural institution.

Great strides have been made in the past decade in design education, even though it has been faced with its greatest challenges. It is important that we recognize the wealth of experience and knowledge that designers have acquired and build upon it. Designers need empowerment, and knowledge is power. The design educator's job is to make graphic designers smarter. However, practicing "professionals" are not only needed to support design education, but to encourage it to go further. With the help of real-world practitioners, design educators must work toward establishing design as a vital part of cultural communication that is integral to, but not submerged by, the new global information environment. Graphic design is bigger than any one of us, so let's start acting like we believe it.

Traversing the Edge and Center:
A Spatial Approach to Design Research

Katie Salen

A story:

I sit at my computer but compose first on paper with furtive scribbles, marking and re-marking words until they lay flat and still as if they were meant to be there—here— in this exact location. The page darkens and fills with unexpected arrows and numbers and lists as I try to say this connects to that to this. Soon I am lost. The computer beckons, but I resist its organizational charms. I cannot find the ideas when I have to concentrate on the keys, hunting for single letters when I am thinking in complete thoughts. I return to my notebook and realize that its structure is inadequate for the shaping of my thoughts—the regularity of the lines patterns in predictable ways, yet my mind wanders another, more dimensional path. This dilemma has been with me for years, and, with deference to my childhood, I have taken up a method of research and composition akin to pin the tail on the donkey. I tear apart my notebook and begin to notate on small scraps of paper, soon taped together along the wall beside me. White, yellow, and brown papers help me to distinguish between ideas. Lists become constellations, numbers neighboring galaxies. Soon layers appear, and string is added to facilitate connection. It is a thing of beauty.

But beauty is not my objective, and I move to the computer to try and bring order to my precious model of words and string. The cursor blinks patiently at first, but I detect a hidden urgency in its intermittent posture. At times I believe it is watching me, daring me to enter its dark field to trace an alphabet of stars that will illuminate distant readers. But my words resist the uniformity of the typewritten lines as well, and soon the string is back, taped from screen to wall, a tiny tightrope my thoughts navigate freely and without fear. I traverse the potential intersections at a fiendish pace, editing with Scotch tape and mind alike, order growing among the apparent chaos. I note its likeness to a model of entropy moving toward a condition of rest.

While few would argue that this method of composition is appropriate for all writers, I would like to suggest that, as an idea, it offers a valuable model for design research occurring during the latter stage of the design process. At this juncture, the literal search for information has concluded and the race to shape the mass of data into some semblance of a coherent argument begins. Upon reflection, the student/designer may raise the question, What does it take to define and defend an idea? Certainly, the answer is variable and dependent upon the specifics of the design problem. But a general strategy of problem assessment, definition, and argument can be facilitated by a spatial approach to research that is rooted in a metaphor of travel, dwelling, and interaction.

In one sense, research (or a quest for knowledge) begins at the level of experience, the given, or data, of any problem. The Latin *experientia* speaks of a voyage across knowledge or a venturing out to the boundaries. Its Greek counterpart connotes a similar venture to the outer bounds but also implies a return home. Homer's *Odyssey* offers an appropriate metaphor for this spatial conceptualization of research as a search for knowledge that marks both profound and articulate connections between concepts traversing edge and center.

To extend this philosophical thread, we can examine Aristotle's classification of knowledge into three general categories—*theoria, praxis,* and *poeisis*—as a way of linking visual and verbal spatial research strategies. *Theoria* is defined as an abstract or cognitive knowing, while *praxis* is a practical knowledge that comes from doing, from activity or the development of a manual skill. *Poeisis,* on the other hand, is defined as knowledge that is involved in making, producing, or creating something. With *poeisis,* research is the creative act.

With this said, what, then, are the implications of Aristotle's *poeisis* to the model of design research that I am proposing? If we are to conceive of research as moving beyond a method of collection into the realm of connection and creative endeavor, then the act of designing becomes primarily an act of research—of travel defined as exploration and transforming encounter. Knowledge gained, manifest in terms of the clarity of the communication, is directly attributable to the process of making—a process involving all three of Aristotle's delineations.

Further, such a concept of design as research, and research as travel, evokes an architecture of joinery and kinetics situating sites of encounter within an evolving information structure. These sites, conceived as places of collection and juxtaposition, assist both problem assessment and problem definition, two integral aspects of the design process. Through this model, students are led to ask, How do concepts negotiate themselves in external relationships, how is one concept a site of travel for another? Instead of focusing on ideas as separate and integral, an approach to design that functions at the component/product level, this spatial conceptualization of research provides a structure for problem solving at the systems/community level. Research is transformed from a simple connect-the-dot activity to a strategy of multilinear systems analysis.

While many students understand that research can be categorized by intent—historical, analytical, descriptive, or experimental[1]—few conceive of research as anything beyond mere data collection. Despite the rhetoric of the so-called MTV generation, it is the rare student that actively thinks laterally or is able to make connections between what they are learning in the classroom and what they are experiencing outside of it. As a result, the concept of design as the sum total of the varied experiences (cultural, political, technological) they confront each day must be brought into their design process. Alternative methodologies that link visual and verbal research strategies in the act of making work can facilitate these connections. Such methodologies look at the relationship between multiple experiences and points of view as well as propose critical perspectives that encourage the designer to spatially conceptualize both historical and cultural contexts in ways that allow for the development of effective communication strategies. The idea of a "wanderground" between here and there marked by an insistence on multiple, external connections further allows for the inclusion of a discussion of the cultural, technological, and visual contexts in which the research is occurring. Numerous concepts provide sites for the departures, arrivals, and transits that take place during any research program—identifying their value at the systems level is critical to an understanding of the design process as a mechanism for organizing essential experiences.

Yet, an emphasis on design process can produce a challenging dilemma: travel to the edge of anything and the path becomes much more seductive than the noted destination. The process adapts itself to the pleasures of the path—to the pureness of discovery—and the process of journey extends into oblivion. A delineation of the boundaries of the design question at hand is both necessary and critical for establishing, and maintaining, focus. Assessment and problem definition involve identifying a set of parameters within which the work will be made and evaluated. Once these parameters have been defined, the important question then becomes, What does it mean to be articulate within those parameters? Articulation requires strategy—clarity is no simple task.

What, then, are strategies for making work that explores process as an extension of experience? First, two questions must be posed: Is the work of value? and To whom? Establishing the significance of the work will help to situate communication objectives within meaningful contexts. Second, consume in a radical way. Read, see, and experience everything through the lens of the design question at hand. When design is reconsidered as a negotiation and exchange of experiences, the process of making work becomes a notation on connections across, among, and between. Third, come to an understanding of what compels and what persists. Treat the work like a memory that cannot be shaken. Uncover the ache of the question and soothe it by giving it form. Begin with the smallest piece of the equation and allow it to grow unencumbered by the weight of the whole. Take small steps, fumble if necessary, but return and try again. Persist. Compel. Consume.

Last, nurture an appreciation of the mundane. Forego singular visions of the sublime—at least in the beginning. Sometimes it is simply the making that is the required strategy—momentum must begin somewhere. Make and measure, and do not be surprised if the poetic emerges from deep within the bowels of the ordinary.

Design as research. Research as travel. Travel as experience. Experience as design and a return to the beginning where words and string continue their movement toward a condition of rest.

NOTES

1. Meredith Davis, "What's So Important about Research?" *Statements,* American Center for Design (ACD), vol. 6, no. 1 (fall 1990). Davis, in a recent ACD article, argues for four distinct kinds of research:

- *Historical research*, which seeks to reveal meaning in events of the past. Historical researchers interpret the significance of time and place in ways that inform contemporary decision making or put current practices into perspective.
- *Descriptive research* observes and describes phenomena.
- *Analytical research* generates quantitative data that requires statistical assistance to extract meaning. Analytical research requires testing and estimation and is particularly concerned with relationships and correlations in an attempt to predict outcomes.
- *Experimental research* attempts to account for the influence of a factor in a given situation. Experimental research defines relationships of cause and effect by changing the factor to be studied in a controlled situation.

The Problem with Problem Solving

Julie Lasky

I know a designer whose working habits were shaped by years at a daily newspaper. "I can't get out of the habit of just solving the problem and moving on to the next thing," she once confided. Though she has weeks, not hours, to do layouts now, she is panicked by the thought of lingering experimentally over her designs. To her, "solving the problem" means arranging words and images so that they are reasonably visible, reasonably legible. She doesn't feel she has the luxury to dally with process. She doesn't take delight in running the obstacle course of size, budgetary, or time constraints. She doesn't think of decision making as a smorgasbord of possibilities, each imparting its own subtle flavor. Instead, she reaches for a layout scheme the way one reaches for the first container at hand to collect water from a leaky roof: a stainless-steel bowl, a mixing bowl, a pitcher, the aquarium tank you put away after the tropical fish died—no, not the Ming vase; that's inappropriate. Any of the others can do the job, though. The problem's solved, move on.

I think of this woman whenever I encounter those well-worn graphic design metaphors "problem" and "solution." They're legacies of the days when designers needed to persuade clients that their work was scientific and required special skill. This analytical language has been useful for design educators too; classroom problems are intellectual training wheels before students tackle problems in the real world. Out there, the goal-directed arrow of problem/solution suggests that design produces results. From the client's point of view, results are what really matter. Clients aren't much interested in the road between problem and solution. But are designers also running the danger of losing sight of process? Do the ideas of problem and solution help the end overshadow the means?

When I first encountered the term "problem" applied to graphic design, I was a staff editor for a publisher of professional books. My background had been in English literature and academic publishing. I circled the word and stuck a gummed flag to the manuscript with a question mark, just in case the author had made a mistake.

It was jarring because "problem" carries two associations, and neither seemed to fit. The first is a puzzle. There may be different means of getting to the solution, but ultimately every square must be filled in with the right letter, every jigsaw piece locked into the right place, or a physical law or formula must be derived correctly. Only one right solution. Hardly an appropriate metaphor for design.

Second is "problem" in the sense of problem child—something troublesome. It's the leaky faucet keeping us awake at night. If we can solve the problem, we can put the world back in order, and it hardly matters whether we replace the washer on the faucet or wrap a rubber band around the spigot and tap, so long as the infernal thing stops dripping. There is a goal here. It is very simple and clear. Stop that obnoxious sound. I don't care how you do it, just do it. Designers care very much how they solve problems, however, and they're not often troubled by the conditions that gave rise to them.

Here's the funny thing. Problem solving is basically what any person with a social security number does, from a waiter figuring out how to balance a dozen trays on his arm, to a biologist trying to understand why a cancer cell divides uncontrollably. Yet designers are alone in claiming it as a job description. Isn't the surgeon in the operating theater solving a problem? Of course she is, but the problematic nature of her profession is taken for granted, and it seems foolish to mention it. Years ago, a friend announced that she planned to enroll in law school because she "liked solving problems." "You could always hang wallpaper," I offered. "We've got a problem, Houston," means that something is wrong, not that a cosmonaut has punched the time clock.

Designers need not insist so much on the intellectual rigor of their work. Design is analytical. It doesn't have laws, exactly, but a lot of rules and limitations narrowing the creative pyramid from infinite possible ways of completing an assignment to, say, only a few hundred thousand. Problem: Design, on a budget of $18,000, a brochure that will be distributed to 30,000 tree surgeons at a convention. Solution: Could you predict one in your wildest dreams? Winnowing down the possibilities through the sifters of finance, audience, materials, suppliers' capabilities, time, appropriateness, and personal taste, one arrives at something that is probably not printed on virgin paper. But who knows? Maybe it is. In the meantime, the effective designer has put a great deal of thought into the matter.

My problem with the publication designer's use of the word "problem" is that she doesn't have a problem. There is no negative situation that requires redressing through any possible means. Careful trial and deliberation may be called for, but a layout isn't a puzzle. The "problem" is filling up the page with words and images that elucidate the content and complement one another and inspire readers to continue reading. Now tell me, when will we know that those conditions have been met? Define, if you will, "elucidate," "complement," and "inspire." Or for that matter, define "words," "images," and "read"? Does skimming count?

I am not a total relativist. I agree that it is possible to say when pages are well designed and when they are not. It is even possible to reach a consensus. But to cast this elusive scheme, with its many opportunities and outcomes, into the language of problem/solution is to risk defining the problem too broadly or narrowly and solving it too hastily. When one is facing a problem, constraints are roadblocks that must be knocked down, rather than a kind of gentle pressure fostering creativity. One is, almost by definition, in a negative state that needs solving, though it might be better to think of it as an indeterminate state that needs resolving. It's fine to be goal oriented in our description of what designers do, but there are so many goals. Can't we also say, "exercise taste," "flaunt imagination," "organize data," "leave a mark," "take a stand," "raise curiosity," "heighten senses"?

Does anyone see a problem in that?

Ricochet Critique: Improvisation in Design Teaching

Roy R. Behrens

In the late 1970s, while teaching at a large urban university in the Midwest, I invented the following teaching device, called the "ricochet critique."

A graphic design problem is presented, and the work is completed outside of class during a period of a week or ten days. On critique day, the solutions, unsigned and hidden by cover sheets, are stacked on a table and then randomly unveiled for viewing. During the critique, each student, in turn, is required to choose any single solution, with the exception of his or her own, and to talk about it in detail, extemporaneously, pretending that he or she created it.

"These are the steps that I went through in solving this problem," the student hypothesizes, "and these are the reasons I did what I did." Or, "I am largely pleased with this solution, but there are certain aspects, as I want to explain, that remain unresolved." As the critique progresses, other members of the class are encouraged to make observations or ask questions, including the work's actual creator, providing that he or she doesn't reveal who made the work.

The ricochet critique was a fascinating gamelike teaching method—the results were inevitably surprising—but it was exhausting for everyone involved, and to critique a problem was almost as challenging as to solve one. Throughout these sessions, nothing was said directly; everything was an indirect ricochet. As a result, the students spoke more freely about the work of their peers, were less offended by open criticism, and were forced to concentrate not on their animosity toward the person next to them, but on tangible qualities of the work itself: How effective is the solution? What are its most conspicuous strengths and weaknesses? At the same time, through improvisational role-playing, they had to empathize with another (albeit anonymous) person, and to reconstruct what had gone on in the mind of the student designer whose work they had arbitrarily chosen.

Prior to inventing this method, as an artist, graphic designer, and writer, I had found that solutions to problems arise, with reliable frequency, not only by grappling with problems directly, but by working indirectly, by delaying closure and purposely browsing or fooling around on the fringes of an idea. I was often reminded of my childhood experience of looking up at the night sky and discovering that faint stars appear more distinct when, paradoxically, I looked to the side of them, rather than staring straight on.

As a teacher, I had also concluded that the content one intends to teach and what students actually learn are often, perhaps inevitably, two different things. Looking back on my own education, I remembered least the factual information that was presented sternly by unimaginative teachers. What stood out instead were moments of self-discovery, inside and outside the classroom, unresolved questions, and a sequence of odd and amusing mistakes or pedagogical bloopers. If education, as someone said, is what remains after you have forgotten what you were taught, what stayed in my mind was the opposite of the stuff of textbooks. And in the end, I decided to invent problems in design to which I truly didn't know the answers; to conduct class in an animated, comic, and often erratic style; and to devise methods of class discussion—like the ricochet critique—that were as provocative, unpredictable, and puzzling as were the original problems themselves.

I thought about all this a few years ago when I ran across an unattributed aphorism about teaching: "The key to teaching is to appear to have known all your life what you learned this afternoon." How wrong, I thought. It should be the exact opposite: "The key to teaching is to appear to have learned this afternoon what you have known all your life."

When students in his life-drawing class became complacent, the Austrian painter Oskar Kokoschka would arrange for the model to suddenly "die" in front of them. William James delivered his Harvard lectures dressed in multicolored ties, red-and-black checkered trousers, and riding boots; he laughed so frequently and was so full of antics in the classroom that his students pleaded, "Please, Doctor, to be serious for a moment." When the naturalist Louis Agassiz lectured to teachers—ostensibly about grasshoppers but really about teaching—he insisted that each of them hold in their hands throughout his lecture a live squirming grasshopper. "Habitualization devours works, clothes, furniture, one's wife, and the fear of war," said Victor Shklovsky, and art exists—and isn't it also a reason we teach?—so that "one may recover the sensation of life; it exists to make one feel things, to make the stone *stony*."

Twenty years ago, I owned nearly a hundred neckties. One semester I offered a modest award to the design student who was first to notice when I wore the same tie twice in a single course. This was complicated, as it meant that I often switched ties as I walked from one class to the next, and I constantly had to make note of the ties that I wore from day to day, from class to class. Some of them were highly similar (six similar but different camouflage patterns, for example), which led to the need for alternative ties in my briefcase, to prove that I wasn't repeating one.

When students resorted to sketching my ties instead of concentrating on my lectures, I was reminded of Søren Kierkegaard's "The Rotation Method," in which he describes his experience as a college student in a course that was taught by a terrible bore. Kierkegaard was determined to drop the course when he suddenly noticed that the man perspired profusely when agitated. Perspiration would form on his forehead as he lectured, stream down to his brow, and collect as a drop at the tip of his nose. Kierkegaard became fascinated. The man's perspiration, instead of his endlessly boring harangue, became the object of Kierkegaard's attention. Instead of leaving the course, he began to invent more provocative questions to ask the teacher, to see if he could cause the sweat to flow more rapidly.

In a demonstration of innate form responses, I once brought a large live chicken into the classroom and attempted to get it to freeze at the sight of a stuffed owl. I prepared artichokes for my students to demonstrate how to eat one and to show them the beautiful pattern that's found on the top of an artichoke heart (based on the Fibonnaci number series, like that of sunflowers and pinecones). I invited a biologist to come to our class to talk about the mating behavior of roadrunners. And, as an excursion into clothing design, I persuaded my students that I had a pet monkey, listed its measurements, and asked that they create a miniature vest (displayed on a stylistically appropriate coat hanger) that epitomized a certain period of design history.

Improvisational teaching has never been easy because it requires resourcefulness, quickness, and wit on the part of the teacher. It is even more difficult now because colleges and universities throughout the country are being dismantled and quickly transformed into compliant, unimaginative trade schools. Job training and cosmetic accountability have become as sacred as collegiate football, and it is unthinkable, even subversive, that a teacher would "fool around" in the classroom with taxpayers' money. Nevertheless, for those who have witnessed the richness it brings to the ambiance of the classroom and to problem solving, the virtues of improvisation are undeniable. And among its chief virtues are the humor and freshness that ricochet from the students themselves.

In the 1970s, I dressed almost daily in a corduroy sports jacket with elbow patches, which back then was the virtual uniform for a rookie college professor. My students found this amusing, and one day when I arrived at typography class, they were already seated and staring at me. I became suspicious. They looked different, in part because somehow they all looked the same. A moment later, the answer became apparent: They were all wearing identical typographic T-shirts, each bearing the same printed message, impeccably lettered and perfectly spaced—it read, CORPS DE ROY.

Memory, Instinct, and Design:
Beyond Paul Rand's "Play Principle"

Michael Golec

He wonders also about himself—that he cannot learn to forget, but hangs on the past: however far or fast he runs, that chain runs with him. It is a matter for wonder: the moment that is here and gone, that was nothing before and nothing after, returns like a specter to trouble the quiet of a later moment.

—Friedrich Nietzsche (1873)

So, we are haunted. Nietzsche's "specter" delivers the "chain" of memory to an unsuspecting subject. The reception of a variety of experiences and images, real and/or imagined, remains always and forever with that person. We do not forget. We cannot put aside, overcome, or disregard anything, especially that which is conveyed to us through experience and education. As Nietzsche proposes, it is not possible to completely deny our past. Yet, there are those of us who wish this were possible; they desire a loss of memory so that they may return to some primal state, so that they might act on instinct alone. Granted, the world in Nietzsche's day was no more civilized than today, but somehow, in our current postindustrial/information society, we too feel that instinct escapes our grasp. We cannot fail to remember our civilized selves.

The question is, Do we possess any less instinct than our forbearers? And if so, How is it that we have lost our capacity for free activity? Can it be that the accumulation of experience and information pushes instinct aside? Indeed, Nietzsche goes on to write that learning banishes the free spirit and annihilates instinct. But still, we dream of a state where, unencumbered by trained responses and conditioning, we engage the world directly like a child or an animal. We know that to do so would entail a willful loss of memory.

Nietzsche suggests that to forget is to return to a time before learning. Forgetting is to revive the child or the purely instinctual animal who is not bound to repeat all that is learned. Yet, Nietzsche states that we "cannot learn to forget. . . ." Is forgetting then impossible? Coincidentally, it is Nietzsche who forgets, as the French philosopher Jacques Derrida notes in his exegesis of Nietzsche's writing. Derrida quotes a fragment from Nietzsche's *Joyful Wisdom*. The German philosopher writes, "I have forgotten my umbrella." By his own inscription, Nietzsche remembers that he forgets. There is a momentary lapse of memory, but it is not absolute—erasure, for Nietzsche, and for us, is never complete. This is the acute paradox of Nietzsche's specter. If we cannot learn to forget, and that which is not learned is instinctual, then forgetting must be instinctual. And memory, a capacity we are born with, works in much the same way. By Nietzsche's logic, recollection must be instinctual because if it is not taught, thus it must be innate. Essential to this essay is, however, a reading of Nietzsche's assertion as a remembrance of a past before learning, before the annihilation of instinct. My intention is to reveal that most important specter—instinct—which cannot take solid form, yet is ever ready to remind us that we can remember to forget. This activity, furthermore, is necessary to learning.

So, what of learning? Particularly, and this is straight to the point, what of design and learning? As expected, the graphic designer is not exempt from Nietzsche's spectral phenomenon, from momentary loss and subsequent reclamation. On the contrary, he or she engages the ghostly visage that is memory, and, most importantly, the designer uses Nietzsche's spook to a single purpose, that is, in the process of designing.

Learning to design is, on a fundamental level, a matter of trial and error. To discover what works best, the designer arranges his or her materials until the appropriate solution is found. But from what place does a designer draw material? Of course, the exterior world. The things a designer sees excite and inspire. The world is overstuffed with stuff, and designers are contracted to venture out and make sense of the proliferation of images and ideas. What prepares a designer for such a task, for organizing a number of communicative morsels that ideally impact a targeted audience? A number of factors come to mind: life experience, university or college education, vocational training, apprentice-ship, art and design history, and instinct. What most consider to be second nature—the apprehension of an object, or an idea, sans reason—is Nietzsche's spectral manifestation of deposited history. That is to say, what was once dormant rises like Nikolai Gogol's ghost of Akakii Akakievich, to startle and inform the designer. It is a memory (inscribed upon the subject through education, experience, and conditioning) that surfaces in direct relation to a project, or problem, at hand. Nonetheless, if we continue to adhere to Nietzsche's spectral manifestations, then, as the designer continues to hone his or her craft, instinct vanishes. But not completely. As we will see, instinct reasserts itself, much like a playful ghost might appear, to contribute to the designer's education and practice.

There remains, within the field of graphic design, an expectation on the part of clients and designers toward innovation. It is thought that a designer—forgetting the rules, forgetting history—forges ahead and creates new forms that, in turn, contribute to the designer's growth within his or her field. Yet, how can unique solutions to design problems exist if the designer is simply the product of a design education? If, as Nietzsche proposes, one cannot forget, then how is it possible to ditch the rules that govern good design? It seems essential to the cultivation of a design practice that experimentation must continue so that yet another experience is added to the designer's arsenal of maneuvers.

At best, the idea of innovation assumes an overturning, or questioning, of what was learned. But prior to this anticipated usurpation, a designer is given a project, the details of which are spelled out in a brief. When given an assignment, a designer is sup-plied a set of rules that are intended to govern a coherent outcome. For example, in the summer of 1990, I was one of twenty students who traveled to Brissago, Switzerland, in order to embark upon a five-week program to study design with Armin Hofmann and Paul Rand. It was the first week of class and Rand assigned his Léger project. After a brief slide introduction, which focused on the French artist's production (a vividly colorful, tubular, transparent style), the students were instructed to develop a series of typographic images (the word "Léger" was used) that evoked the economy of the painter's oeuvre. Simple. I had at my disposal the name Léger and a rudimentary understanding of the painter's work, plus Rand's outline. This is what I knew. These were the rules. Yet, how was I to impress, surprise, and delight my instructor? Was I to forget all that I knew of the design process?

Now, according to Rand, in order to innovate—to construct a thing that is unique—the designer must enact a scene of play. Apparently, this activity allows a designer to freely explore a myriad of possibilities. Nevertheless, every game has its rules, and, as the saying goes, the rules are made to be broken. Play creates boundaries, which, in turn, are breached—this is innovation. In other words, the given structure of a project, which is dictated by previous design successes as determined by an instructor (or client), is challenged and invigorated by a designer's instinctual maneuvers. Rand writes in "Design and the Play Instinct," "a problem with defined limits, with an implied or stated discipline (system of rules) that in turn is conducive to the instinct of play, will most likely yield an interested student and, very often, a meaningful and novel solution." The scene of play, or what Rand calls the "play principle," is a discourse between the objects (typography, illustration, and photography) at hand and their multiple relations. The rules are important, and, as Rand asserts, without them "there is no motivation, test of skill, or ultimate reward—in short, no game." Rand continues his formulations in "Intuition and Ideas":

> Without regard to available systems . . . the designer works intuitively. . . . Very often a system is used merely as a crutch . . . regardless of need. . . . A system can be applied either intuitively or intentionally, interestingly or tediously. There is always the element of choice, sometimes called good judgment, at others good taste.

Rand makes clear that instinct is outside the system, that it is not part of, but is in certain circumstances drawn to, the system. By understanding this, we comprehend yet another aspect of Rand's game. He implies that rules are broken, that boundaries are tested and crossed, by his desire for a design student to achieve a "novel solution." The rules, in and of themselves, are not sufficient. There must be an added element. Play, then, is a means to forget the rules if only for a moment, to return to instinct. The designer then remembers this moment of forgetting, this breaking of the rules, and applies this memory to the project at hand. Whether the playful moment leads to a good or a bad design is not important; on the contrary, what is essential is that the designer retains this moment, which is stored for use. Therefore, we can conclude that play always leads to learning, and can be considered, as Rand believes, an implement for design education. While the "game" functions as a tool for learning, it also serves to suggest alternatives to the rules; it "is an equally effective means for exploring the use of unorthodox materials. . . ." Ultimately, the play principle should result in the rupture of the given structure, while retaining the instructor's (or client's) primary goals.

Rand's serious play as problem solving is, as most design students will agree, an established mode of education. As such, Rand's play principle establishes any number of specters that will surely, and by his own educational purpose, intentionally "trouble the quiet of a later moment." What may very well be an instinctual questioning of a project's structure is retained as memory and thus ceases to be instinctual. If indeed there can be an instinctual maneuver, it is but a flicker that is apprehended by the designer and stowed away for subsequent appearances. The play principle constructs a scene of remembrance of forgetting.

To further elucidate Rand's play principle, I will introduce yet another figure. When playing, as the psychoanalyst Sigmund Freud asserts, the subject is removed from the everyday—he or she forgets daily concerns, restrictions, rationalizations, etc. The subject acts instinctually. Now, when the designer plays, he or she also forgets—forgets the rules of the game. Again, if play leads to an exciting and new solution to the problem at hand, the designer learns from the game. To be even more specific, I might add, Rand's instructional theory is a tool for learning, it is not, as Rand proposes, learned. The play principle delivers what cannot be forgotten, what is relegated to some buried place—memory. But first it draws an intuitive response, that which is outside of, or beyond, the play principle. The action beyond learning is actually before learning. Furthermore, if instinct is likened to a child's response, then what is beyond the play principle is actually before Rand's scene of play. Returning to the time before learning allows the designer to continue learning, thus the play principle is not a model for memory per se, rather it accesses the very root of creation, which soon becomes just that which cannot be forgotten. This is precisely why play is a tool for learning, or, in other words, play is situated toward learning.

Again, participation in Rand's designer's game promotes unique solutions that challenge the original restrictions of a project. It is not too surprising to find that Rand is not alone in his idea. By attempting to explicate artistic genius, Freud suggests that play, fantasies, and daydreaming account for creativity. As Freud explains in "Creative Writers and Daydreaming," play is unreal and is unconnected to the concerns of the everyday. Therefore, play is not bound by social or historical constrictions or preconceptions. As one grows older, however, one ceases to play, hence play is exchanged for daydreams and fantasies. Moreover, Freud believes that daydreams and fantasies bear the trace of an originary moment. Freud writes that a subject who daydreams regains "what he possessed in his happy childhood." But the subject's gain, as Freud states, is predicated on a wish, which "makes use of an occasion in the present to construct, on a pattern of the past, a picture of the future." Taking a cue from Freud's essay, and addressing Rand's play principle, I propose that a designer's innovation (future) is predicated on the interplay of pre-memory (instinct), memory (past), and the rules of the assignment (present). In other words, Freud's notion of the conjured past influences the present, which, in turn, determines the future. For Freud, creation is a continuation of child play, not the child playing, which overcomes the barriers that inevitably constrict creative solutions. But pre-memory is most important to this essay's assertions, for it is here that I locate, as does Freud and Nietzsche, instinctual activity. The experience of instinctual moments, however, is soon relegated to memory. And it is the conjured past—the return of the dormant child, or animal—that is the specter. In the end, instinct always succumbs to memory, and the childlike act is learned and cannot be forgotten. As this specter is present during the problem-solving process (Rand's game), it ruptures the stasis of the assignment. This is how a designer overcomes the inevitable constriction of the instructor's (or the client's) brief. It is the specter, the memory of the game, that allows the designer to push elements around, to determine compositional quality, to become aware of the boundaries. That sudden spark that sets him or her to push things around, like the attention-starved spook who flings the family heirlooms and furniture, the unforgotten often provokes spectacular rearrangements. Confronted by the specter of design education, the designer is compelled to act, to question, and to achieve fresh forms.

During the summer of 1990, I had the opportunity to see one of these ghosts. Keenly aware of the blank white sheet that lay before me—it literally reflected the void that was my mind—I was struggling with Rand's Léger project. I just didn't know where to start. Yes, of course, one begins with pencil and paper. One sketches. At least that is what I had been taught. Ideas are generated in this manner. The freedom of drawing, the mind unencumbered by preconceptions, and the ability to discern that which is useful all add up to the scene that Rand refers to as the play principle. I should have been playing. Instead, I was "angsting." I had no idea.

Then Rand came to my little table (the class convened in a primary school lunchroom). He sat down beside me and surveyed my desert. Picking up a stray pencil and pulling at a pad, Rand set to play. After a moment, he rose and moved on to the next little table, and I was left with a charming sketch of a ghost with "LE" hovering just to the left of Rand's apparition—*le spectre,* or the specter.

Some Things Change . . .

Chris Pullman

In the past decade, we have witnessed a series of amazing changes in the way we think about the profession of graphic design. Here is my short list.

2-D → 4-D

Once graphic design meant flat, static, two-dimensional.

Now it encompasses multiple, hybrid media. It is not just visual, but involves a variety of the senses, more like life itself, which plays out in a four-dimensional world.

object → experience

Once what you were making was an object.

Now it is more often an experience.

composition → choreography

Once the designer's art was composition.

Now it is choreography. In a fluid, four-dimensional world, the problem is not so much to get the fixed thing right as to find an elegant sequence of evolving relationships. This involves understanding how the conventions of typography and the dynamics between words and images change with the introduction of time, motion, and sound.

fixed → fluid

Once you made it stay put. Great care was taken to get everything in just the right spot, just the right relationship.

Now, increasingly, the output is a variable, not a constant. Think of the way your Web decisions look on somebody else's screen. The new problem is to design the *rules* for the relationship of things, not a single predictable outcome.

craft based → technology based

Once the profession was genetically linked to the ancient crafts of hand typesetting, bookbinding, drawing, and cutting.

Now it no longer is so physical, mediated by technology that can make it feel almost virtual. The basic tools are suddenly so different that, as McLuhan predicted, the things we can make, or even dream up, will be different.

cheap → expensive

Once for a few hundred dollars and some dumb tools you could open up a shop.

Now the cost of entry is much higher and the overhead never stops.

isolated, solo → collaborative, team

Once you could do just about everything yourself. Paul Rand ran a one-and-a-half-person shop for most of his professional life.

Now the paradox is that while the personal computer and plunging software costs have revitalized the tradition of the one-man band (a publishing house or a postproduction studio on your desktop), the trend is toward collaborative, multidisciplinary teams of people pushing toward a common goal. It's not just *your* opinion anymore. Collaborating calls for a different set of genes, a different kind of ego, a tolerance for complexity and consensus.

one voice → many voices

Once it was possible to assume that there was one language (yours), one culture, one set of meanings.

Now "mass communications," which were based on that notion, have given way to targeted communications; broadcast shifts to narrowcast; one-to-many becomes many-to-one. And the visual and verbal language of the end user is almost certainly different from your own.

piecework → strategic thinking

Once most of us did piecework, making a new thing to fit within a small universe of other things.

Now, while piecework won't disappear, the new focus is on strategy: design as strategic planning, design as a business resource. This implies a different level of thinking and participation, even a different vocabulary.

naive → self-aware

Once design didn't have much conscious history. You just did it.

Now we *have* a history and people are actually *writing* about it. Ironically, few young people know anything about it.

neutral → personal

Once the designer's role was thought to be a neutral mediator between the message and the recipient. This was the modernist way: to stay *out* of the way, to be clear, to be unobtrusive, to facilitate.

Now there is a tolerance, even an appetite for interpretation. Theoreticians point out that since it is next to impossible to *not* bring your baggage to the transaction, one might as well recognize or even celebrate one's intrusion on the message.

These shifts have vastly expanded the expressive options for visual communications and fundamentally altered the way graphic designers practice. But while much has changed, many of the essential qualities of being a designer have stayed the same.

For example:

Design is different from art

I have always felt that being a designer and being an artist are quite distinct activities, attracting people with different goals and preferences. Where a person ends up on this continuum is more a matter of chromosomes than anything else. Someone who becomes a successful painter or sculptor or performance artist is likely to be a person who derives their energy and intellectual satisfaction from solving problems that come from inside *themselves*. In contrast, someone who ends up as a successful designer is probably a person whose energy and intellectual satisfaction comes from solving someone *else's* problems. Each of us inevitably brings to the task of designing a unique load of experience and bias, which can and should express itself in our work. But the current attention paid to the importance of "authorship" in design shouldn't mask the underlying distinction between personal expression and the puzzle of figuring out a problem posed by others.

Design is content independent

One of the great satisfactions of being a designer is that the core skills of problem solving and storytelling are not linked to any one range of content. What are you interested in? How wide and deep is your life experience? The thing most likely to constrict one's range of content options within the profession is a limited personal repertoire of formal or stylistic expression.

Design isn't necessarily a pro-social profession

In the early days of the modernist movement, design was seen as an agent of positive social change. But then, as now, the seeming pro-social acts of facilitating communication, providing access to ideas, and promoting understanding don't necessarily assure a positive outcome. It depends on what the message is. Throughout one's professional life, the key decision is: *Which* problems will you use your skill to help solve?

Graphic design has its roots in language

Graphic design is unique among all design disciplines because of its deep roots in language. Graphic communications rely on the interaction of words and images to convey a message that is almost always dependent on language and its cultural context. As a consequence, the heart of our practice is typography, a set of conventions that allow us to represent, however crudely, the rich inflections and rhythms of spoken language.

The visual power of design derives from the idea of contrast

If you ask why something works and you push back far enough, eventually everything seems to be based on contrast: the ability to distinguish one thing from another. Composition, sequencing, even legibility all rely on devices that affect the contrast between things. Contrast seems to control many of the phenomenon essential to visual communication: grouping things into families, creating theme and variation, establishing hierarchies, and providing interest.

Nothing happens out of context

Few things we make have no precedent. It is important to understand how one thing fits into the larger family of things to which it belongs. You can't enjoy the variation if you don't know the theme.

The goal of design education is resourcefulness

A good education is one that gives you the resourcefulness to solve the problem you haven't anticipated. It should provide experiences that give you the ability to express yourself in a variety of media. And with the inevitability of change in both the tools and the scope of design, it should probably keep focusing back on the fundamental mechanisms that control what makes an experience authentic, accessible, and understandable.

Computers Don't Speak, Type Does

Michael Worthington

In his 1974 book, *Compendium for Liter-ates,*[1] Karl Gerstner recorded the possible variations of how words may exist in the printed medium. His approach was clinical, his observations were ordered logically and delivered scientifically. Gerstner's writing made me wonder how these rules, or set of possibilities, for printed typography would be different for the screen and for motion-based typography—how they might be explored and exploded, surpassed or confirmed, and how teaching screen-based typography differs from teaching traditional print-oriented typography. Most graphic designers understand how printed type conveys its message to an audience, what its form signifies, but few understand how that differs in the environment of the screen. In the screen-based world of typography, what was stable in the print world becomes movable, alterable, and temporal. Some of Gerstner's possibilities for static typography seem irrelevant, restrictive, or untranslatable in this new world. If his rules have been made anachronistic by current technology, I found myself questioning whether the written word should still be such a major part of our communication process. Should there be a new system of communication for new media? Why use type at all when you will be able to have live video, computer animation, constant audio, icons, and digital imagery that merge into a mass of navigable online space—and maybe even thinking, talking computers?

The prospect that typography and the written word might evolve into something more—i.e., with motion and sound becoming an integral part of the alphabetic system—is extremely seductive; a new "alphabet" that combines its audio and visual representations. A "magical" form of communication. Consider how writing has evolved through various technological advances (carving in stone, painting on paper, mechanized printing, etc.). It has always been a magical tool: has always had the ability to reconstruct images, meaning, events, from an abstract platform across space and time, between best friends or total strangers. Even though the letterforms themselves—and their means of production and dissemination—have altered wildly, the magic of the written word as communication has remained. This alphabetic magic differs from the communicative magic of the image. Chris Crawford succinctly sums up the difference between pictorial and textual elements in reference to game design.[2] He defines depiction as "being intrinsically direct" (i.e., pictorial elements) and representation as "being intrinsically indirect," needing interpretation to reach the entity represented (i.e., text). Traditionally, depiction lends itself to visually dense or obscure problems (a picture paints a thousand words); information that might be gathered by reading page upon page of descriptive text can be conveyed instantly in a pictorial screen. The problem of depicting complex concepts—such as, for example, society, respect, or even new media—may be solvable by a series of images or icons, but they have nowhere near the specificity, or speed of understanding, that text has in conveying these constructs (a word paints a single picture). There are situations when type is the logical choice (for example, when you have a list of four hundred similar items from which to choose) because it functions in ways that other media cannot and at times when nontypographic media is more suitable (for example, in relation to speed of access, the two-hour movie versus the book that takes two days to read).

Language has poetic qualities—the ability to create different images within the minds of different readers—which may be impossible to represent visually. Crawford gives us the example of Bob Dylan's "Mr. Tambourine Man": "And take me disappearing through the smoke rings of my mind, down the foggy ruins of time, far past the frozen leaves, the haunted frightened trees, far past the twisted reach of crazy sorrow." Crawford writes, "Consider the futility of trying to communicate these phrases with depiction. What would 'the twisted reach of crazy sorrow' look like?" And to whom? The poetics of language can act as a gateway to a myriad of meanings (a word paints a thousand pictures), yet can be specific enough to feel personal to an individual (a word paints your very own picture).

The functionality and poetic possibilities of the alphabetic system mean that the written word will not disappear in the environment of new media—though when to use which means of representation should be a considered decision—the future won't be devoid of the written word and dominated by talking computers. Yet, type does speak. Typography's "voice" is apparent in the forms of the letters themselves. The variations allowed within the limits of legibility give room for some emotive form, some "reading" of the font itself: a secondary signifier (the primary signifier being the representation of a mental image conjured up by the sound of the word). This is apparent when watching children draw letters that enforce the word's primary signified by use of the secondary: making words look "short" or "tall," "thin" or "fat." Set in a certain typeface, the word can be more specific in its communication. A "dog," for example, can be a happy tail-wagging dog in Keedy Sans, a vicious dog in Crackhouse, a mongrel in Dead History, or a thoroughbred in Univers. Suddenly, the words have character; they are read visually as well as literally.

This reading of the expressive qualities of type spans beyond the choice of typeface. In print, we read the composition, the format, and the context before we even get to the content. We hear the tone of voice before we understand what it is saying. These elements come into play on the screen too, though in screen-based typography we are given ancillary information through the relationship the text has with time and motion. By virtue of its existence in a time-based medium, type has further expressive possibilities, further layers of signification. Words are given life, characters are given character: motion gives more information. The onscreen typographer is armed with additional communicative ammunition; but haven't time and motion always been present in print design? Well-designed print typography uses hierarchy and composition to create a rhythm that leads the eyes: headlines to pull you in, bodies of text to slow you down, pictures and type to skip over or return to. The difference is that on the screen both the reader's eyes and the media's surface (the screen) are in motion. Our preconceptions of reading can be challenged: left to right, top to bottom, no longer has to be the norm. Motion can become a tool of hierarchy. Like color, our eye is drawn to it, even when it is applied to a small area. Motion can be used as a structural device. Words can appear from any direction, prompting the reader through a text.

The screen introduces possibilities for a three-dimensional typographic environment, fully navigable and interactive. At present, creating these "hypertypographic" environments is time consuming, and often the end result seems to be hackneyed cinematic flying type. A structural rethinking of the way typographic information works, along the lines of Muriel Cooper's work at MIT,[3] is needed, but with the inclusion of typography's connotative aspects, rather than using typography only as a means to structure information.

Within the two-dimensional flat-screen space, depth is offered by the representation of three-dimensional worlds, but there is also another depth: the fourth dimension, time. Time can be used to create multiple layers of meaning (without adding formal confusion) through devices such as hidden text and multiple readings. Wordplay can be layered over time; critical or supportive subtexts can be hidden in one moment and apparent in the next; different voices can be housed around the same core content. An intrinsic part of onscreen typography is that the designer becomes more involved with the text (both editing and creating): perhaps this is because the text feels fluid and unfinished in the digital realm, hence it has less authority, is less threatening, and designers are more willing to become involved not only with the form of the words, but with the words themselves.

Because there are few models or standards for interactive work, it should still be viewed as a platform in flux. It provides an opportunity for form and content (typography and writing) to merge into something specific to the realm of the screen, a place where the collapse of the idea that a designer is merely an addition to the writing/meaning of others might seem natural.

Critical analysis of motion typography for computer screens is difficult because, even now, few people have seen a substantial body of interactive work. Every critique is a virgin critique—comments naive and uninformed—because comparisons are difficult to make, there is no scale to form a system of judgment, and there is little discourse beyond asking what program the work was made with. The increased capabilities of the Web have made it easier to view the work of others, but, unlike in the print world, there is no canon of work, no "good reference" section, no historical genres into which work can be categorized. In one respect, this is liberating; there are no limits to what can be done, no creative restrictions, no formal preconceptions of the end result. In other respects, it is less wonderful. Seeing what already exists is vitally important—to gain a perspective on the plethora of motion-based typography as a whole and try to make sense of it on a global rather than on a local scale, or even to rebel against and to reinvent it.

New media develops in an exponential manner. It builds on the previous at a furious rate. Each interactive creative experience is not just a lesson for the individual maker, but also a work that is assimilated into a broader understanding of screen-based digital work. Rather than a total loss of authorship, there is a sense of sharing. You have to make this stuff and put it out there—let it have a life of its own, be altered by others (particularly on the Net), be toyed with and abused. Like a typeface, it only really comes to life when it is used by someone or, rather, in this case, experienced by someone. There is a liberalism that is essential to this production, leaving both design and text open to alteration and multiple interpretation is intrinsic to new media: the idea of creating a "readable" experience rather than a scripted space. The thinking and conceptualizing of these new spaces is more appealing than constructing well-styled possibilities with the available tools. Until the discipline of onscreen design stabilizes, you can always wish for it to be easier, for the technology to be ahead of what is currently possible. However, advances in technology will not substantially alter the fundamental energy of a piece. How the graphic form communicates the idea—including notions of function, appropriateness, and style—is still paramount, though new media designers also have to work on developing the concepts of experience and interaction. At the moment, "the future of new media design is in the hands of game designers making worlds rather than graphic designers making interfaces."[4]

Karl Gerstner's *Compendium for Literates* provides an excellent catalog of typographic possibility for the time when it was written, but times, typography, and the nature of graphic design have changed since then. As new media moves away from mimicking print into its own unique territory, it becomes clear that the rules, metaphors, and processes of print cannot be imported wholesale into the interactive realm, nor can they be taught in the same way. Typography that exists for print and typography that exists for screen are different: after all, they are functioning in different contexts. That is not to say that all the typographic knowledge that has been acquired by graphic designers should be abandoned. The process is selective. Some information is relevant. Some is not. Typography in new media need not look like a book page, but ignoring all typographic convention is premature too. The fundamentals of expression and hierarchy, which often seem at odds with the medium, will be necessary until text and new media reach a stable point where new conventions will be born. Meanwhile, creators of new media will have to learn to write differently, to design differently, and to use the technology to expand typography's expressive voice. To stay ahead of commerce and avoid becoming redundant, design students must become versed in a more varied set of skills than previously required. To cope with this, design education must incorporate subjects traditionally seen as the property of other disciplines: the techniques of animation, timing, and sequencing for motion; the fundamentals of narrative structure; a creative attitude toward working with audio and video; and an openness to experimenting in order to design the future. These skills should not be tacked onto the end of conventional typographic training. They should be informed by and mixed with traditional knowledge at all levels of design education and thereby made an intrinsic part of typographic education.

NOTES

1. Karl Gerstner, *Compendium for Literates*, trans. D. Q. Stephenson (Cambridge: MIT Press, 1974). [*Kompendium für Alphabeten: Systematik der Schrift Arthur Niggli* (Teufen, 1972).]

2. Chris Crawford, *Representation versus Depiction: Interactive Entertainment Design*. Chris Crawford's writings can also be found at *www.erasmatazz.com/Library.html*

3. William Owen, "Design in the Age of Digital Reproduction," *Eye* 4, no. 14 (autumn 1994).

4. In conversation with Brett Wickens, a graphic designer and contributing editor for *Eye* magazine, Los Angeles, 1997.

Have Sign, Will Travel: Cultural Issues in Design Education

Ellen McMahon and Karen White

If you watched American television in the late afternoons in the early sixties, you might associate the first part of the above title with a man named Paladin. His calling card inscribed with the motto Have Gun, Will Travel expressed his position (armed) relative to his changing surroundings. This essay is about a project intended to disarm design students by making them more conscious of their assumptions and more aware of the instability of signs as they travel between maker and receiver. This project, called "Exchanges: Culture, Place, Identity, Memory," was designed to reveal how graphic design functions as a transmitter of cultural information, personal biases, and social values and to bring students face-to-face with the complex issues surrounding representation and interpretation.

"Exchanges" is a postcard exchange project that originally took place between our senior design classes at the University of Arizona and the University of Hawaii. Students researched their own histories and selected events that were significant in laying the groundwork for their sense of personal and/or group identities. They then collected (from memory, family interviews, and a variety of readings) verbal and visual material relating to those events. We encouraged them to work with a visual language based on metaphors, icons, symbols, indexes, and signs, and discouraged them from relying on direct literal narratives. The resulting materials were used to create postcards that were sent to exchange partners from the other class. The postcards were discussed with the entire class, and interpretations were mailed back to the designers of the cards. These were followed by e-mail responses and, in some cases, extended conversations between the exchange partners.

The exchanges covered a wide range of subjects from day-to-day concerns to the long-term ramifications of sociopolitical phenomenon, adopted identities, and cultural assimilations. Through extended conversations, students discussed the differences in their design educations, the pros and cons of computers, the relationship between style and meaning, the commodification of images, and sexual stereotyping. Through the family stories of their peers, they learned about forced immigration, political exile, internment camps, and the Holocaust.

Students compared modes of communication used in the cards, from literal descriptions that did not invite receiver participation, to messages that offered some information but left room for interpretation, to those that were too obscure to hold interest. The compelling content of many of the postcards stimulated an urgency to understand the message in full. Suddenly, many students found themselves firmly on the side of legibility in the ubiquitous form-versus-function debate. Others enjoyed the more open cards that triggered a variety of interpretations and speculation. When the designers of these cards responded by e-mail, it became obvious how the meanings of a particular sign shifted because of individual and cultural experience. The following interpretation illustrates this point:

> We first noted the symbols: a background of blue sky, some incense sticks, a wood frame, and a black-and-white photocopy of a bald figure. We noticed these symbols and the absence of any type, and concluded that this piece seems to be about the senses: the smells of incense, the peaceful freedom of an open sky, and the claustrophobic positioning of the figure. All I can think of is that this piece is about some sort of Buddhism. The incense, the bald Buddhist-like figure, and the sky create an image of what a Zen experience is like.
>
> There are some questions that I'd like answered. First of all, is our interpretation correct? Also, what is the figure and why is it crafted in such a manner? The numbers of the incense sticks vary. Is that in any way meaningful? We've noticed the intertwining of the sticks with the sky, but the numbers create some confusion. Finally, the wood frame: it cramps an otherwise open-feeling piece, and we are not sure why.
>
> This was an interesting postcard. It's good that it was not too straightforward because it forced us to look into it more deeply and really search for your story. I cannot wait for a response from you, complete with a story or an explanation about your card.

The eagerly awaited e-mail response from the designer read:

> I find your interpretation of my postcard quite interesting. I guess I should start by explaining to you the story behind my postcard. My mom is a traditional Chinese who believed in ancestral worship. My postcard is about my grandfather, who passed away when I was two. We had an altar at home where my mom put my grandfather's picture along with a plaque with ancestor's names, incense, flowers, and fruits. The figure in the card is my grandfather. I only showed the top part of his head because that is what I saw when I looked up at the altar as a child. The incense represents my grandfather in heaven. You commented that the frame cramps an otherwise open feeling. The frame is about the portrait of my grandfather as it serves as a way to save his memories. By putting a frame around the card, I am also trying to preserve the memories of my grandfather because it is like another portrait of my grandfather. I thought a lot about putting text on

the card, but I thought the "to:" was enough because it signifies my grandfather's journey from one world to the next. . . .

Two of the Japanese Americans from the class in Hawaii devoted their cards to very different aspects of their cultural pasts. One student raised in Hawaii focused on her Issei (first-generation) grandmother who was a picture bride from Okinawa. A map of the Pacific, a photograph of her grandmother in a traditional Japanese wedding gown, and a lock of her long black hair depicted the common practice of Hawaiian Japanese plantation workers arranging marriages with Japanese women through photographs.

Another Japanese-American Sansei (third-generation) student explored her mother's internment during World War II. On this postcard, the war is depicted through images of soldiers and the proclamation number that forced Americans of Japanese descent into internment camps. Through the visual juxtaposition of American icons and imprisonment, she expressed the personal and cultural tragedy of this historic moment. The following interpretation from the student in Arizona reveals his perspective.

> It appears you are someone of Japanese descent whose parents or grandparents spent some time in an American reeducation camp. It seems that innocent Japanese people were sent to these camps to get educated about American politics and so forth. Many of the Japanese people probably felt as though they were being locked up (which the chain link represents on the postcard). I felt that the use of black and white to represent the whole issue was very effective. Black and white can say many different things, and I believe that what you are saying with your piece is that Americans saw it one way and the Japanese being locked up saw it completely differently.
>
> I also noticed on the back of the card that there was no return address or anything. It just had the word "to" printed on it. I don't know if this was intentional, but if I was going into one of these camps I wouldn't know if I was coming back, where I was, or even how to get mail. So, I think that not putting a return address is equally effective at carrying out the whole idea of being stuck somewhere. . . .

The e-mail response from the designer clarifies the original message and provides a different perspective based on her family's history.

> For the most part, you knew exactly what I wanted to say. The camp that the Japanese Americans were sent to was not an American reeducation camp, it was a relocation camp that these Americans were sent to because the government was afraid they might leak out secret information to Japan about the U.S. Military. They were innocent people who were herded into these camps because they were easily recognized as being different looking. . . . What's funny to me (not really) is that my mom was there too. She doesn't even speak Japanese. . . . Right now, I

work part time in a Japanese restaurant, and most of our customers are tourists from Japan. They don't even consider American Japanese as Japanese. They consider us Americans.

In the process of creating representations of personal and cultural experience, many students developed insights into their relationships to one or more cultures. A student raised in Phoenix, Arizona, the son of Czech political exiles, constructed his card out of rusted metal grating smeared with dark red paint—a reference to his parents' suffering. The back side of the card spoke of his visit to Czechoslovakia where he found a cherry tree his mother had described to him as a child. The simple act of picking a cherry himself helped him understand his parents' difficult past and reconcile his own position caught between two cultures.

Two other cards from the class in Arizona addressed the immediate influences of commodity culture. One student who felt his main influences were television and product advertising identified himself with a Universal Product Code and created a postcard that was an elaborate and seductive package containing nothing but a relatively small photograph of himself. Another student presented a dismal picture of his roots in "techno-burbia," with rows of identical little gray houses, and the only distinctive symbol a looming McDonald's sign. The former celebrated his freedom to create himself as a commodity, the latter lamented his isolation and separation from his ethnic history.

One student from the class in Arizona received a card made of woven vellum strips covered with gritty crescent-shaped black-and-white imagery and Chinese characters. Since no one in the class read Chinese, another student took the card home to his Chinese paternal grandmother for a translation of the writing. It turned out to be a recipe for (very) American macaroni salad (lots of mayonnaise). This new information allowed us to see the forms as elbow macaroni. The interpretation of the card dramatized the investigative aspects of the project, turning the reading of signs into the solving of a mystery and also pointed out the unintentional effect that the method of production can have on the message. The designer's name was Carmen, which inspired the opening line, a reference to the children's show on PBS, *Carmen Sandiego*.

> So, Carmen—if that is your real name—thought you could throw a smart guy
> like me for a loop using incongruous formats, illegible hieroglyphs, and cloaked
> subject matter, huh? Well, it didn't work. I see through your pseudotechnical
> presentation in diffusion dither and right to the heart of your fetish for macaroni
> salad. Never mind all your efforts to sidetrack me into thinking this is a piece
> about scanning electron microscopy or germs or viruses or any other creepy-
> crawly things unnoticed by the naked eye. . . . It was so simple, a lesser-trained
> eye may have missed it. Your computer is a Macintosh SE, SE/30, Classic, Classic
> II, or PowerBook running a Chinese Language Kit, with no color capabilities.

Many issues were raised about culture and design as these diverse student bodies participated in "Exchanges." Throughout the research phase of the project, students discovered the roots of their own perspectives; through the design phase, they enriched their own visual vocabularies by translating this information into form; and in the exchange phase, they learned about diverse cultures on a one-to-one basis.

As design educators, our role is not to censor or ban our students from using any particular kind of imagery, but rather to foster an understanding of the ways that images carry meaning. The bonds that formed between students in the process of "Exchanges" created a personal interest in some of the important issues presently facing professional design practice, like stereotyping, appropriation, and the commodification of ethnic images. Through direct interaction, students got a sense of what they don't know about the experience of others. Our hope is that the humility gained will make our students more responsible visual communicators, and more responsive to the complexities of representation and interpretation.

Special thanks to Stacie Widdefield for her thoughtful suggestions about this essay.

Searching for a Black Aesthetic
in American Graphic Design

Sylvia Harris

What influence have African Americans had
on contemporary graphic design? Is there such a thing as an African-American design
aesthetic? These are questions that I have been asking designers and art historians for the
last ten years. The answer I am usually given is, "I don't know." The relationship of ethnic
minorities to the development of American graphic design is rarely discussed or documented by our profession because of the historic lack of racial diversity in the field.
However, increasing numbers of African Americans entering the profession are calling for
a fresh look at graphic design history in order to discover the aesthetic contributions of
their people.

In 1971, when I entered design school, there was only one other black student in
attendance. Twenty-five years later, this situation has improved slightly. Today, I teach
graphic design at the university level and have one or two black students in my department
each year. Those students often exhibit insecurities that negatively affect their performance. In fact, they experience a problem common to many black design professionals: the
feeling that they are not completely welcome in the profession. Lack of exposure to the
prevailing aesthetic traditions also puts them at a disadvantage. This outsider posture leads
many black designers to compulsively imitate and assimilate mainstream aesthetic traditions in order to feel accepted and be successful. More often than not, black designers and
students are trapped in a strategy of imitation rather than innovation.

The graphic design profession is driven by visual innovation. The most visible and
celebrated designers are those who are continuously innovating within, or in opposition
to, the prevailing schools of design thought. Black designers are working at a disadvantage
when they do not feel a kinship with existing design traditions and also have no evidence
of an alternative African or African-American design tradition upon which to base their
work. In 1995, Claude Steele completed groundbreaking research on the links between
performance and self-esteem, which indicated that self-confidence may be the single most
important influence in the lives of successful African Americans. For instance, the spectacular success of black musicians demonstrates the relationship between confidence,
leadership, and success. Black musicians have been successful because they feel confident
and secure about their work. They are secure because they are working within intimately

known traditions built by others like themselves, and they are motivated by the thrill of adding to that successful body of work.

Is there a potential design tradition that can fuel black designers in the same way that black music traditions fuel black musicians? By "black tradition" I do not mean black subject matter or imagery, but the styling and expressions common to people of African descent. I believe this tradition does exist, but black contributions to America's rich graphic design history have been overlooked, so far, by design historians who have focused either on European influences or on the current phenomenon of cultural hybridity. Buried in libraries and design journals is evidence of black graphic styles and influences stretching from the New Negro movement of the 1920s through the hip-hop aesthetics of the latest generation of designers. I believe that this material, if uncovered, has the potential to nurture a new generation of designers.

How do we construct and document a black design tradition? There is already a small body of research on the lives of America's first black designers. Chronicling the work of these pioneers is an important first step, but most of these brave people were so concerned with surviving within a hostile profession that their work expresses little that is uniquely African American. I believe that the building blocks of a black design aesthetic are scattered across many disciplines and will be found in unlikely places. For instance, some of the best examples of the potential for a black design vocabulary are found in the work of white designers who have been inspired by black culture and take advantage of the market for black expressive styles.

We must also look outside the design disciplines to the performing arts and to fine arts movements, such as the Afri-Cobra, which have based visual explorations on African and jazz rhythms. We can study these disciplines for characteristic black expression (improvisation, distortion, polyrhythms, exaggeration, call and response) that can be translated into graphic form. Black design traditions must be pieced together from a variety of sources to make a complete canon of black expression.

In discussion with design educators (both black and white), many argue that to focus too much attention on black aesthetics will limit the full creative expression of black designers. They argue that black designers have spent the last twenty years working to erase race and class bias in the profession; to them a focus on blackness invites discrimination. I disagree. Black designers have access, training, and opportunity; what they lack is the drive that comes from innovation. And in order to thrive, innovation requires a tradition to either build on or oppose. It is up to us as historians and educators to research and teach in a way that addresses the unique cultural experience of all our students. Right now, black design students would benefit greatly from a study of their design traditions. Otherwise, they may be doomed to a future of bad imitations.

The notes below are excerpts from my ongoing search for black influences in American design.

NOTES ON AFRICAN-AMERICAN STYLE IN AMERICAN GRAPHIC DESIGN

1920s: The New Negro Movement

In his first design history book, *A History of Graphic Design,* Philip Meggs stated that "a collision between cubist painting and futurist poetry spawned twentieth-century graphic design." Early twentieth-century cubist artists were obsessed with visualizing modern technological and social freedom. The style of the non-Western people of the world, particularly those who had perfected forms of abstraction and symbolism, were quickly drawn into the stylistic vortex created by this modernist revolution. In this way, black graphic expressions made their debut in the Western world indirectly, through the works of cubist artists such as Georges Braque, Pablo Picasso, and Fernand Léger. All these artists later acknowledged the significant impact of African art on their work; however, most scholarly writing about cubism has obscured its African roots. Postmodern art scholarship, starting with William Rubin's book *"Primitivism" in Twentieth-Century Art: Affinity of the Tribal and the Modern,* has begun to record and study the role of African art in the invention of cubism and the success of the modernist movement.

By the 1920s, "jazz" became not only a musical term, but a stylistic one. European designers, who were influenced by the pioneering work of cubist painters, struggled to capture the spirit of modernism through the expression of jazz rhythms and motifs. The expression of jazz style in the design of popular communications in the 1920s represents the first appearance of what can clearly be considered a black-inspired graphic design style. The jazz-era climate of relative freedom in the North created an environment for blacks to publish and design their own publications. During this "renaissance," Alain Locke cited the emergence of the "New Negro" and declared that black culture was the appropriate source of inspiration and content for African-American artists. He argued that the art of black people was a powerful inspiration to successful white artists, so why shouldn't black artists also work with this powerful force. One of the first designers to give graphic expression to this call was a European modernist, Winold Reiss, who created African-inspired logotypes and titles for the book *The New Negro.* Young black artists, most notably Aaron Douglas, were encouraged by Reiss and Locke to expand the emerging modernist trends and lead the emerging New Negro art and design movement.

The line between artist and designer was still blurred in the 1920s. Many artists were illustrators, and illustrators were often typographers. The best examples of the African aesthetic in the designs of the 1920s are seen in black-owned journals. The designers of these publications were often black artists, influenced by European cubist painters, who were, in turn, influenced by African art. Artists such as Aaron Douglas, one of the best of these artists/designers of the time, learned to recognize and resonate with the African in cubism. Douglas and other black designers had a unique opportunity to express black style in a world that was starved for fresh, anti-Victorian imagery. Douglas's covers for the quarterly magazine *Fire!!* show the emergence of a unique graphic design expression that combines the syntax of cubism with the forms of African art.

1930s: Revival of Black Folk Traditions and the Iconography of Black Labor

The prolific jazz-age production of black art and design was cut short by the depression of the 1930s. However, during the thirties and early forties, a revival of black folk traditions occurred, prompted by the direct observations of anthropologists and folklorists such as Zora Neale Hurston, Southern white writers such as DuBose Heyward, and interviewers for the WPA oral history project on slavery. Artists supported by federal arts programs and socialist groups interpreted black folk and labor themes in programs, posters, fliers, and other printed materials. It is not clear how much of this material was designed by blacks; examples buried in archives await inspection, interpretation, and inclusion in the design history texts.

1940s to 1950s: Commercial Art

Printing and publishing before and during World War II were significantly segregated. Unlike the fine arts professions, publishing institutions were restricted by racism and classism. Most printed publications and commercial art that circulated in black communities was generated by white-owned presses and designers. However, we do know that some black printers and photographers worked successfully in black communities; their products, including letterpress posters for popular music performances, were based on vernacular traditions and contributed directly to a continuing black graphic aesthetic.

1970s: The Aesthetics of Black Power

It is interesting to note that the bursts of black graphic production in the twentieth century occurred during eras in which young people were preoccupied with concepts of freedom. It is no surprise that the 1960s saw a renewed interest in African-American visual expression fueled by black cultural nationalism. Some of the work of this period combined socialist protest-art forms with black in-your-face bodaciousness to create a graphic design product that was uniquely African American. This decade of black graphics reflects the aesthetics of resistance and black power.

1980s to 1990s: Tribal Chic

Popular designers and illustrators such as Keith Haring and David Carson benefited from the lack of black participation in the design profession during the late 1980s surge of interest in rebellious urban style. They shaped new styles and lucrative careers based on bold public vernacular expression such as graffiti and rap, class rebellions and black rhythms, and tribal symbolism. At the first Organization of Black Designers conference, filmmaker Arthur Jaffa cited David Carson's *Ray Gun* magazine as offering the best example of a visual jazz aesthetic.

1990s: The New *New Negro Movement*

There are a handful of black designers who are designing for black audiences and, in doing so, are continuing black visual traditions into the next century. For instance, designers for new black media, including the magazine *YSB,* give graphic form to contemporary black culture. Like the artists of the original New Negro movement of the twenties, these designers use black vernacular stylings and African expression to inform their aesthetic decisions. The designers of this new generation are not isolated. They are working within a long tradition that, though they may not be aware of it, stretches across the century.

These notes are presented as snapshots and pointers to the research waiting to be undertaken. It is my hope that American designers and scholars will contribute to this body of knowledge and support a generation of designers hungry to see their people and experience reflected in the mirror of our profession.

History with Attitude: A Subjective Tour of Studies in American Graphic Design Education

Ellen Mazur Thomson

In his *Theatres of Memory*, the Oxford historian Raphael Samuel reaffirmed the power of the present in directing our understanding of the past: "History is an argument about the past, as well as the record of it, and its terms are forever changing, sometimes under the influence of developments in adjacent fields of thought, sometimes . . . as a result of politics. . . ." History, he argued, must continually be revised, "stamped with the ruling passions of its time," yet to be convincing it must create "a consecutive narrative out of fragments, imposing order on chaos, and producing images far clearer than any reality could be." Historical studies that engage and excite us use the past to inform our present preoccupations and interests. Unlike critical appreciations of designers and objects (works of connoisseurship) or chronicles of styles and schools, recent studies in graphic design education have posed questions and constructed versions of the past that lend depth and complexity to contemporary issues.

These studies have re-created histories of graphic design education that confront issues of interest to contemporary practitioners: the status of graphic designers in American society; the benefits of establishing a core curriculum to define the professional; what is, or should be, the relationship between classroom instruction and the needs of design firms or advertising agencies. These issues are rooted in the history of the profession. They pose significant questions about the relationship between graphic design and the larger society. In addition, and not, I would argue, incidently, these studies are based on a wide variety of primary documentation, published and unpublished, that falls outside the scope of what is currently considered design history. This essay touches briefly on some of the studies that ask interesting questions about these materials.

One of the most engaging of these recent works was based on children's drawings, student artwork, magazines, ledgers, and instruction books the author found in the collection of the Cross family. In *Drawn to Art: A Nineteenth-Century American Dream* (Hanover, N.H.: University Press of New England, 1985), Diana Korzenik followed the members of a New England family as they moved from rural New Hampshire to careers in Boston's printing establishment and art schools. She was able to show that the Crosses, like many others between 1850 and 1900, saw art education as preparation for work in a new economic system. Drawing was "an avenue by which industrialization could be integrated into culture." (p. 22)

The value of design to society has been a perennial topic in design education. Educators and design professionals alike have written about the graphic arts' contribution to the economic well-being of the nation—or, conversely, the degree to which the arts are corrupted by commercialism and democratization. In the nineteenth century, this was a central issue for those in the industrial drawing movement, a movement of importance to graphic design history because it shaped the training of illustrators, engravers, type designers, and printers. In William Minifie's *Popular Lectures on Drawing and Design* (Baltimore: School of Design of the Maryland Institute, 1854), he contended that the study of drawing and design is "not as a mere accessory that may be dispensed with at pleasure, but one of the fundamental branches of education." Minifie maintained that design education would directly increase opportunities in manufacturing and cure unemployment. Similarly, Walter Smith, an Englishman trained in the Arts and Crafts system, was hired by the state of Massachusetts to administer its 1870 law that required instruction in industrial or mechanical drawing for all students in the public school system. Smith's *Art Education: Scholastic and Industrial* (Boston: Osgood, 1873) is a fulsome justification of this provision. A decade later, the federal government sponsored Isaac Edward Clarke's six-volume *Art and Industry* (Washington, D.C.: U.S. Office of Education, 1885–98). Perhaps the first great work on art education for industry, it was appropriately monumental. Clarke passionately believed in the importance of instruction in the applied arts and gathered vast amounts of data and documents that he reproduced with detailed curricula of individual design schools, many of which began during this period.

Twenty years later, Charles R. Richards's *Art in Industry* (New York: Macmillan, 1922) combined in one volume information on design education, based on a survey of close to six hundred instructional programs throughout the United States and Europe. He described trade schools, schools connected with colleges and museums, and art schools that gave instruction in graphic design.

Modern studies of design schools go beyond institutional histories to explore the impetus for their creation and the context in which they operated. Nancy Austin in "Educating American Designers for Industry, 1853–1903" (*Proceedings of the American Antiquarian Society* 105, 1 [1995]: 211–30) uses the early history of the Rhode Island School of Design as a model to examine the beginnings of design schools in the United States—as institutions created during the industrial revolution to transform the training of artists to meet the needs of machine manufacturing. Austin's thesis—based in part on this material—is that the origins of consumer culture and the commercialization of art lie in the late eighteenth and nineteenth centuries and occurred as part of the industrial revolution.

Not surprisingly, feminism has also contributed to the focus of contemporary art-education history. Using admissions records, published catalogs, census data, and personal interviews, Nina de Angeli Walls analyzed changes (over nearly a century) of the class and geographic origins, ethnicity, age, and aspirations of the women who attended the Philadelphia School of Design. "Educating Women for Art and Commerce: The Philadelphia

School of Design, 1848–1932," (*History of Education Quarterly* 34, no. 3 [fall 1994]: 329–55), unlike so much design history, combines statistical data with other materials, enabling the author to describe both quantitatively and qualitatively the women who attended professional design schools and the reasons they did so. Walls demonstrates that despite the change in student population, women used vocational training in the applied arts to gain entry into the middle class or maintain their status within it.

The Hochschule für Gestaltung in Ulm (1953–68) is the subject of an unusual study that uses documents of the period and comments on them by presenting—on the bottom half of the same page—contemporary interviews and essays by former teachers and students. *Ulm Design: The Morality of Objects*, edited by Herbert Lindinger (Cambridge: MIT Press, 1991), not only describes the school's curriculum, but the theory behind it and how the experience, in both personal and political dimensions, was perceived by participants then and thirty years later.

THE IMPORTANCE OF THEORY

Education theories are ultimately based in the philosophies of knowledge—explanations of visual perception, how we see, and how we understand and use what we see. Successive theories are based on new understandings of the way humans learn. The education philosophies of Johann Heinrich Pestalozzi, Friedrich Froebel, Arthur Wesley Dow, John Dewey, and, in the mid-twentieth century, Victor Lowenthal set the terms of the American art curriculum. Yet, design historians have, for the most part, ignored them. Arthur Wesley Dow (1857–1922) is the exception. Dow's emphasis on formal elements and his direct influence on advertising photography give his theoretical writing contemporary interest. In his hugely popular *Composition: A Series of Exercises Selected from a New System of Art Education* (New York: Baker & Taylor, 1899), Dow emphasized the application of abstract visual principles rather than technique. Two of Dow's pupils, the photographer Clarence White and painter Max Weber, incorporated Dow's theory into the curriculum of the Clarence H. White's School of Photography, where pioneers in advertising photography, including Anton Bruehl, Paul Outerbridge Jr., and Margaret Watkins, studied.

Most recently, Dow, White, and the school have been the subject of several studies written by historians of photography interested in White because he represents an alternative to the aesthetic tradition of Alfred Stieglitz and the photo-secessionists. Bonnie Yochelson's "Clarence H. White Reconsidered: An Alternative to the Modernist Aesthetic of Straight Photography" (*Studies of Visual Communication* 9, 4 [fall 1983]: 23–44), Susan Doniger's essay, "The Clarence H. White School of Photography" in *Collective Vision* (Athens: Ohio University Art Gallery, 1986) and *Pictorialism into Modernism: The Clarence H. White School of Photography*, edited by Marianne Fulton (New York: Rizzoli, 1996), trace the application of Dow's philosophy.

INSTRUCTIONAL TEXTS

Perhaps nothing goes out of style more quickly, or is more revealing of its period, than the instructional text. For historians, they are invaluable to understanding how design was taught, what topics were included, what skills were considered important, and what styles were favored. Yet, most of these texts have not been subjected to scholarly analysis.

The exception is a fascinating study based on nineteenth-century instructional texts that focused on the early proponents of the industrial drawing movement. Peter Marzio examined the dilemma faced by late-eighteenth- and nineteenth-century art educators who wanted to find a role for the visual arts in a young democracy. His *The Art Crusade: An Analysis of American Drawing Manuals* (Washington, D.C.: Smithsonian Institution Press, 1976) describes the controversy over drawing instruction in the public schools.

As part of this movement, Louis Prang, the great chromolithographer and publisher, worked with Massachusetts commissioner of art education, Walter Smith, in developing a series of teachers' manuals. Prang expanded his operation to publish a large number of graduated lesson plans for both elementary and high school classes. Michael Clapper's "Art, Industry, and Education in Prang's Chromolithograph Factory" (*Proceedings of the American Antiquarian Society* 105, 1 [1995]:145–62) analyzes Prang's publishing company as it influenced ideas about the use of art in industry and as a business enterprise.

Unlike Prang's publications, which were written for public school teachers and students, the United Typothetae of America sponsored a series of texts for use in trade schools. Originally entitled "Typographic Technical Series for Apprentices" and later the "U.T.A. Library," these publications provided technical information on machinery and materials, presswork, binding, printing history, accounting practices, and English grammar. They also addressed topics in design as in Laurence B. Siegfried's *Typographic Design in Advertising* (Washington, D.C.: Committee on Education, United Typothetae of America, 1930). The influence of these texts has yet to be explored.

If many of the studies cited seems to use design textbooks to illuminate cultural and social history, Edward R. Tufte's *Visual Explanations: Images and Quantities, Evidence and Narrative* (Cheshire, Conn.: Graphics Press, 1997) may be said to reverse the process and focus on the graphic strategies of nondesign texts. Tufte shows, among much else, how illustrations in textbooks on magic, dating from the sixteenth to the twentieth century, could add the element of time or multiple points of view, could "make verbs visible." Using books that were written to induct the would-be conjuror into the routines and skills of the magician, Tufte demonstrates how their graphics went beyond mere description to show both the trick as seen by the audience and the sequence of operations the magician used to achieve his illusions.

AUTOBIOGRAPHY AND BIOGRAPHY

Autobiographies almost always include accounts of the writer's education. Subjective by their very nature, they cannot be taken as a general picture, but they often give insights into the learning process that more objective studies miss. Unlike most histories, they trace the change from apprenticeship to school instruction.

Some of the earliest books describe apprenticeships rather than schooling. John Thayer, in *Astir: A Publisher's Life Story* (Boston: Small Maynard, 1910), recalls his training as an apprentice in a Boston print-shop composing room and how he expanded his skills by moving to Chicago to work and train in larger printing establishments. Will Bradley, in *Will Bradley: His Chapbook* (New York: Typophiles, 1955), recounts how, starting as a twelve-year-old in a small Michigan printing plant, he rose from printer's devil to master printer to self-taught designer, pouring over magazine illustrations and exchanging ideas with friends. A rarely cited Goudy biography, Bernard Lewis's *Behind the Type: The Life Story of Frederic W. Goudy* (Pittsburgh: Department of Printing, Carnegie Institute of Technology, 1941), was written in cooperation with the subject and shows that Goudy learned many type production and printing skills by working with craftsmen in a variety of trades.

This transition from apprenticeship to school is explored by several authors in "The Cultivation of Artists in Nineteenth-Century America," a special issue of the *Proceedings of the American Antiquarian Society* (105, 1 [1995]). Donald C. O'Brien's "Training in the Workshop of Abner Reed" (pp. 45–69) uses three generations of family records, including unpublished diaries, letters, trade cards, and copperplate engravings, to reconstruct "the sequence and nature of the work of apprentices" in an engraving shop. David Tatham examines "The Lithographic Workshop, 1825–50" (pp. 71–78) to show that master craftsmen were forced to assume a teaching role because of the tremendous need for skilled draftsmen. Ann Prentice Wagner's "The Graver, the Brush, and the Ruling Machine: The Training of Late-Nineteenth-Century Wood Engravers" (pp. 167–92) describes the gender differences in training engravers as well as the consequences of introducing photographic methods of reproduction.

CONCLUSION

Taken together, these studies create a very different sense of American graphic design from that presented in standard works on the subject. The impact of Ruskin and Morris in the nineteenth century or European modernism in this century are not ignored, but they are shown to be only a part of a complex evolution. This evolution is complex because no single narrative thread ties graphic design history from its past to the present. It is complex also in that the influences operating at any particular time on education and on design came from a wide variety of forces both within and outside the profession.

Tear It Down

Virginia Smith

Art education from the famous past came out of a solid foundation of ideas. During the Russian Revolution and the Weimar Republic artists brought their worldview into their classrooms. Can we teach graphic design today without such a foundation?

Graphic design today acknowledges two influential schools of style: the Bauhaus style of geometric abstraction, and constructivism, the expression of Russian revolutionary theory. Both schools based their courses on theories of art developed by original thinkers such as Oskar Schlemmer in Germany and Varvara Stepanova in the Soviet Union. What those two shared was an overflowing richness of mind. From the depth of thought that motivated their own lives and actions, theoretical richness overflowed into teaching. At the Bauhaus it was intellectual-spiritual-mystical-rational; at Vkhutemas it was polemical-political. Both ideologies arose from allegiance to grand ideas that existed before any curriculum.

Schlemmer was the master considered by some to be closest to Walter Gropius's thought in founding the Bauhaus. So, it is not surprising that a month after Schlemmer joined the Bauhaus in Weimar Gropius asked him to develop a curriculum. Schlemmer wrote his wife: "Gropius says he would like to start drawing from the nude for sculptors and would I take it over. I have agreed gladly and he says he will propose it. They should study the nude. Something may come of this. I am pleased about it."[1] What came of it was one of the most remarkable classes in the Bauhaus or any art school curriculum— Schlemmer's course on "Man." As a platform for this course, the theoretical foundation on which his lectures and twice-weekly classes were based, Schlemmer drew upon philosophers, poets, psychologists, and natural scientists all the way back to Heracleitus, with stops at Voltaire and Lao-tzu or any other thinker that had something to say to him. Over two hundred pages of notes—some of them typed syllabi, some of them charts and diagrams—survived, and were later published.

"Man," as a course, is a richly confusing attempt to divide the study of a human being into areas of the natural sciences, philosophy, and psychology, based on man's trinity of mind, nature, and soul or mind, nature, and psyche (sometimes called normative, biological, and philosophical)—and a tumultuous outpouring of notes and sketches.

Impossible to follow as a curriculum, the notes Schlemmer left indicate the intensity of his interest in the subject and his will to completely rethink the education of artists through drawing. Schlemmer endorsed the Bauhausler's cry, "We the modern moderns," and accepted the challenge of defining the "new life" of modernism.

A goal of early European modernism was to improve the life of humanity through art. Modernism was, in part, and for Bauhaus masters like Gropius, a reaction against the war, poverty, and class divisions of the past. The human being was at the center of modernism. Schlemmer's course, intellectually based and creatively inspired, had nothing to do with the craft interests of the Bauhaus and everything to do with Schlemmer's views on the human body in relation to the universe, views derived from study with his teacher Adolf Holzel and obviously acceptable to Director Gropius.

Schlemmer thought man a "cosmic being." This means that he saw the human being as both a world in itself and as a unit in relation to the world. For an artist to draw this grand and cosmic creature, the draftsman needed to understand the history of mankind, the origin of man, the theory of race. His biology must be understood, also his sexuality; his relationship to air, light, warmth, and clothing; his anatomy; his nervous system; and his capacity for movement—this last especially interested Schlemmer, who directed the Bauhaus theater and taught in the theater department. Man as a philosophical creature must be shown, through an awareness of materialism, realism, idealism, concepts of God, and insights into the psyche, the will and the imagination. All this exists in Schlemmer's notes—the basis for his classes. The lists of books he consulted are by German authors whose names are not common to Americans: Ranke, Sachs, Schider, Dubal, Buschan, Hufeland—unless I'm alone in not knowing them. We know some of the philosophers he listed in his syllabus for studying the origins of life and "substances": Locke, Pascal, Descartes, Giordano Bruno, Hume. The corpus in Schlemmer's cosmos was no simple bag of bones.

To vary teaching possibilities, the class moved to the Bauhaus stage. There, dramatic contrasts of light and dark could be achieved with theatrical spotlights and shadows. The drawings from the course show fluid, strong abstractions of the figures. What seems remarkable is that the students themselves served as models, and in the nude. As much as anything else, the existence of nude drawings of students testifies to the total commitment of the Bauhaus community to the primacy of art over convention. Female models seem to have worn underpants, while male models are seen fully nude. The drawings are abstract, rather than realistic.

Schlemmer himself made drawings. In translucent renderings of the human body, he showed the organs nestling within; in some, the skeleton neatly inhabits the flesh, and in others, the musculature strolls along with the skin.

Though the course "Man" was based on a long bibliography, it must have motivated students mainly through the force of Schlemmer's charm as a person. All photographs of him—in costume for his *Triadic Ballet,* fencing on the roofs—and the diaries and letters he left reveal a playful, tolerant man with passionate convictions. With Itten, Kandinsky, and Klee, Schlemmer was part of the mystical faction that influenced the

Bauhaus before the communism of Hannes Meyer or the avaricious intellectuality of Mies. In his notes on the "Man" course, Schlemmer quotes Goethe's vision of an ideal community from *Wilhelm Meister's Travels* (a book I read at the Yale School of Art in a desperate, but unconscious, attempt to compensate for the intellectual barrenness of classes at that school). *Wilhelm Meister* is the story of a young German student's search for meaning through his *Wanderjahre* around Europe. The paragraphs Schlemmer extracted describe an ideal atmosphere for learning, a vision of what the Bauhaus could be. In Goethe's community, the facial expression of the inhabitants, the gravity of their manner, revealed "a secret spirit leading towards one great goal." Did the Bauhaus house such spirits? I think so.

Itten, who dressed in monk's clothes and demanded vegetarianism in the kitchen, was the most influential on the early Bauhaus, though not as well known as those masters who emigrated to America (Albers, Gropius, Mies, etc.). As one of the first masters appointed in 1919,[2] he originated the famous Foundation Course, the model at many art schools to come, through the influence of his book.[3] Itten was a mystic who believed in the liberation of the creative artist through exercises on the roof and in the classroom, swinging the hand before picking up a pencil. Itten's method of teaching was intuitive, contrasted with Schlemmer's, which was based on summarizing the intellectual thought of all the ages. But both were powerful influences at the early Bauhaus.

At the other major school of art to which graphic design is connected, through constructivism, the spiritual was less important than the political. This art school was the state arm of the Russian Revolution. Malevich said in 1919 that "cubism and futurism were revolutionary movements in art, anticipating the revolution in the economic and political life of 1917." Artists such as Rodchenko, Tatlin, and Stepanova thought they had gone as far as they could by the early 1920s with Malevich's abstract painting, "reducing form to zero," and they turned to the useful task of teaching art to implement the ideals of the revolution. The school, called Vkhutemas (initials of the Vysshie Khudozhestvenno-Tekhnicheskie Masterskie or Higher Artistic Technical Studios), was an arm of the People's Commissariat for Enlightenment. The radical teaching faculty[4] held conflicting opinions about the goal of the people's revolution, but aspects of constructivist theory such as composition, construction, and facture were settled in the 1921 debates among Varvara Stepanova and Aleksei Gan (later executed in a gulag) and radical artists Ossip Brik and El Lissitzky. In addition to creating curricula at Vkhutemas, constructivist thinker Stepanova formulated theoretical key issues of constructivism, namely, facture.

Facture, also called tectonics, derived, she said, from the "structure of communism and the effective exploitation of industrial matter." A rough surface demonstrated anti-elegance, the anti-aesthetic of the people. Fine printing was disdained as expression of a corrupt bourgeois who valued finish over content, the superficial over the deep truths of the text. Glossy paper, embossing, other luxurious traditions of printing were seen as demonstrations of wealth and exploitation of labor. Facture was a way of turning "art" into "production" by Stepanova and the constructivists. Her influential lectures resolved the matter that constructivism was "intellectual production."[5]

Stepanova wrote that the constructivists' cry (did everyone have a cry?) was,

"Down with aesthetics and taste." Facture had no taste, it showed material honestly and showed the hand of the worker who had made it. His labor was evident in his work; the work a tribute to himself. Book covers and posters were not designed under orders of rich industrialist oppressors. Imperfect type, rough paper, foreign materials, exemplified facture. There is no "quality control" in communism; it must be a capitalist concept. The style of constructivist graphic design resulted from available paper, found art, and the constraints of the letterpress printing presses in and around Vkhutemas.

What is the ideological foundation supporting graphic design programs today? It's not political, it's certainly not spiritual, and can we say it's intellectual? No, it must be technological. Everyone has a computer, more and more time is spent before the screen. As Americans, we have always excelled in technology, and perhaps we should accept that our basis for doing everything is faith in technology and let go of imitating alien styles; tear down the foundations that really don't reflect who we are. We should be confident in the profundity of our contemporary style; it reflects our true ideology. As the Apple (you recall that eating the apple gave the secret of knowledge to Eve) gets stronger and faster, we'll spend more time before the electronic altar. We are building on a sophisticated technical foundation; it is our intellectual base. Let us adopt the cry, "Up with the mouse and on with the millennium," and construct our curriculum on that mighty piece of plastic.

NOTES

1. Oskar Schlemmer to Tut Schlemmer, May 1, 1921, in *Diaries and Letters,* ed. Tut Schlemmer (1958; reprint, Middletown, Conn.: Wesleyan University Press, 1972).

2. With Lyonel Feininger and Gerhard Marcks.

3. *Design and Form: The Basic Course at the Bauhaus and Later,* rev. ed. (New York: Van Nostrand-Reinhold, 1975).

4. Kandinsky was the crossover figure, living in Moscow, Munich, at the Bauhaus, and in Paris, teaching at the Bauhaus in 1922–33, overlapping with Schlemmer, Klee, and Itten. A spiritual figure, he remained Russian Orthodox throughout his life and wrote *The Spiritual in Art,* expressing his mysticism.

5. Alexander Lavrentiev, *Varvara Stepanova: The Complete Work* (Cambridge: MIT Press, 1988).

Writing Now: Journalism, Criticism, Critical Journalism

Rick Poynor

This is the opening broadside from a review of the book *Barthes for Beginners,* published in Britain's weekly design magazine:

> The last time I checked everybody I knew had studied Roland Barthes at art college. From media studies to graphic design courses, the theory lectures were full of words like "semiotics" and "structuralism," usually taught by someone in unmatching socks. If there was a single culprit for this drivel then his name was Roland Barthes.
>
> Those of us who actually attended the lectures might remember that Barthes also has much to say on the nature of pleasure and sexual non-conformity, and applied his ideas on communication to every area of culture and life—from fashion and popular culture to classical French literature and homosexuality. . . .
>
> If all that sounds interesting but a bit too much like hard work, there's a new book . . . that should get you through the most demanding cross-examination on the man's life and works.[1]

Note how the writer tries to have it both ways. She wants us to appreciate that she knows about Barthes and takes it for granted that her reader will know about him, too: Oh yes, we have all studied Roland, but only the kind of nerd who is so out to lunch he can't even match his socks would take the man and his confreres so seriously. Our reviewer affects an air of superiority to Barthes, putting him squarely in his place for his "drivel," yet she and her editor seem to feel the need to inform us about this book. Overall, despite the ambivalence of its opening paragraphs, the review is fairly positive.

The most interesting aspect of an extract that is in tone by no means untypical of Britain's design press is the would-be flattering but ultimately patronizing way in which it pictures the reader. It appears to offer insight, but declines to risk anything like a genuine discussion by someone with something worth saying about Barthes and design, preferring to play it for laughs. Who, one wonders, does this publication suppose are its readers, and what does it think they know already, or would like to learn? Slightly rephrased, these are two key questions now facing graphic design criticism as it struggles to be born: Who is the emerging criticism for? And what is it for?

The answers used to be breathtakingly straightforward. Here is the British designer Ashley Havinden, addressing the question, "Does Today's Criticism Help Design?" in 1952:

> The role of the serious critic is that of an educator. By searching out the many examples of good design and appraising them constructively, he may convince the manufacturer or the printer of the merits of good design associated with his product. In the same way he may succeed in inspiring the shopkeeper with the desire to offer good design to the public. Such constructive criticism in the press would teach the public, not only to appreciate, but to demand good design in the products they buy.[2]

At no point in this short article does the writer define his conception of "good design." There was no need to because he could take it for granted that his readers— fellow professionals—would know exactly what he meant. Havinden's concern was with the world beyond the profession, the realms of industry, retail, and the client. The task, as he and other design leaders saw it, was simply to get everyone else to fall into line with their manifestly correct views. To achieve this end, he advised, design would need to receive weekly, nonspecialist press coverage of the kind routinely given to art, music, literature, film, the theater, and "ladies' fashions"—as Havinden so gallantly put it.

Forty-five years later, almost nothing has changed. Ladies' fashions are covered to excess in the generalist press, while poor old graphic design must make do with only the occasional review for a rare exhibition or an exceptionally noteworthy book. The primary limitation facing today's design criticism is that its placement in professional magazines— still the primary outlet—means that it consistently preaches to the converted.

This is not to deny that such writing, at its best, retains an educational purpose, though in a narrower, more professionally focused sense than Havinden intended when he described the critic as an "educator." The critical awareness advocated by a small minority of magazines encourages critical reflection in the designer's personal practice, while an acquaintance with design history develops an awareness of the profession's internal dialogues and broadens the designer's sense of the possible, or the no longer viable. Perhaps these are some of the pragmatic goals that Massimo Vignelli had in mind when he observed a few years ago that "criticism is the instrument that sharpens our tools."[3] Andrew Blauvelt, writing in *Eye*, puts a 1990s spin on this way of thinking:

> The notion of design as a field of study without practical application is unlikely and undesirable. After all, it is the practice of graphic design—no matter how wanting or limiting—that provides the basis for a theory of graphic design. This is not to say that the education of graphic designers needs to be tied so intimately to professional practice that it cannot engage in activities which challenge design's social function, historical understanding, or professional legitimacy. The calls for graphic design to be a liberal art . . . need to be supplanted by strategies which foster "critical making," teaching when, how, and why to question things.[4]

At root, though, despite a much enlarged sense of what might be professionally possible, design commentary remains, even here, at the service of design. Its purpose is still, ultimately, to create "better" designers, even if the conception of "better" has changed.

There is another, more combative view of criticism, however, summarized in an essay by Anne Bush, writing in *Emigre* in 1995:

> Criticism in its most rigorous form is analytic contestation. Its goal is not to reinforce, but to reveal. As an interaction between internal disciplinary conditions and outside influences, it must ultimately eschew consensus to maintain its critical eye. Thus to promote pragmatic criticism because it appeals to a professional body actually thwarts analytic introspection. . . .
>
> By separating reflection and action, a singularly professional criticism depoliticizes graphic design. Preferring to focus on internal questions, it implies that design is only important to itself, privileged and immune, distanced from social and cultural conditions that it actually has a hand in constructing.[5]

Exactly how radical Bush envisages such a criticism to be remains unclear. One of her sources, literary critic Terry Eagleton's *The Function of Criticism*, ends with the proposition (not quoted by Bush) that "Modern criticism was born of a struggle against the absolutist state; unless its future is now defined as a struggle against the bourgeois state, it might have no future at all."[6] In this view, criticism breaks free from narrow professional goals and becomes an instrument of radical social transformation. One could indeed imagine design criticism as part of a wider cultural criticism conducted along such lines, but given graphic design's intimate role, as usually taught, in serving the bourgeois state, one supposes such an approach would be highly critical of many of the institutions, practices, and beliefs that design holds dear. I don't intend to pursue this here, but I do want to suggest that there is a need for much greater clarity on the part of graphic design criticism's more radical exponents when it comes to design's sociopolitical dimension.

Anne Bush's analysis is valuable as one of the few recent attempts to explore issues surrounding the development of a graphic design criticism, but it stops at the point where it might more fruitfully have begun. Bush does not tell us which audience or audiences she envisions for her brand of "analytic contestation," what the vehicles—real or even hypothetical—would be for this kind of writing, who is going to write it, or how it would be funded. She offers only the vaguest sense of what such a graphic design criticism would be like to read and mentions no one who is actually doing it. The lack of examples in her essay makes it almost impossible to test the cogency or viability of a position with which, in outline, I have a great deal of sympathy.

I will return to some of the practicalities that Bush overlooks because they offer the best guide we have to the state of graphic design criticism today. First, though, I want to look in broader terms at the relationship between academic writing and journalism on the subject. Here, there is a long-standing tension that can also be seen in many other subject areas, but this need not be a case of either/or. Both kinds of writing have their purpose and their place; both kinds of writing have their problems and their pitfalls. The inadequacies of much design journalism hardly need spelling out. The quotation with which I began exemplifies its anti-intellectualism and compromise, and the way it consistently underestimates its readers. But nor is academic publishing completely untouched by external factors. Academia has its politics, its personality clashes, its career paths, its tendency on occasions to encourage orthodoxy or to domesticate dissent, all of which exert a subtle influence on what gets written.

Neither of these positions, however, represent the ground we have attempted to occupy with *Eye*. As an editor, what I tried to encourage and develop is a "critical journalism" positioned somewhere between the two poles. The choice of term is deliberate because most journalism on the subject is not critical at all. But the concept is hardly new: broadsheet newspapers and magazines, such as *Harper's, New York Review of Books* (and its London counterpart *London Review of Books*), and the British film monthly *Sight and Sound*, all publish critical journalism.

Many of *Eye*'s writers are academics. The style and presentation of this writing is, however, journalistic—up to a point. If someone submits a piece titled "Figurative Boundaries: The Body in Early German Graphic Design," we will probably suggest something colon-free and snappier, such as "The Modernist Body."[7] It looks better on the page and is a much stronger hook for the uncommitted reader. If writers are overfond of jargon or needlessly circuitous, we will encourage them to rephrase, or make some suggestions. Most professional magazines ban footnotes, which are seen as distracting to nonacademic readers. *Eye* is sparing in their use, but retains them where a piece would be compromised without, or where they will be helpful to readers with research interests. We have always published lists of suggested further reading if it seemed useful to do so. Aesthetically, *Eye* has elements of the bookishness and sobriety found in an academic journal, but combines this with the visual resources of a professional magazine. The politics of reproduction makes an interesting subject in itself, but we can at least show the reader clearly what our writers are talking about.[8]

The point of these techniques is to attract readers and hold their attention. I have sometimes been challenged for the assumptions I make about what readers will or won't accept, but unless you are going to commission detailed market research, this is all you can do. Editors navigate by instinct, experience, and the feedback their magazines receive. An editor's guiding sense of the "ideal" reader—a composite individual made up of many actual people—helps to give a magazine its coherence and shape. In *Eye*'s case, this notional reader was also, to a large extent, myself, and many an editor has admitted as much. We hoped to appeal to a mix of designers, educators, students, and anyone with a wide-ranging interest in contemporary visual culture, and as far as we can tell, this is *Eye*'s readership.

I would like now to change the angle of view and take a look at the individual on whom the development of design criticism must necessarily depend: the critic. Without people consumed by a regular urge to write, there can be no writing or criticism. The presence of committed critics in reasonable numbers, as well as their availability to do the job, is the real measure of graphic design criticism's state of health.

When we started *Eye* in 1990, I had a clear sense, from reading American publications, that the United States was ahead of Britain in developing an English-language criticism of graphic design. It would be satisfying to report, after seven years of concerted effort, that there had been real developments in this area. In the United States, there has undoubtedly been progress. Existing writers have grown stronger. Ambitious new writers, would-be critics, have arrived on the scene. Anthologies of critical writing are being published. Graphic design conferences include discussions of criticism. In Britain, however, despite the undeniable buoyancy of the graphic design scene, we still lag behind. More people are writing about graphic design, but, disappointingly, the standard of this writing has not, on the whole, improved. It lacks breadth and ambition and even the best of it is journalism, not criticism. I am not sure how to account for this. With *Eye*, we created a platform, issued frequent invitations, showed we were ambitious for the writing to develop and that we would give it the freedom and space to do so, but eager, would-be critics did not come flocking to join the cause. With a few exceptions, British academics teaching in humanities departments (as opposed to design schools) have not seen *Eye* as a place they want to publish; and not every academic writer is, in any case, a critic.

Perhaps I should define what I think it takes to be a critic and achieve a critical presence.

1. The critic needs to be identified with a strong personal point of view or position. This is one of the factors that sets the critic apart from the journalist. One of Britain's best-established graphic design journalists once told me that he liked to sit on the fence. So far as I know, he's still there.
2. The critic will probably be identified with a particular area or subject matter. This is the most obvious way of distinguishing yourself from other writers. It can only be achieved over time and it is harder than it sounds.
3. As a sign of seriousness, the critic will need to publish in the right places. This sounds horribly snooty, but it is a fact of life. Some publications have critical credibility and others don't.
4. In time, the critic will certainly publish books as well as articles.
5. The critic will almost certainly need to stick his or her neck out. Not everyone is going to like what critics have to say, but their willingness to do this and risk the possible consequences is another mark of their critical seriousness.
6. Last, but absolutely central to the enterprise, the critic will need to be an exceptionally good writer.

This is what a critic needs in outline, but there is more to be said about the last two points. First, sticking your neck out. My disappointment with some academic writing about graphic design is that, while it can be very outspoken when addressing general issues or abstract ideas, it is not nearly so brave when criticizing individuals or institutions—in other words, when it involves saying something that could entail some personal cost to the writer, if not now, then at some imagined future point. It is the difference between calling for "analytic contestation" as a desirable goal and actually practicing it by analytically contesting real design phenomena out there in the world. Academics writing for *Eye* could be surprisingly gentle even when, for instance, reviewing a book. Their real opinions, which sometimes emerged in conversation after the writing was done, were not vigorously reflected in the writing itself. But why not? This is why we went to them in the first place. If I single out academic writing, it is only because the ambition to develop a graphic design criticism is coming principally from that direction. If we are to have it, it will need to grow sharper teeth.

Second, the need for talent. As an editor, I was looking for opinionated writers who were not shy of telling us what they really thought, but I was also searching for a much harder-to-define quality that I will call a writer's sensibility. By this I am trying to suggest the manner of thinking, the areas of personal emphasis, the unique life experiences, the peculiarities of outlook, perhaps even the tics and quirks that inform a writer's writing and help to set it apart. The medium of an individual sensibility is, to a large degree, a writer's style and its resulting tone. This is one of the problems with jargon: it is the language of a certain kind of officialdom. By using it, you join the club and make yourself intelligible to other members, but you make it hard for nonmembers to enter and you also surrender something of yourself. It takes a fine writer to incorporate a professional jargon and transcend it. The British writer on popular culture, Dick Hebdige, dean of the School of Critical Studies at CalArts, has achieved this brilliantly. At a lower intellectual level, the same problem affects large tracts of graphic design journalism. Many journalists write with an interchangeable vocabulary and the same tone of voice. But journalism doesn't have to conform to a single style any more than academic writing does. Good writers can satisfy commercial and generic requirements while bringing something of their own to the writing. Mark Dery, for instance, an American writer on cyberculture, is a first-rate practitioner of an informed, incisive, always personal, critical journalism.

One of the ironies of recent design writing is that designer-writers who are sensitive to every tiny nuance of style in a piece of design sometimes forget (or perhaps never really understood) that writing is just as much a craft as design, and that style in writing is just as much a medium of meaning and a means by which you seduce and hold your reader as it is in design.

There has been a lot of straining after the grand effect in recent design writing—small or medium-sized ideas eked out to would-be definitive bulk until the whole construction, or perhaps the reader, collapses under a weight that simply cannot be supported by the material's level of intrinsic interest. But writing does not always have to be about the huge, world- or epoch-transforming idea. Most writing is far more quotidian. Whatever its field, it makes a modest contribution to a cultural dialogue in which we are all, as readers, already taking part. It deals with smaller but still significant things, new information, new angles and interpretations of familiar issues. The best writing pays careful attention, as it proceeds, to the little observations that lead to a sense, as they connect with each other, of how things are. An insight doesn't necessarily need a whole paragraph—it can be imparted in a sentence, a clause, a parenthesis. It is the accumulation of little insights that gives strong writing its density. As an editor, I was less interested in the ponderous application by a writer of someone else's theories than I was in the writer's original perceptions and freshness of insight. Until we produce such a writing, we will never appeal to the world of potential readers outside the profession.

The necessity for craft is equally true of another recent tendency, the "essay," which aims to readjust the conventional boundaries between writing and design and allow design to take a more active and discursive role in the articulation and framing of the content. As a genre, such experiments are intriguing, but that doesn't rule out critical appraisal of the results. A collaboration between a London-based design educator and John Warwicker of Tomato in *Emigre* (still the main outlet for such experiments) showed how the process can go awry. The piece's claim, made near the beginning, is that ordinary publishing formats and editorial frameworks would be inadequate for what it has to say. The writer explains:

> I knew that it could not be constructed as a conventional interview. Tomato, and John himself, had been instrumental in building a reputation for developing a philosophy concerning, new approaches to thinking about, design and communication. To settle for a simple question/answer would not do. . . . We agreed the piece should provide the "evidence" which mapped the developmental process of discussion, through our individual and collective journeys.[9]

In terms of its informational content, the fourteen-page piece, constructed as a patchwork of statements and quotations, contains little from Warwicker that is not available elsewhere. A "simple question/answer," skillfully conducted, might have elicited new insights into his background and motivation. (Anyone who imagines there is anything simple about seeing an interview through from the formulation of appropriate questions to its final appearance in print should try it.) But the main problem lies not so much in the conceptual framework, which might have been made to work, as in the unconvincing tone of the writing and the lack of critical distance the writer brings to an undeniably timely subject. The pair meet in the Rose Garden in London's Holland Park, where the "tranquillity is shattered," we are told, by the arrival of "London's infamous graphic design anarchist." John—it is first-name terms throughout—is wearing a pair of "all-essential" Arnett sunglasses, and he is in an "upbeat and chatty mood indicating that things were going very well for him." It seems that for Tomato, the paragraph concludes, "everything is coming up roses." Even journalists who prefer to sit on the fence would have avoided a corny punch line like this.

It is unnecessary, perhaps, to go into further stylistic analysis of this piece. A much higher degree of writing competence is needed before such an exercise lives up to its claim of offering forms of insight that are inaccessible—in some way that is never properly explained by the author—to more conventional means. The brevity of the individual text components calls for, if anything, a particularly concentrated and specialized form of writing—almost a screenwriter's skill. The larger question that might be asked is whether real critical detachment is possible when a writer allows the critical framework to be determined at the outset by the personal preferences of the subject.

One of the factors shaping this piece, I suspect, is the writer's desire to become at least half of its subject. "I was of the opinion," the author says, "that the process of us working together on this piece in a collaboration would ultimately lead to a positive exploitation of each person's cognitive abilities and personal viewpoints." What we are increasingly seeing, as the new graphic design criticism unfolds, is writing by writers who wish they were the star of the show. Unless the author is a Garrison Keillor, whose life is his subject matter, readers aren't reading because they want to know about the writer, but because they want to know about the writer's subject. Naturally, readers do get to know some—though by no means all—writers over time by what they choose to write about, by their point of view, by their writing style, and by personal details they sometimes let slip where appropriate, but it can take years, and a lot of writing, to build up such a relationship with an audience. It is a big mistake to imagine that just because you suddenly find yourself in print, you are instantly fascinating to readers as a subject in your own right.

And yet, having sounded this cautionary note, in a much subtler and more positive sense, the most compelling critical writing is a journey of self-discovery in which the critic is at times quite nakedly exposed. Critics undertake a prolonged and sometimes profound dialogue with their own instincts, sensibility, understanding, and intellect in the hope of discovering what they think in the first place and why, precisely, they think it. They are learning in public. Readers come to criticism for very similar reasons, to take part in this dialogue, using the writing as guide, touchstone, and punching bag. With so much at stake, critics need a nose to uncover the truth and a willingness to speak as they find; not truth in some absolute sense, but truth to their own experience and perceptions. The most valuable criticism does not simply sharpen our tools, it *is* a tool—a tool for revelation, analysis, and reflection. As such, it should occupy a place at the very heart of the educational process.

NOTES

1. Yolanda Zappaterra, "The Art of Barthes," *Design Week* (February 28, 1997): 32.
2. Ashley Havinden, "Does Today's Criticism Help Design?" *Printing Review*, no. 60 (winter 1952–53): 36.
3. Massimo Vignelli, foreword to R. Roger Remington and Barbara J. Hodik, *Nine Pioneers in American Graphic Design* (Cambridge, Mass., and London: MIT Press, 1989), ix.
4. Andrew Blauvelt, "Dumb," *Eye* 6, no. 22 (autumn 1996): 54–57.
5. Anne Bush, "Criticism and the Politics of Absence," *Emigre*, no. 36 (fall 1995).
6. Terry Eagleton, *The Function of Criticism: From* The Spectator *to Post-Structuralism* (1984; reprint, London and New York: Verso, 1996), 124.
7. See *Eye* 6, no. 24 (spring 1997): 57.
8. For a brief discussion of the implications of high-quality reproduction in the context of *Eye*, see Robin Kinross, "In the Same Bed" (letter to the editor), *Eye* 3, no. 12 (1994): 3.
9. Teal Triggs and John Warwicker, "Inthisworldtogether," *Emigre*, no. 40 (1996): 33–47.

Thanks to Eric Kindel

Graphic Authorship

Michael Rock

What does it mean to call for graphic designers to be authors? "Authorship," in one form or another, has been a popular term in graphic design circles, especially those circles that revolve around the edge of the profession, the design academies, and the murky territory that exists between design and art. The word has an important ring to it, and it connotes seductive ideas of origination and agency. But the question of how designers become authors is a difficult one, and exactly who are the designer/authors and what authored design looks like depends entirely on how you end up defining the term and criterion you chose to determine entrance into the pantheon.

In order to subject the problem of design authorship to close examination, it is first necessary to dispense with some definitions before moving on to more specific design examples and suggestions for possible theories of graphic authorship. It may also be useful to reexamine the preconceived qualities we attribute to this powerful figure, the author, and wonder how those attributes apply to a profession traditionally associated more with the communication than with the origination of messages. Finally, it is interesting to speculate about how theories of authorship can serve to legitimize marginalized activities like design and how authorial aspirations may actually end up reinforcing certain conservative notions of design production—notions that might contradict the stated goals of the budding designer/author.

WHAT IS AN AUTHOR?

The issue of the author has been an area of intense scrutiny over the last forty years. The meaning of the word itself has shifted significantly over history. The earliest definitions are not associated with writing per se, in fact, the most inclusive is, "the person who originates or gives existence to anything." But other usages clearly index the authoritarian—even patriarchal—connotations: the "father of all life," "any inventor, constructor, or founder," "one who begets," and "a director, commander, or ruler."

Basically, all literary theory, from Aristotle on, has in some form or another been theory of authorship. This paper, however, is not a history of the author, but a discussion of author as metaphor, so I start with recent history. Wimsatt and Beardsley's seminal text,

The Intentional Fallacy (1946), drove one of the first wedges between the author and the text, dispelling the notion a reader could ever really "know" an author through his or her writing. The so-called death of the author, proposed most succinctly by Roland Barthes in 1968,[1] is closely linked to the birth of critical theory, especially theory based in reader response and interpretation rather than intentionality. Michel Foucault used the rhetorical question, "What Is an Author?" as the title of his influential essay of 1969, which, in response to Barthes, outlines the basic taxonomy and functions of the author and the problems associated with conventional ideas of authorship and origination.[2]

Foucaultian theory holds that the connection between the author and the text has transformed and that there exists a number of author-functions that shape the way readers approach a text. These stubbornly persistent functions are historically determined and culturally specific categories.

The earliest sacred texts were authorless, their origins lost in ancient history (e.g., the Vedas and the Gospels). In fact, the ancient, anonymous origin of the text served as a certain kind of authentication. The author's name was symbolic, never attributable to an individual. (The Gospel of Luke, for instance, could be a diversity of texts gathered under the rubric of Luke.)

On the other hand, scientific texts, at least through the Renaissance, demanded an author's name as validation. Far from objective truth, science was based in personal invention and the authority of the scientist. By the eighteenth century, Foucault asserts, the situation had reversed; literature was authored and science became the product of anonymous objectivity. When authors came to be punished for their writing—i.e., when a text could be transgressive—the link between author and text was firmly established. Text came to be seen as a kind of private property, owned by the author, and a romantic criticism rose up that reinforced that relationship, searching for critical keys in the life and intention of the writer. With the rise of scientific method, on the other hand, scientific texts and mathematical proofs were no longer authored texts, but were seen as discovered truths. The scientist revealed an extant phenomena, a fact that anyone faced with the same conditions would discover. Therefore, the scientist and the mathematician could claim to have been first to discover a paradigm, and lend their name to the phenomena, but never claim authorship over it. (For instance, the astronomer that discovers a new star may name it, but does not conjure it.)

Ownership of the text, and the authority granted to authors at the expense of the creative reader, has fueled much of twentieth-century obsession. Poststructuralist reading of authorship tends to critique the prestige attributed to the figure of the author and suggest or speculate about a time after his fall from grace. The focus shifts from the author's intention to the internal workings of the writing itself; not *what* it means but *how* it means. Barthes ends his essay supposing "the birth of the reader comes at the cost of the death of the author."[3] Foucault imagines a time when we might question, "What difference does it make who is speaking?"[4] All attempt to overthrow the notion that a text is a line of words that releases a single, theological meaning—the central message of an author/god—and refocus critical attention on the activity of reading and readers.

Postmodernity began to turn on a "fragmented and schizophrenic decentering and dispersion"[5] of the subject, noted Fredric Jameson. That sense of a decentered text—i.e., a text that is skewed from the direct line of communication from sender to receiver, severed from the authority of its origin, and existing as a free-floating element in a field of possible significations—figured heavily in recent constructions of a design based in reading and readers. But Katherine McCoy's prescient image of designers moving beyond problem solving and by "authoring additional content and a self-conscious critique of the message . . . adopting roles associated with art and literature"[6] was, as often as not, misconstrued. Rather than working to incorporate theory into their methods of production, many self-proclaimed deconstructivist designers literally illustrated Barthes's image of a reader-based text—"a tissue of quotations drawn from innumerable centers of culture"[7]—by scattering fragments of quotations across the surface of their "authored" posters and book covers. (The technique was something like, theory is complicated, so my design is complicated.) The rather dark implications of Barthes's theory, note Ellen Lupton and J. Abbott Miller, were fashioned into "a romantic theory of self-expression."[8]

Perhaps, after years in the somewhat thankless position of the faceless facilitator, many designers were ready to start speaking out. Some designers may be eager to discard the internal affairs of formalism—to borrow Paul de Man's metaphor—and branch out to the foreign affairs of external politics and content.[9] In that way, by the seventies, design began to discard the kind of scientistic approach that held sway for several decades. (Even as early as the twenties, Trotsky was labeling formalist artists the "chemists of art.")[10] That approach is evident in the rationalist design ideology that preached strict adherence to an eternal grid and a kind of rational approach to design. (Keep in mind that although this example is a staple of critiques of modernism, in actuality, the objectivists represented a small fragment of the design population at the time.)

Müller-Brockmann's evocation of the "aesthetic quality of mathematical thinking"[11] is certainly the clearest and most frequently cited example of this approach. Müller-Brockmann and a slew of fellow researchers like Kepes, Dondis, and Arnheim worked to uncover preexisting order and form in the manner a scientist works to reveal a natural "truth." But what is most interesting in Müller-Brockmann's writing is his reliance on tropes of submission; the designer "submits" to the will of the system, "forgoes" personality, and "withholds" interpretation.

In his introduction to *Compendium for Literates,* which attempts a highly rational dissection of writing, Karl Gerstner describes the organization of his book, claiming "all the components are atomic, i.e., in principle they are irreducible. In other words, they establish a principle."

The reaction to that drive for an irreducible theory of design is well documented. On the surface, at least, it would seem that contemporary designers were moving from authorless, scientific text—in which inviolable visual principles were carefully revealed through extensive visual research—toward a more textual position in which the designer could claim some level of ownership over the message. (This at the time that literary theory was trying to move away from that very position.) But some of the basic, institutional features of design practice have a way of getting tangled up in zealous attempts at self-expression. The idea of a decentered message does not necessarily sit well in a professional relationship in which the client is paying a designer to convey specific information or emotions. In addition, most design is done in some kind of collaborative setting, either within a client relationship or in the context of a design studio that utilizes the talents of numerous creative people, thus the origin of any particular idea is increasingly clouded. And the ever-present pressure of technology and electronic communication only further muddies the water.

IS THERE AN AUTEUR IN THE HOUSE?

It is not surprising to find that Barthes's *Death of the Author* was written in Paris in 1968, the year students joined workers on the barricades in the general strikes and the year the Western world flirted with real social revolution. To call for the overthrow of authority in the form of the author in favor of the reader—read that "masses"—had real resonance in 1968. But to lose power, you must have already worn the mantle. Thus, designers had a bit of a dilemma overthrowing a power they may have never possessed.

The figure of the author implied a total control over creative activity and seemed an essential ingredient of high art. If the relative level of genius was the ultimate measure of artistic achievement, activities that lacked a clear central authority figure were necessarily devalued.

Almost ten years earlier, film critic and budding director François Truffaut had proposed *La politique des auteurs*, a polemical strategy developed to reconfigure a critical theory of the cinema. The problem facing the auteur critics was how to create a theory that imagined the film, necessarily the work of broad collaboration, as a work of a single artist and thus a work of art.

The solution was to develop a set of criteria that allowed a critic to decree certain directors as "auteurs." In order to establish the film as a work of art, auteur theory held that the director—heretofore merely a third of the creative troika of director, writer, and cinematographer—had the ultimate control of the entire project.

Auteur theory—especially as espoused by American critic Andrew Sarris[12]— speculated that directors must meet three essential criteria in order to pass into the sacred hall of the auteur. Sarris proposed that the director must demonstrate technical expertise, have a stylistic signature that is demonstrated over the course of several films, and, most importantly, through choice of projects and cinematic treatment, demonstrate a consistency of vision and evoke a palpable interior meaning through his work. Since the film director often had little control of the material—especially in the Hollywood studio system that assigned directors to projects—the signature way he treated a varying range of scripts and subjects was especially important in establishing auteur credentials.

The interesting thing about the auteur theory was that, unlike literature, film theorists, like designers, had to construct the notion of the author as a legitimizing strategy, as a method of raising what was considered low entertainment to the plateau of fine art. By coronating the director as the author of the film, the *critics* could elevate certain subjects to the status of high art. That elevation, in turn, would facilitate new freedoms granted to the director in future projects. (Tantrums could be thrown in the name of artistic vision. "I'm an artist, dammit, not a butcher!" Expensive wines could be figured into overhead to satisfy rarefied palates.)

The parallel to design practice is quite striking. Like the film director, the art director or designer is often distanced from his or her material and often works collaboratively, directing the activity of a number of other creative people. In addition, over the course of a career, the designer works on a number of diverse projects that have widely varying levels of creative potential, so any inner meaning must come through the aesthetic treatment as much as it does from the content.

If we apply the auteur criteria to graphic designers, we yield a body of work that may be elevated to auteur status. For instance, technical proficiency could be fulfilled by any number of practitioners, but couple technical proficiency with a signature style and the field narrows. The list of names that could fill those two criteria would be familiar, as their work is often published, awarded, and praised. (And, of course, the selective republishing of certain work, and exclusion of other, constructs a unified and stylistically consistent oeuvre.)

But, great technique and style alone do not an auteur make. If we add the third requirement of interior meaning, how does the list fare? Are there graphic designers who, by special treatment and choice of projects, approach the issue of deeper meaning the way a Bergman, Hitchcock, or Welles does?

Of course, how do you compare a film poster with the film itself? The very scale of a cinematic project allows for a sweep of vision not possible in graphic design. Therefore, as the single design project lacks weight, graphic auteurs, almost by definition, have long-established bodies of work in which discernible patterns emerge. The auteur uses very specific client vehicles to attain a consistency of meaning. (Renoir observed that an artistic director spends his whole career remaking variations on the same film.) Think of the almost fetishistic way that a photographer like Helmut Newton returns to a particular vision of class and sexuality no matter what he is assigned to shoot.

However, many great stylists don't seem to make the cut, as it is difficult to discern a larger message in their work, i.e., a message that transcends the stylistic elegance. (You have to ask yourself, What's the work about?) Perhaps it's the absence or presence of an overriding philosophy or individual spirit that diminishes some designed work and elevates other.

We may have been applying a modified graphic auteur theory for many years without really paying attention. What has design history been if not a series of critical elevations and demotions as our attitudes about style and inner meaning evolve? In trying to describe interior meaning, Sarris finally resorts to "the intangible difference between one personality and another."[13] That retreat to intangibility—the "I can't say what it is, but I know it when I see it" aspect—is the Achilles' heel of the auteur theory, which has long since fallen into disfavor in film criticism circles. It never dealt adequately with the collaborative nature of the cinema and the messy problems of moviemaking. But, while the theory is passé, its effect is still with us; the director is, to this day, squarely in the middle of our perception of film structure.

The application of auteur theory may be too limited an engine for our current image of design authorship, but there are a variety of other ways to frame the issue. There exist a number of paradigms on which we could base our practice: the artist book, concrete poetry, political activism, publishing, illustration, and others.

The general authorship rhetoric seems to include any work by a designer that is self-motivated, from artist books to political activism. But artist books easily fall within the realm and descriptive power of art criticism. Activist work may be neatly explicated using allusions to propaganda, graphic design, public relations, and advertising.

Perhaps the graphic author is actually one who writes and publishes material about design. This category would include Josef Müller-Brockmann and Rudy VanderLans, Paul Rand and Erik Spiekermann, William Morris and Neville Brody, Robin Kinross and Ellen Lupton—rather strange bedfellows. The entrepreneurial arm of authorship affords the possibility of personal voice and wide distribution. The challenge is that most split the activities into three recognizable and discrete actions: editing, writing, and designing. Even as their own clients, design remains the vehicle for the written thought. (Kinross, for example, works as a historian, then changes hats and becomes a typographer.) Rudy VanderLans is perhaps the purest of the entrepreneurial authors. *Emigre* is a project in which the content is the form—i.e., the formal exploration is as much the content of the magazine as the articles—the three actions blur into one contiguous whole. VanderLans expresses his message through the selection of material (as an editor), the content of the writing (as a writer), and the form of the pages and typography (as form giver).

Ellen Lupton and partner J. Abbott Miller are an interesting variation on this model. A project like *The Bathroom, the Kitchen, and the Aesthetics of Waste*, an exhibition at the MIT List Gallery, seems to approach a kind of graphic authorship. The message of the exhibit is explicated equally through graphic/visual devices as well as text panels and descriptions. The design of the show evokes the design issues that are the content; it is clearly self-reflexive.

Lupton and Miller's work is primarily critical; it forms and represents a reading of exterior social or historical phenomena and explicates that message for a specific audience. But, there is a subset of work that is often overlooked by the design community, the illustrated book, which is almost entirely concerned with the generation of creative narrative. Books for children have been one of the most successful venues for the author/ artist, and bookshops are packed with the fruits of their labors. But many illustrators have used the book in wholly inventive ways and produced serious work. Illustrator/authors include Sue Coe, Art Spiegelman, Charles Burns, David MacAulay, Chris Van Allsburg, Edward Gorey, and Maurice Sendak. In addition, the comic book and the graphic novel have generated a renewed interest both in artistic and critical circles. Works like Spiegelman's *Maus* and Coe's *X* and *Porkopolis* extend the form into new areas and suggest expanded possibilities.

If the ways a designer could be an author are complex and confused, the way designers have used the term and the value attributed to it are equally so. Any number of recent statements claim authorship as the panacea to the woes of the browbeaten designer. In an article in *Emigre,* author Anne Burdick proposed that "designers must consider themselves authors, *not facilitators.* This shift in perspective implies responsibility, voice, action. . . . With voice comes a more personal connection and opportunity to explore individual options."[14] A recent call for entries for a design exhibition entitled *designer as author: voices and visions* sought to identify "graphic designers who are engaged in work that *transcends* the traditional service-oriented commercial production, and who pursue projects that are personal, social or investigative in nature."[15] (italics mine) In the rejection of the role of the *facilitator* and in the call for *transcendence,* there is the implication that authored design holds some higher, purer purpose. The amplification of the personal voice compels designers to take possession of their texts and legitimizes design as an equal of the more traditionally privileged forms of authorship.

But if the proclivity of the contemporary designer is toward open reading and free textual interpretation—as a litany of contemporary theorists have convinced us—that desire is thwarted by oppositional theories of authorship. The cult of the author narrows interpretation and places the author at the center of the work. Foucault noted that the figure of the author is not a particularly liberating one. By transferring the authority of the text back to the author, by focusing on voice, presence becomes a limiting factor, containing and categorizing the work. The author as origin, authority, and ultimate owner of the text guards against the free will of the reader. The figure of the author reconfirms the traditional idea of the genius/creator, and the esteem or status conferred on the man or woman always frames the work and imbues it with some mythical value.

While some claims for the value of authorship may simply call for a renewed sense of responsibility, at times they seem to be ploys for property rights, attempts to finally exercise some kind of agency where traditionally there has been none. Ultimately, author equals authority. The longing for graphic authorship may be the longing for a kind of legitimacy, or a kind of power, that has so long eluded the obedient designer. But do we get anywhere by celebrating the designer as the central character? Isn't that what fueled the *last* fifty years of design history? If we really want to move beyond the designer-as-hero model, we may have to imagine a time when we can ask, What difference does it make who designed it?

Perhaps, in the end, authorship is just not a very convincing metaphor with which to describe the activity we understand as design. There are few examples of work that is clearly the product of design authors and not designer/authors, and the few clear examples tend to be the exceptions to the rule.

I propose three alternative models for design that, rather than glorify the act and sanctify the practice, attempt to describe the activity as it exists and as it could evolve: designer as translator, designer as performer, and designer as director.

The first model, designer as translator, is based on the assumption that the act of design is essentially the clarification of material or the remodeling of content from one form to another. The ultimate goal is the expression of the content rendered in a form that reaches a new audience. (I am drawn to this metaphor by Ezra Pound's translations of poetry composed in Asian characters. Pound translated not only the literality of the character, but the visual component of the poem as well. Thus, the original is rendered as raw material reshaped into the conventions of Western poetry. The translation becomes a second art.)

Translation is neither scientific nor ahistorical. Every translation reflects both the character of the original and the spirit of the contemporary as well as the individuality of the translator. (An 1850 translation of *The Odyssey* will be radically different from a 1950 one.)

In certain works, the designer remolds the raw material of given content, rendering it legible to a new audience. Like the translator of poetry, the designer not only transforms the literal meaning of the elements, but must translate the spirit as well. For example, Bruce Mau's design of a book version of Chris Marker's film *La Jetée* attempts to translate the original material from one form to another. Mau is certainly not the author of the work, but the translator of form and spirit. The designer is the intermediary.

The performer metaphor is based on the traditional performing arts of theater and music. The actor is not the author of the script, the musician not the composer of the score, but without actor or musician, the art cannot be realized. The actor provides the physical expression of the work. Every work could have an infinite number of physical expressions. Every performance recontextualizes the original work. (Here, imagine the range of interpretations of the plays of Shakespeare.) Each performer brings a certain reading to the work. (No two actors play the same role the same way.)

In this model, the designer transforms and expresses content through graphic devices. The score or script is enhanced and made whole by the performance. And so, the designer becomes the physical manifestation of the content—not author, but performer: the one who gives life to (who speaks) the content, who contextualizes the content and brings it into the frame of the present.

Examples abound, from early dada, situationist, and fluxus experiments to more recent typographic scores like Warren Lehrer's performance typography or experimental typography from Edward Fella or David Carson. The most notable example is perhaps Quentin Fiore's performance of McLuhan. It was Fiore's graphic treatment as much as McLuhan's words that made *The Medium is the Massage* a worldwide phenomenon. (Other examples include any number of "graphic interpretations," such as Alan Hori's reinvention of Beatrice Warde's "Crystal Goblet" essay or Scott Makela's improvisation on a Tucker Viemiseter's lecture, both originally printed in Michael Bierut's publication *ReThinking Design*.)

The third model is the designer as director and is a direct function of bigness. This model is possible only in projects of a large-enough scale that the meaning can be manufactured by the arrangement of the project's elements. It is only in large-scale installations, advertising campaigns, mass-distribution magazines, and very large books that we see evidence of such a paradigm.

In such large projects, the designer orchestrates masses of materials to shape meaning from given content. Working like a film director who oversees a script, a series of performances, photographers, artists, and production crews, the meaning of the work is a product of the entire production. Large-scale, mass-distribution campaigns, like those for Nike or Coca-Cola, are examples of this approach. Curatorial projects such as Sean Perkin's catalog *Experience,* which creates an exhibition of other design projects, is another example of this model.

But perhaps the clearest paradigm is Irma Boom's project for SHV Corporation. Working in conjunction with an archivist for over five years, Boom shaped a narrative out of an undifferentiated lump of raw data. The meaning and narrative of the book is not a product of the words, but almost exclusively the function of the sequence of the pages and the cropping of the images. It is a case of the designer creating meaning almost exclusively through the devices of design. The scale of the book allows for thematic development, contradiction, and coincidence.

The value of these models is that they accept the multivalent activity of design without resorting to totalizing description. The problem with authorship is that it encourages both ahistorical and acultural readings of design. It grants too much agency, too much control to the lone artist/genius, and discourages interpretation by validating a "right" reading of a work.

On the other hand, work is made by someone. And the difference between the way different subjects approach situations, the way different writers or designers make sense of their worlds, is at the heart of a certain criticism. The challenge is to accept the multiplicity of methods that comprise design language. In the end, authorship is only a device to compel designers to rethink process and expand their methods.

If we really need to coin a phrase that describes an activity that encompasses imaging, editing, narration, chronicling, performing, translating, organizing, and directing, I'll conclude with a suggestion: designer = designer.

NOTES

1. Roland Barthes,"The Death of the Author," in *Image-Music-Text,* trans. Stephen Heath (New York: Hill and Wang, 1977).

2. Michel Foucault, "What Is an Author," in *Textual Strategies,* ed. Josué Harari (Ithaca: Cornell University Press, 1979).

3. Barthes, 145.

4. Foucault, 160.

5. Fredric Jameson quoted in Mark Dery, "The Persistence of Industrial Memory," *ANY,* no. 10.

6. Katherine McCoy, "American Graphic Design Expression," *Design Quarterly,* no. 148 (1990): 16.

7. Barthes, 146.

8. Ellen Lupton and J. Abbott Miller, "Deconstruction and Graphic Design: History Meets Theory," *Visible Language* 28.4, ed. Andrew Blauvelt (fall 1994): 351.

9.   Paul de Man, "Semiology and Rhetoric," in *Textual Strategies,* ed. Josué Harari (Ithaca: Cornell University Press, 1979), 121.

10. Leon Trotsky, "The Formalist School of Poetry and Marxism," in *Literature and Revolution,* trans. Rose Strumsky (Ann Arbor: University of Michigan Press, 1960), 110.

11. Josef Müller-Brockmann, *Grid Systems in Graphic Design* (Stuttgart: Verlag Gerd Hatje, 1981), 10.

12. Andrew Sarris, *The Primal Screen* (New York: Simon and Schuster, 1973).

13. Andrew Sarris, "Notes on the Auteur Theory in 1962," in *Film Culture Reader,* ed. P. Adams Sitney (New York: Praeger Publishers, 1970), 133.

14. Anne Burdick, "The State of Design History," *Emigre, no.* 27.

15. "Re:Quest for Entries," *designer as author: voices and visions* exhibition.

The Designer as Producer

Ellen Lupton

The slogan "designer as author" has enlivened debates about the future of graphic design since the early 1990s. The word "author" suggests agency, intention, and creation, as opposed to the more passive functions of consulting, styling, and formatting. Authorship is a provocative model for rethinking the role of the graphic designer at the start of the millennium; it hinges, however, on a nostalgic ideal of the writer or artist as a singular point of origin.[1] The avant-garde movements of the 1910s and 1920s critiqued the ideal of authorship as a process of dredging unique forms from the depths of the interior self. Artists and intellectuals challenged romantic definitions of art by plunging into the worlds of mass media and mass production. As an alternative to designer as "author," I propose designer as "producer." Production is a concept embedded in the history of modernism. Avant-garde artists and designers treated the techniques of manufacture not as neutral, transparent means to an *end,* but as devices equipped with cultural meaning and aesthetic character. In 1934, the German critic Walter Benjamin wrote "The Author as Producer," a text that attacked the conventional view of authorship as a purely literary enterprise.[2] He exclaimed that new forms of communication—film, radio, advertising, newspapers, the illustrated press—were melting down traditional artistic genres and corroding the borders between writing and reading, authoring and editing.

Benjamin was a Marxist, committed to the notion that the technologies of manufacture should be owned by the workers who operate them. In Marxist terminology, the "means of production" are the heart of human culture and should be collectively owned. Benjamin claimed that writing (and other arts) is grounded in the material structures of society, from the educational institutions that foster literacy to the publishing networks that manufacture and distribute texts. In detailing an agenda for a politically engaged literary practice, Benjamin demanded that artists must not merely adopt political "content," but must revolutionize the means through which their work is produced and distributed.

Benjamin attacked the model of the writer as an "expert" in the field of literary form, equipped only to craft words into texts and not to question the physical life of the work. The producer must ask, Where will the work be read? Who will read it? How will it be manufactured? What other texts and pictures will surround it? Benjamin argued that artists and photographers must not view their task as solely visual, lest they become mere suppliers of form to the existing apparatus of bourgeois publishing:

> What we require of the photographer is the ability to give his picture the caption
> that wrenches it from modish commerce and gives it a revolutionary useful value.
> But we shall make this demand most emphatically when we—the writers—take
> up photography. Here, too, therefore, technical progress is for the author as
> producer the foundation of political progress.[3]

Benjamin claimed that to bridge the divide between author and publisher, author and reader, poet and popularizer is a revolutionary act because it challenges the professional and economic categories upon which the institutions of "literature" and "art" are erected. To enact this revolutionary shift, the author must embrace the new technologies of communication.

Benjamin's Marxist emphasis has a tragic edge when viewed from the vantage point of today. By the time he wrote "The Author as Producer," abstract art was already at variance with Stalin's state-enforced endorsement of social realism. Benjamin applauded dada and surrealism for challenging the institutions of art, and yet, such experimental forms were forbidden in the Soviet state he so admired. Benjamin's theory of the author as producer remains relevant today, however, as writers, artists, designers, and editors challenge the existing structures of media and publishing, opening new paths of access to the means of manufacture and dissemination.

In the 1920s, Benjamin met László Moholy-Nagy, the Hungarian constructivist who had become a prominent figure at the Bauhaus. Benjamin's 1928 collection of essays *One-Way Street* reflects on experimental typography and the proliferation of such commercial forms as the pamphlet, poster, and advertisement, which were upending the classical book as literature's sacred vessel. Benjamin wrote, "Printing, having found in the book a refuge in which to lead an autonomous existence, is pitilessly dragged out onto the street by advertisements and subjected to the brutal heteronomies of economic chaos. This is the hard schooling of its new form."[4] Describing the relation of authorship to technology, Benjamin predicted that the writer will begin to compose his work with a typewriter instead of a pen when "the precision of typographic forms has entered directly into the conception of his books. One might suppose that new systems with more variable typefaces might then be needed."[5]

Such "new systems" are, of course, ubiquitous today in the form of software for word processing and desktop publishing. These tools have altered the tasks of graphic designers, enlarging their powers as well as burdening them with more kinds of work to do. Such is the rub of despecialization. Benjamin celebrated the proletarian ring of the word "production," and the word carries those connotations forward into the current period. Within the professional context of graphic design, "production" is linked to the preparation of "artwork" for mechanical reproduction, rather than to the intellectual realm of "design." Production belongs to the physical activity of the base, the factory floor: it is the traditional domain of the pasteup artist, the stripper, the letterer, the typesetter. The "desktop revolution" that began in the mid-1980s brought these roles back into the process of design. The proletarianization of the editorial process offers designers a new crack at materialism, a chance to reengage the physical aspects of our work. Whereas the term "author," like "designer," suggests the cerebral workings of the mind, "production" privileges the activity of the body. Production is rooted in the material world. It values things over ideas, making over imagining, practice over theory.

When Benjamin called for authors to become producers, he did not mean for them to become factory workers alienated from the form and purpose of the manufactured thing. Likewise, the challenge for educators today is to help designers become the masters, not the slaves, of technology. There exist opportunities to seize control—intellectually and economically—of the means of production and to share that control with the reading public, empowering them to become producers as well as consumers of meaning. As Benjamin phrased it in 1934, the goal is to turn "readers or spectators into collaborators."[6] His words resonate in current educational models, which encourage students to view the reader as a participant in the construction of meaning.

How can schools help students along such a path at this critical juncture in our history?

- Language is a raw material. Enhance students' verbal literacy, to give them the confidence to work with and as editors without forcing them to become writers.
- Theory is a practice. Foster literacy by integrating the humanities into the studio. Infuse the act of making with the act of thinking.
- Writing is a tool. Casual writing experiences encourage students to use writing as a device for "prototyping," to be employed alongside sketching, diagramming, and other forms of conceptualization.
- Technology is physical. Whether the product of our work is printed on paper or emitted from a screen, designers deal with the human, material response to information.
- The medium is on the menu. Familiarize students with the many ways that information and ideas are disseminated in contemporary life. Give them the tools to find their rightful place in the food chain.

The power of the term "author"—its cultural authority—lies in its connection to the written text. In order for designers to take charge of the content and social function of their work, they need not become fluent writers, no more than an art director must become a professional photographer or illustrator in order to use these media effectively. In the business of film, a producer brings together individuals with a broad range of skills—writing, directing, acting, cinematography, editing, and so on—in a work whose authorship is shared. For the designer to become a producer, he or she must have the skills to begin directing content, by critically navigating the social, aesthetic, and technological systems across which communications flow.

NOTES

1. Michael Rock offers a critical history of "authorship" in "The Designer as Author," originally published in *Eye* 5, 20 (spring 1996): 44–53 and reprinted in this volume.

2. Walter Benjamin, "The Author as Producer," in *Reflections: Essays, Aphorisms, Autobiographical Writings,* ed. Peter Demetz (New York: Schocken Books, 1978), 220–38.

3. Benjamin, 230.

4. From "One-Way Street," in *Reflections: Essays, Aphorisms, Autobiographical Writings,* 77. My attention was drawn to Benjamin's acquaintance with Moholy-Nagy in a lecture given by Frederic Schwartz at the Victoria and Albert Museum, London, March 21, 1997.

5. Benjamin, 79.

6. Benjamin, 233.

Design Studies: Proposal for a New Doctorate

Victor Margolin

Today, visual communication design and the design of industrial products are undergoing a profound transformation as new technologies continually challenge the way images and things are produced. The results of this transformation are both salutary and alarming. Regarding visual communication, we can recognize as salutary a widening of the project field in which visual communicators work. Graphic designers now routinely design websites, arrange exhibitions, contribute to interactive software design, and engage in the production of moving-image sequences that include sound. The boundaries between graphic design and other media such as film, video, and product design have begun to blur, and many crossovers are occurring. On the alarming side, one notes that all these changes are happening with insufficient reflection concerning which past ideas and methods of practice might be preserved as sites of resistance to a powerful technological determinism.

Not only is the actual practice of design becoming more complex, but there is also a recognition that design does not occur in a neutral space; it is an activity that produces messages and objects in a social sphere that is highly charged with differing values. To better understand the implications of their work, designers therefore need to know more about this sphere and how it determines the conditions for their work.

Given the profundity of the changes that confront design, is it any wonder that the traditional foundations of design education are now being severely questioned and in many cases being found inadequate? My own engagement with this situation has been one of reflection on design rather than the practice of it. I teach design history to future designers, conduct seminars on issues in contemporary design, and participate as an author and editor in the production of design writing. I have long been interested in the prospects of a doctoral program to study design as a cultural activity, but have yet to find an institution to undertake such a program. But at this stage of design's development, it is better to talk about new doctoral programs, regardless of the immediate opportunity to make them happen, than to defer such discussion to a more propitious time.

Until a few years ago, most educators, whether in visual communication or product design, would have been skeptical of the idea that a doctorate in design could be of any relevance to the design professions or that a doctorate in a design-related field could open up a new space for research not already covered by existing disciplines such as art history or sociology. Today, things are different. In the United States, the Institute of Design in Chicago and the University of Minnesota have doctorates in design, and one is being planned at North Carolina State University, while the Bard Graduate Center in New York City is planning a Ph.D. in the history of the decorative arts, design, and culture. In Germany, there are doctoral programs at the University of Wuppertal and in Hanover; in Italy there is one at the Milan Politecnico; in England, a doctoral program exists at the University of Reading; and in Finland there is one at Helsinki's University of Art and Design, where students are working primarily on issues related to theory, philosophy, and management. There are Ph.D. programs in design at Istanbul Technical University and Bilkent University in Turkey, a new design doctorate, combining studies in design history and practice, is on the drawing board at the Higher Institute of Industrial Design (ESDI) at the University of Rio de Janeiro in Brazil, and another is being developed at the National University of Mexico in Mexico City.

Interest in design doctorates is particularly strong in the United Kingdom where the recent transformation of the polytechnics into universities has generated a need to justify this new status by upgrading study courses so that faculty can compete in national competitions for research funds. This has produced an intense exploration of different models of doctoral study, such as practice-led degrees in which the documentation of art or design production, rather than scholarly writing, is at the core of the program.[1]

Design studies, the research area about which I want to speak here, is the study of design in and as culture. Just as cultural research, in the broadest sense, is neither the exclusive purview of the social sciences nor the humanities, so ought the case be similar for the more narrowly focused study of design. Therefore, my definition of design studies includes but goes beyond the traditional history, theory, and criticism approaches to art, architecture, and design in order to incorporate the social sciences as well.[2]

To distinguish my approach to a design studies doctorate from the various doctoral programs in design already in existence and in preparation, I want to relate it to three models of research described by Christopher Frayling, rector of the Royal College of Art (RCA).[3] They are research *into* art and design, research *through* art and design, and research *for* art and design. Frayling's research *into* art and design comes closest to my own ideas about design studies. In this category he includes the traditional history, theory, criticism triumvirate, but also incorporates aesthetic or perceptual research and research into technical, material, and structural perspectives on art and design.

Research *through* art and design, Frayling's second category, is centered on the studio project and relates to what is being called, elsewhere in the United Kingdom, practice-led research. As examples, Frayling cites research into the behavior of materials, customizing a piece of technology to accomplish new tasks, or documenting a practical studio experiment. In this type of research, documentation of what is done is an essential component.

According to Frayling, the third category, research *for* art and design, is the most difficult to characterize. It is an area where the primary conveyor of research accomplishment is an art or design object or a body of such objects. At the RCA, says Frayling, research *for* design is not currently an option, although higher or honorary doctorates are given as honors to individuals for distinguished bodies of exhibited or published work.

The scope of design studies, considered within Frayling's first category of research *into* art and design, is quite broad. At a conference entitled "Discovering Design" that Richard Buchanan and I organized at the University of Illinois, Chicago, in November 1990, a small group of scholars and practitioners presented and discussed papers on design with the aim of creating a space for productive conversation. The conference was successful because the participants, who included historians, sociologists, psychologists, political scientists, cultural studies theorists, philosophers, designers, and marketing experts, had a stake in exploring common themes rather than defending disciplinary boundaries. They heard and responded to each other in an atmosphere of mutual respect and shared inquiry. This is the spirit in which I see design studies developing at the doctoral level.[4]

Although design history is a central practice for design studies, I have argued for its inclusion within a wider field of research because I believe that history, if brought into relation with other disciplines, can contribute much to the study of design in contemporary culture as well as to its role in the culture of the past.[5] While I don't wish to subsume historical or theoretical research under research for practice, I do believe that it can both inform and be informed by practice if the two are considered more closely. When this is not so, as has sometimes been the case in the United Kingdom, where design history has a strong relation to cultural studies, the emphasis on practice can be diminished and replaced by a focus on consumption or use.

A good example of how history and theory can productively inform each other is to be found in sociology, where the history of sociological thought, though a study in its own right, remains a strong force in the formation of practicing sociologists. Sociology has developed in such a way that some scholars do their primary research in the field of history while others make theory or field work their central focus. Yet, the sociologist R. Stephen Warner notes the potential relation of these different interests when he states:

> The skills of the historian, while requiring practice, are not wholly esoteric, and
> the nearer in time the object of our explanations the more nearly those skills
> approximate those of the anthropologist or sociological field researcher.[6]

To facilitate the relation of reflection to practice, I believe design studies would be strongest as a field organized by topics rather than by methods. This would encourage more interdisciplinary study than if methodological training were foregrounded. Within a university setting, design studies might therefore be housed in a flexible interdisciplinary center rather than a department, although such a center should be able to grant its own degrees.

To avoid characterizing "design" too precisely, I have been working with a definition that includes the entire artificial world.[7] While this may seem too comprehensive to some, I find it useful because it emphasizes the open horizon of design activity in addition to the existing artifacts that already represent that activity. Design is a practice that continues to redefine itself. Designers invent new subject matter as they take on unprecedented projects. Once considered to be primarily about images and things, design is now also concerned with projects that are about processes and organization.[8] It therefore makes sense for design studies scholars to remain open when considering their field's subject matter. In *Design Issues*, the academic journal that I coedit, my fellow editors and I are consistently pushing the subject matter boundaries to include such topics as the design of aquariums, software, artists' books, typefaces, and even entire organizations. We choose our articles carefully and use their inclusion in the journal polemically, to broaden the idea of the artificial world with which the journal is concerned. A similar strategy could work in design studies where the field's subject matter would be grounded in a core curriculum, but continually defined by the completion of research projects that push the field's boundaries.

As a prelude to my discussion of topics within design studies, I want to note that "design" refers to both an activity and a product; hence, design studies has relations to disciplines that study human action such as sociology and those that study objects such as art history or material culture. The product itself, whatever its form, is bracketed by its conception, planning, and making, on one side, and by its reception, on the other. A design studies scholar may emphasize the conception and planning of objects, which could involve research into invention, production, or design policy. Or research could be done on product reception, using reception theory or rhetoric.

I propose four core topics, or *topoi,* for design studies: design practice, design products, design discourse, and one more that is different from the other three—metadiscourse, which is the reflexive investigation of the field itself. I intend these four topics to embrace the complexity of design culture and the roles that its different actors—designers, managers, theorists, critics, policymakers, curators, and users—play in it. The topics arise from a recognition that design is a dynamic activity whose methods, products, and discourse are interactive and constantly changing.

The study of *design practice* includes those activities related to the conception, planning, and making of a product, and here I define a product as a Web page or a book as well as a lawn mower or a chair. Design practice refers to the people, processes, and organizations that are involved in product planning and production as well as those organizations involved with design policies. Design practice belongs to the realm of social action, which has traditionally been studied by sociologists, anthropologists, psychologists, and other social scientists. Here I would include books such as Donald Schon's *The Reflective Practitioner,* Lucy Suchman's *Plans and Situated Actions,* and Donald Norman's *The Psychology of Everyday Things.*

The study of *design products* emphasizes the identity and interpretation of products and their role in culture. Methods germane to this area are first of all theories of interpretation such as semiotics and rhetoric, but also aesthetics and interpretive methods that may be drawn from structuralism, poststructuralism, or psychoanalysis. The study of products includes the ways that people give meaning to them as objects of contemplation as well as function. Links in this area would be made with scholars in art and design history, philosophy, cultural studies, material culture, technology studies, and related fields. Representative books include *The Meaning of Things* by Mihaly Csikszentmihalyi and Eugene Rochberg-Halton, *The System of Objects* by Jean Baudrillard, *Doing Cultural Studies: The Story of the Sony Walkman* by a group of colleagues at the Open University and the University of Leicester, and Steve Baker's *Picturing the Beast: Animals, Identity, and Representation.*

The study of *design discourse* is concerned with the different arguments about what design is and might be, as these are embodied in the literature of design. This area is the locus for design philosophy and theory as well as criticism. The literature of design is the record of how judgments about design practice and products have developed historically. It includes works by John Ruskin and William Morris, Sigfried Giedion, Jan Tschichold, Herbert Read, and Reyner Banham, as well as Tomás Maldonado, Gillo Dorfles, and Paul Rand, to name some of the more prominent writers. There has been all too little study of design literature, and more work in this field would help to set standards for future authors. Links to this area might be made with literary theorists, philosophers, and critics of art and architecture.[9] I consider this topic to be particularly important as it is the one that should provide the frame for contemporary discourse. All too often, designers make pronouncements about their practice without a knowledge of how their concerns form part of arguments that have a long historical tradition.

The last topic is the *metadiscourse* of design studies. It is the place for reflection on the field itself and the location of the field's self-awareness. It embraces historiography as well as other writings about the study of design. Examples would include Clive Dilnot's seminal two-part article on design history in *Design Issues* and Cheryl Buckley's critique of design history's patriarchal underpinnings in the same journal.[10]

Besides outlining a range of topics, it is also important to address the questions of who might be attracted to a design studies doctorate and what someone might do with it. First, it would be a degree that provides a reflective framework for design practice. Design studies can certainly contribute to the formation of an informed and critical practitioner and might point the way, depending on a student's research, to the development of new forms of practice. Second, a doctorate in design studies would be a useful degree for a design educator who could then bring the relation of reflection and practice into the classroom. This model has been well developed in architecture where it is common for architects or planners to seek doctorates in the history, theory, and criticism of their field. Third, individuals such as design managers, museum curators, or policymakers could use such a degree to explore and refine their understanding of design and culture in order to deepen their own practices. And fourth, as a field, design studies could be a place where historians, anthropologists, sociologists, or political scientists might work on design's place in culture as they earn their doctorates in established disciplines. It could serve as a site to explore and develop research projects and location where this research could be shared and disseminated. I don't imagine that design studies doctoral programs will be pervasive in academia, but certainly a few such programs would provide centers where new knowledge about design in culture could be developed. This knowledge would gradually make its way into design classrooms, studios, publications, and exhibitions and would have the function of raising issues and provoking questions. Such knowledge is badly needed at this critical moment in design's history when designers are faced with eroding divisions of practice as well as the challenge of new social tasks.[11]

The time is right to organize design studies as an academic field. This is a moment when the traditional boundaries in the humanities and social sciences that were established in the nineteenth century are collapsing. As a recent book entitled *Open the Social Sciences: Report of the Gulbenkian Commission on the Restructuring of the Social Sciences* notes: "We are at a moment when the existing disciplinary structure has broken down. We are at a point when it has been questioned and when competing structures are trying to come into existence."[12]

The report makes four recommendations that support the type of academic arrangement I propose for design studies. The authors urge the following changes in the structure of doctoral and postdoctoral research: the expansion of institutions that can bring scholars together for short periods of time to explore specific themes, the establishment of integrated research programs within universities that cut across traditional lines and have funding for limited periods of time; the appointment of professors in more than one department, and the same recommendation for graduate students. Regarding these students, the authors ask:

> Why not make it mandatory for students seeking a doctorate in a given discipline to take a certain number of courses, or do a certain amount of research, that is defined as being within the purview of a second department? This too would result in an incredible variety of combinations. Administered in a liberal but serious fashion, it would transform the present and the future.[13]

Therefore, I do not advocate separate tracks for design historians or critics at the advanced degree level. Instead, I prefer to see scholars develop who can bring different methods of inquiry to bear on a single problem related to design.

Although the focus of design studies is research *into* design rather than *through* or *for* design, the field, nonetheless, has the potential to contribute to the improvement of design practice as part of its purpose to explain how design and designing operate in contemporary culture. This capacity gives design studies a broad mission. Until now, the richness and complexity of design culture have been all too invisible to scholars, practitioners, and the public alike. Design studies, more than any intellectual strategy we have devised thus far, has the potential to remedy this situation.

NOTES

1. A good example of a practice-led doctoral degree in art and design exists at the Robert Gordon University in Aberdeen, Scotland.

2. Art history, once a discipline practiced exclusively by historians, is now being transformed into a discipline of history, theory, and criticism that includes doctoral degree holders who are being asked in some cases to teach theory *rather than* history. In architecture, history, theory, and criticism, doctoral degrees are well established. Among the leading programs are those at MIT and Princeton.

3. Christopher Frayling, "Research in Art and Design," *Royal College of Art Research Papers* 1, no. 1 (1993/94). Frayling derives his distinction of three kinds of research from Herbert Read. On the development of pedagogical methods for advanced research degrees at the RCA, see Alex Seago, "Research Methods for M.Phil. and Ph.D. Students in Art and Design: Contrasts and Conflicts," *Royal College of Art Research Papers* 1, no. 3 (1994/95).

4. The "Discovering Design" conference grew out of several prior meetings in Chicago organized by Victor Margolin and Marco Diani, and sponsored by the Center for Interdisciplinary Research in the Arts (CIRA) at Northwestern University. The first meeting, held in February 1988, was entitled "Design, Technology, and the Future of Postindustrial Society." The second, "Design at the Crossroads," took place in January 1989. Both events included participants from a number of disciplines and practices. The proceedings of the second meeting were published as *Design at the Crossroads* (Evanston: CIRA Monograph Series, 1989). A French translation appeared in a design journal published at the University of Montreal, *Informel* 3, no. 1 (winter 1989).

5. I first discussed the relation of design history to design studies in my article "Design History or Design Studies: Subject Matter and Methods," which was initially published in the British journal *Design Studies*. It was subsequently reprinted in a special History number of *Design Issues* as an argument to which a group of scholars were invited to respond. See *Design Issues* 11, no. 1 (spring 1995).

6. R. Stephen Warner, "Sociological Theory and History of Sociology: Autonomy and Interdependence," *Sociological Theory: A Semi-Annual Journal of the American Sociological Association* 3, no. 1 (spring 1985): 22.

7. My conception of the artificial follows the extremely broad definition introduced by Herbert Simon in his MIT Compton Lectures of 1968, *The Sciences of the Artificial* (Cambridge: MIT Press, 1969). In those lectures, Simon defined the artificial as everything that is human-made. However, unlike Simon, I don't consider design to be a science, nor do I see design studies as a discipline that emulates scientific practice.

8. The argument for an expanded design practice has been cogently made by Richard Buchanan in two articles, "Wicked Problems in Design Thinking," in *The Idea of Design*, ed. Victor Margolin and Richard Buchanan, (Cambridge: MIT Press, 1995), 3–20, and "Branzi's Dilemma: Design in Contemporary Culture," in *Design—Pleasure or Responsibility?* ed. Paivi Tahkokallio and Susan Vihma (Helsinki: University of Art and Design, 1995), 10–29.

9. The number of books and articles that might be listed here is vast. It should be noted, however, that, unlike architecture, there has been no history of design thinking, something that is badly needed. For a listing of sources, see my bibliographic essay "Postwar Design Literature: A Preliminary Mapping," in *Design Discourse: History Theory Criticism*, ed. Victor Margolin (Chicago: University of Chicago Press, 1989), 265–88.

10. Clive Dilnot, "The State of Design History, Part I: Mapping the Field," and "The State of Design History, Part II: Problems and Possibilities," in *Design Discourse: History Theory Criticism*, 213–50, and Cheryl Buckley, "Made in Patriarchy: Toward a Feminist Analysis of Women and Design," in the same volume, 251–64. See also John Walker, *Design History and the History of Design* (London: Pluto Press; New York: Unwin Hyman, 1989).

11. The questioning of existing boundaries of architectural and design practice was central to a symposium on architectural education, organized by Archeworks and the Graham Foundation for Advanced Studies in the Fine Arts in Chicago, March 14, 1997.

12. *Open the Social Sciences: Report of the Gulbenkian Commission on the Restructuring of the Social Sciences* (Stanford: Stanford University Press, 1996), 103. The Commission was chaired by Immanuel Wallerstein and included Calestous Juma, Evelyn Fox Keller, Jürgen Kocka, Dominique Lecourt, V. Y. Mudimbe, Kinhide Mushakoji, Ilya Prigogine, Peter J. Taylor, and Michel-Rolph Trouillot.

13. *Open the Social Sciences*, 105.

The Common Core

Geoffry Fried and Douglass Scott

WHO WE ARE

[Design is] to see things of our world in their interconnection and, where possible, to make things better.

—Armin Hofmann[1]

Design is not the product of an intelligentsia. It is everybody's business, and whenever design loses contact with the public, it is on the losing end. For the first time in history, there is today a total disconnection between art and the people. When I say that design is everybody's business, I don't mean that design is a do-it-yourself job.

—Paul Jacques Grillo[2]

All men are designers. All that we do, almost all the time is design, for design is basic to all human activity. The planning and patterning of any act towards a desired, forseeable end constitutes the design process. Any attempt to separate design, to make it a thing-by-itself, works counter to the inherent value of design as the primary underlying matrix of life.

—Victor Papanek[3]

For some time now, the landscape and boundaries of graphic design have been shifting. In the midst of great turmoil—changing technologies, new working relationships, and ever-increasing access to once specialized tools—many designers and teachers have expressed uncertainty about what graphic design is or should be. As more and more people become involved in activities we once considered exclusive, it seems more difficult to justify the value or define the special nature of what we do.

Since computers have recently made it possible for so many people to manipulate text and images, can everyone claim to be a graphic designer? The answer is both yes and no. In many ways, everyone is a designer, and design is a central activity in our lives.

Anything that involves planning, prototyping, evaluating, and making things—from planning a dinner party to building a bridge—is design at some level. By connecting graphic design to this broader sphere of activities, we will make it easier, in some ways, for people to understand what we do and what it means to do it well.

However, not everyone who uses a computer and a few fonts becomes a professional graphic designer—a good image maker or organizer—just in the way that not everyone who picks up a pencil becomes a professional writer or a good storyteller. The basic values that define our profession must be clearly articulated and constantly renewed if we are to count ourselves as a profession at all, or a worthwhile field of study.

Becoming a professional in any field requires accumulating knowledge and expertise over a period of years. Herbert Simon, social scientist and winner of the 1978 Nobel Prize in economics, suggests a ten-year period of learning in any profession, based on rates of acquiring information and our abilities to retain and process it.[4] He also discusses how the organization of information in our minds increases our level of understanding and creates expertise. It is our ability to recognize patterns, positions, and relationships in large amounts of information that allows us to become experts.

Simon compares the brute-force methods of a chess-playing computer (calculating as many moves ahead as possible) with the pattern recognition skills of the human grand master (recognition of positions and their inherent possibilities). He also describes an experiment in which both beginning players and experts are briefly shown chess positions on a board and are then asked to reproduce them from memory. Beginners try to remember all the squares and all the pieces. Because this means remembering so much information, they tend to make a great number of mistakes. Experts recognize the patterns of play leading to the situation on the board—they only need to remember five or six pieces of information that point to the positions shown—and therefore are able to reproduce the positions more accurately.[5]

In any learning situation, beginners pick up individual bits of information that later organize themselves as sets of relationships. Once we understand the nature or behavior of a particular set, we can forget the individual bits, freeing up space for more learning.

Consider how we, as graphic designers, acquire and use some of our basic visual knowledge. Remember how difficult it was, at some point, to learn about values, sizes, differentiation of type styles (shapes and weights), or the organization of colors? Yet, it is our instant recognition of things light and dark, large and small, bright and dull, smooth or sharp that allows us to make quick judgments about content, emphasis, and visual structure.

Instead of having to remember and catalog every shade of gray, we remember "value" as an axis with varying effects, and we learn many different ways to create those effects. Built one atop another, in increasing complexity, these axes of knowledge define the areas of our expertise within our profession. They support and amplify any aptitudes for visualization, organization, or expression that originally brought us to graphic design.

Another idea Simon discusses is that professions break up into subspecialties, or use new reference tools, when knowledge in a field grows beyond the point of our ability to acquire and use it in a reasonable way.[6] While graphic designers like to see themselves as generalists (and some practice more generally than others), we are now seeing increasing specialization in areas such as environmental graphic design, user interface design, and interactive and information design, in addition to the more traditional areas of print design and books.

All these areas require specific and often distinct professional skills. Work in electronic media requires an attention to time, motion, navigation, and technology that is different from work in print. Print has its own special world of inks, papers, presses, and bindings—with book designers meeting different objectives and using different materials from those who design annual reports, newspapers, or magazines. If you work in exhibit design for any length of time, you learn all about silkscreening on painted aluminum and laminate, but may neglect your paper-sample collection. Most important, you develop a different sense of scale and sequence in each medium that may help or hinder you when moving from one area to another.

Of course, it is possible to make transitions within our field precisely because at its basis all graphic design has a common core. Those who remain generalists in a growing profession take on a new role. Generalists know when to "hand off" a more complex problem, or how to collaborate with those who have complementary professional expertise.

In graphic design, Helvetica gives way to Arbitrary Sans, letterpress gives way to lithography, mechanicals to disks, and who knows what lies beyond. Books and magazines coexist with CD-ROMs and websites, exhibits with virtual reality, flat paper with computer and TV screens. If our work as designers is to have any relevance now and in the future, it will be because we know and understand something about all these things. That, in turn, will only be possible if our basic education exposes the common core of knowledge from which they spring.

WHAT WE TEACH

The graphic designer's expertise can be identified in two ways: (1) that of the "form-giver . . ." (2) that of the "planner . . ." The activities of the form-giver or planner are often inseperable and represent a *range* of practice. Many design problems involve expertise in both.

—Ockerse, Poggenpohl, et. al.[7]

Design that lacks ideas and depends entirely on form for its realization may possess a certain kind of mysterious charm; at the same time it may be uncommunicative. On the other hand, design that depends entirely on content will most likely be so tiresome that it will not compel viewing. "Idea and the form," says James, "are the needle and thread, and I never heard of a guild of tailors who recommended the use of thread without the needle or the needle without the thread." Good design satisfies both idea and form, the needle and the thread.

—Paul Rand[8]

Basic graphic design education should cover subjects relating to perception, concept, and method, with particular emphasis on the relationships among these three things. This provides a broad foundation that can support various specialties and more focused areas of research. It does not limit the method of teaching or prescribe a particular way of organizing curricula; instead, it targets a particular way of understanding our work. Education that is too specialized or that fails to integrate the three areas in a balanced way will limit graphic designers' abilities to adapt to changing circumstances and use their skills in new areas.

Perception refers to visual skills and sensitivities. As one aspect of design education, we try to develop both an ability to see, differentiate, and recognize nuances of shape or form, placement, value, color, and space and an ability to use those characteristics to create specific visual or physical relationships. Contrast, scale, grouping, and proportion are all relationships between things such as pieces of type, images, and the surfaces on which they appear. Our ability to manipulate and relate these things to one another defines one area of our expertise, regardless of the materials being used.

Concepts are visual ideas and the context in which they exist. They are the messages communicated by a specific set of visual relationships in a particular situation (whether intended or not). These are communicated through the organization of the material (structure, emphasis, and hierarchy) and through association with known ideas (symbols, signs, metaphors, and visual language). How things are interpreted is always a function of the context in which they are seen. What is useful in one situation may not be understood or appreciated in another. Part of our job as graphic designers is to know how to generate visual ideas, organize visual material, recognize clear concepts, and know when a concept is appropriate to a specific situation or a particular medium.

Method includes a broad range of skills and activities that allow us to accomplish the tasks described above. At one end of this range are the very specific skills that go with making something in any medium: knowledge of tools, materials, and processes. At the other end are the general problem-solving skills that are common to all areas of design: techniques for problem definition, generation and evaluation of ideas, visualization and prototyping, and implementation, production, and documentation of solutions.

Making something specific is at the heart of the design process, although we ourselves are not always the ones making the final product. We acquire knowledge about how specific things are made, and we also develop methods to test and display the results of our thinking at all stages during the process. Whether you design intuitively or systematically, your problem-solving skills and your interaction with clients and their particular needs are defined by the way you use these methods.

As important as these three individual areas are, perception, concept, and method are most useful when viewed together as an interacting set. Our perceptual skills are intimately related to our methods—our skills at making and manipulating various materials—and are usually developed by practicing those manipulations (just as a musician practices scales). These same perceptual skills must be coupled with the meaning of the things we make and see—the conceptual side of our training—if they are to be used for anything more than simple exercises. Concepts and methods interact when we consider designers' relationships to their clients and society, the meaning or function of an idea, a plan, or an object in a particular situation.

A description of what we should teach, as presented above, in no way limits the number of ways we might accomplish the job. Some teach by example, others by articulating and exploring more specific ideas and techniques. It is clear, however, that in some way education in a profession must define and present basic principles that extend beyond current practices. This is what allows others to understand what you are doing, and what allows you to keep doing it in the face of change.

Imagine a doctor who could not deal with diagnosis in the face of new medicines and new medical techniques, or a lawyer who could not work to establish guilt or innocence in a landscape of changing laws and court reforms. Graphic designers must also be prepared to deal with changing technologies, business conditions, and social structures. While we are teaching students to design a specific thing, we must also be teaching them what it means to design anything.

WHAT WE VALUE

Design is how we continuously express our values and priorities in remaking the world. By connecting vision to action we project ourselves into the future.

—Michael Shannon[9]

Graphic design education is a combination of many subjects, but the first of those is the study of graphic design. When we are asked what we teach, we do not say anthropology, sociology, semiotics, painting, or physics. We answer graphic design, and this is why it is important to carefully define and present the basic knowledge in our field.

That is not to say other subjects are not important in the education of graphic designers. Far from it. Our core of knowledge rests within a larger context of design in general, and is surrounded by the study of art, literature, history, other humanities and social sciences, and the natural sciences as well. We value not only our special expertise, but also our ability to connect that expertise to the social, political, and economic context of the world around us.

It is within the larger context of design that we recognize the nature of our own activities. We see our own efforts to evaluate problems, visualize possibilities, enumerate ideas, mock up solutions and evaluate their effects, mirrored in the efforts of other kinds of designers. We gain an ability to differentiate design from other disciplines: not art, not science, not engineering, but simply design.

The general theories and definitions of this larger field show us ways to ground our work in the concerns of a broader culture. When Herbert Simon says that design "is concerned with how things ought to be, with devising artifacts to attain goals,"[10] he does not specify whose goals are to be obtained in any particular situation. Instead, he and others point to a way of acting—or a posture that prepares us for action—in many different situations.

Studies of disciplines outside of design are equally valuable. This is partly because it is the special nature of our profession to interact with people in many fields. We must be prepared to absorb and respond to information from these varied sources, and to become partners in formulating the content of work we produce. It is also because the purpose of education goes beyond immediate productivity, and because one of its aims should be to broaden our potential for action in the world, not narrow it.

These are the more general goals of any education: the transmission of ideals and values on which a culture and society are based. As we encourage curiosity and experimentation, we also want to foster critical thinking, ethical conduct, and idealism. We want to see these values reflected in the projects our students produce, even as they grapple with the very particular subjects—perception, concept, and method—that we teach.

These subjects have value precisely because their reach extends beyond boundaries of culture, technology, or style. They support the assertion that work of the highest quality is always possible, even as the means for achieving it are in flux.

Bad design will always be with us. We need not fear its spread in an environment where it is easier to make things and easier for people to try their hand at the things we do. Our job is to define and promote the values of good design to those who are disposed to listen, willing to pay, or otherwise eager to participate in the processes that make it possible. These are values that endure through changes of season and fashion, values that include new people and welcome new work, and values that encourage us all to continue learning.

NOTES

1. From the exhibition catalog *universal/Unique*, University of the Arts, Philadelphia, 1988.
2. Paul Jacques Grillo, *What Is Design?* (Chicago: Paul Theobald and Company, 1960).
3. Victor Papanek, *Design for the Real World* (London: Granada Publishing Ltd., 1971).
4. Herbert Simon, *The Sciences of the Artificial* (Cambridge: MIT Press, 1981), 108.
5. Ibid, 105.
6. Ibid, 108.
7. Thomas Ockerse, Sharon Poggenpohl, John Massey, Roger Remington, Gordon Salchow, Michael Vanderbyl, *AIGA Education Report* (New York: American Institute of Graphic Arts, 1985).
8. Paul Rand, *Design, Form, and Chaos* (New Haven: Yale University Press, 1993).
9. Michael Shannon, "Public Design Education: Learning to Design Society" in *Choosing Design* (Minneapolis: the Core of Understanding Book Project, 1991).
10. Simon, 133.

2. How I Learned What I Learned

Louis Danziger

Louis Danziger, graphic designer, art director, and design consultant, is on the faculty of Art Center College of Design in Pasadena, California. An educator since 1956, he is one of the pioneers of graphic design pedagogy.

Where did you go to school?

I assume you mean design education. First, Evander Childs High School in the Bronx. I was an art major taking every course offered including basic design, poster design, stage design, and costume design. The head of the department was an extraordinary woman, Anne Beberfald. We had reproductions of Klees and Picassos around the school at a time when most of America was hostile to modern art. All art majors were given memberships to the Museum of Modern Art and encouraged to go. After military service, I went to Art Center in Pasadena, California, under the GI Bill. Stayed there about a year. When Alvin Lustig left, so did I. I hated Art Center with the exception of one or two teachers; it was too rigid at that time. I returned to New York. In 1948, while working as a designer at *Esquire,* I took Brodovitch's class at the New School. I think it was called Graphic Journalism. He took a liking to my work and sort of made me his protégé—took me under his wing, connected me to Bob Cato, Dick Avedon, and others. He was very helpful and particularly encouraging, which was not characteristic for him. He was a hard one to please.

Did you have any mentors? If so, what did you learn?

From Lustig, I learned that design was important and worth doing well. He was inspiring. He also opened up the design world, introduced us to the work of Jan Tschichold, Max Bill, Hans Hofmann, and others. He would bring books and other stuff for us to look at and made very important connections to the world of architecture, literature, and fine art. From Brodovitch, I learned how important I was; that is, that there was no other me. I'm absolutely the best at that—I have no competition. I also learned to have a proper disrespect for what I did. Although I was never Paul Rand's student officially, the biggest part of my design education was what I learned from his work—his writing as well, but mostly just looking at what he did and thinking about it. I also learned a lot from Charles Eames, who I often saw, especially in the early fifties. We continued to be good friends till his death, and I would see him quite frequently. Although I always got something out of his incredible powers of perception, it was during the early days that I learned the most from him. He gave me a copy of Buckminster Fuller's *Nine Chains to the Moon* (probably around 1950). It was Fuller's first book, and I was greatly influenced by it. Probably the most influential force in helping to clarify one's own ideas were my fellow design students in Alvin Lustig's classes. We formed a design group that met regularly for many years. I still see some of them.

You come out of a modern tradition. Why?

I was interested in lettering from about the age of ten. I'm not completely sure how that happened. It probably had to do with getting positive feedback from friends. I began looking at *Gebrauchsgraphik* magazine. I subliminally absorbed the work of the great German designers. When I started doing design in high school, I immediately produced essentially modern work—never went through the phase of corny illustrations, cartoons, etc. When I became a member of the Museum of Modern Art, while in high school, I took to much of the work immediately.

How do you define "modernism"?

I really have come to dislike the term. I think that most designers today mean something else when they use it. A better term for me is "contemporary" design rather than modern design. Its contemporariness is an important adjunct of what I think of as modernism. The basic premises for me are those of El Lissitzky. The work must be practical, functional, economical, problem- and content-driven; it must use modern means. It must serve, if at all possible, the needs of the audience and society. It should also serve the needs of the client as well as my own. There is always an area where all of those interests and needs overlap, and *there* is where one finds the solution to the problem. From [Paul] Rand's work and writing, I learned that the solution is always found in the problem itself. The "look" is not brought to the work, but rather emerges from the process. This is also a premise of Lissitzky's, but I understood it best from studying Paul's designs.

Is there relevance in teaching modern methods today?

Bad question. There are no methods. There is no system. No rules. You can help students learn how to connect themselves to the task at hand. To connect, not to the world of "dezine," but to the stuff they're working on. You can demonstrate that originality comes from that connection. It's good to know about grids, contemporary design issues, and technology, etc., but that is not what it's all about.

How would you describe an ideal design education?

A great teacher or great designer and some great students hanging out. An environment were students find themselves discussing their work and the design world with each other. I believe, ultimately, that great education is self-education, especially in the arts. The students are not empty bottles waiting to be filled. They're full. What is needed is to get the stuff out. An ideal education develops confidence, ego strength, and a thirst to discover one's possibilities. I think a good teacher doesn't teach, but creates an environment or climate where people learn.

As a teacher, how do you appeal to students?

I mostly like them. By and large, they are all better than they think they are. I seem to be able to get them to see that. They always produce what they think is over their heads but is not. I don't think that Lustig really taught anything specifically about design, but we all wanted to be like him (I didn't care for much of his work, even as his student, but I sure wanted to know what he knew). Perhaps I also impress my students with what I know. I don't do it consciously. My teaching is always improvisational. Much of the creativity in teaching comes from designing the assignment. If I think that this particular group of students is not sufficiently imaginative, I don't try to tell them to be more imaginative. I develop an assignment that can only be solved by being imaginative.

I have been influenced by all sorts of teachers, and since it must have affected who I am, it must influence my teaching. I have no idea how. If I were to try to describe how I teach, I don't really know. I think I help students see the possibilities in any given problem. I do think that all the students are different, they get on the train at their own station and get off at their own destination. Some have to be kissed, some have to be kicked, and only your own intuition tells you which ones and when. I also think if they are better when they leave my class than they were coming in, I've done a good job. For everything I teach them, there is something I have neglected. You can't begin to teach what there is to know. I guess to really find out about the nature of my appeal, you need to talk to my students. I've had over a thousand by now and they are all over the world.

Milton Glaser

Milton Glaser, illustrator, graphic designer, and cofounder of Push Pin Studios, has taught for over thirty years at the School of Visual Arts in New York. His classes and summer workshops have been a mecca for designers the world over.

What school did you go to?

I went to a variety of schools, the first having a relationship to my design career was a Saturday life class at the Fifteenth Street studios of Moses and Raphael Soyer. I was twelve at the time.

A few years later, I entered the High School of Music and Art, a remarkable place that maintained high academic standards at the same time that it encouraged students to pursue a career in art or music. I then failed the entrance examination to Pratt Institute and consequently worked for a year in a packaging studio before I was able to go on to Cooper Union where I received an excellent design education. Some months after graduation, I received a Fulbright grant to Bologna and continued my education at the Accademia di Belle Arti.

What did you learn in design school?

At Cooper Union, I received a general grounding in painting, color theory, architecture, calligraphy, typography, two- and three-dimensional design, but perhaps more significantly, it encouraged my desire to think of design as a broad, encompassing activity that did not have to be narrowly defined by the standards of professional practice. Or put another way, design was not essentially about picking typefaces or cropping photographs, but a way of encountering the social and cultural issues of our time. In fact, now that I think of it, it was the desire to continue the imaginative and optimistic atmosphere of our years at Cooper Union that encouraged Seymour Chwast, Ed Sorel, Reynold Ruffins, and myself to start Push Pin Studios.

You took a sojourn to study in Italy. What was the result?

My time on the Fulbright grant in Italy, shortly after I graduated from Cooper Union, made me aware of how parochial and ignorant I was about almost everything. It was the first time I'd ever been away from home, and the culture shock was overwhelming. The architecture, the sense of history, the food, the landscape, the very rhythm of life challenged my deeply held but largely unexamined beliefs. I went to the Accademia di Belle Arti and learned how to draw academically for the first time. I also had the opportunity to study with a remarkable artist and exceptional human being, Giorgio Morandi. His painting and etchings are among the twentieth century's finest works, but his modesty and generosity were even more impressive.

The early fifties in Italy were a compelling time. The country was poor and still recovering from the war, and the sense of recovery energized the atmosphere. During that time, I traveled throughout Italy and Europe, saw paintings and buildings I never dreamed of (color reproductions will not do), and, like many, became obsessed with the history of the Renaissance. I cannot imagine what my life and work would have been like without my time in Bologna.

Did you have any mentors? Who were they?

I would certainly include Morandi as a mentor (even though our contact was limited), especially if you broaden the definition to include those who have changed your life by providing a behavioral model. At Cooper Union, a teacher named George Salter, a respected calligrapher and book jacket designer, took an interest in me and supported and encouraged my early work.

Salter was part of that European intellectual and artistic community that had escaped Hitler in the forties by coming to the United States. He loved books, paper, letterforms, writing instruments and was a devoted teacher. He transmitted these interests and commitments to all his students. Of course, there are many others who later encouraged my work who are not necessarily teachers. Henry Wolf, a longtime friend, gave me a number of work opportunities that displayed my abilities and shaped my talents at the beginning of my career. Silas Rhodes, the director of the School of Visual Arts, created design opportunities over a period of thirty-five years.

What, if anything, of your own education influenced your teaching?

In addition to the personalities I've mentioned, I studied with a teacher of kundalini yoga named Rudi who was a valued friend as well as a gifted teacher. Like Morandi, he made me aware of the fact that teaching involved the expression of the teacher's view of life; or put another way, what the teacher was, as well as what was said, informs the class.

This may seem self-evident, but I believe most people have the idea that teaching is essentially about transferring a body of facts of technical information to a student. This, of course, is part of teaching, but creating an attitude toward those facts is even more significant.

How do you engage students in learning?

By any means I can. Mostly, by trying to create an atmosphere of inquiry where the class is a safe place to fail. The secret of most successful classes is the presence of a handful of gifted students who respond well to the problems and provide a standard for the rest of the students. Without this core, teaching can be very difficult indeed. I believe the best learning occurs when students become aware that they are responsible for their own education and that the teacher is not the source of all knowledge, but rather an instrument to awaken the students' dormant imaginations. The creation of what could be called a community of inquiry where, to some extent, everyone teaches and learns simultaneously is not easy to achieve, but highly desirable. It takes a long time to recover from bad teaching and convince students that the purpose of an assignment is not to display cleverness, but to learn something they did not already know.

Have your methods of teaching changed or evolved throughout the years?

I hope they have. I think that the most substantive way I've changed my teaching methods is the following. I used to teach more about skill and technique, presuming that after students developed skills, they could apply them to a variety of problems. Now, I teach more from the point of view of objectifying one's intention and assuming that the skill and technique will follow.

Have students changed over the years?

Of course they have, but that is one of those questions that make you sound like a fool if you attempt to answer it. Life has changed, the profession has changed, and inevitably students are responding to those changes. What remains constant is the small number of extraordinary students who are both innately gifted and willing to devote their complete attention to becoming serious practitioners. I use the word "serious" in the Italian sense, as someone who must be paid attention to because he or she has the passion, talent, and persistence to change things.

Can you define or describe what the best design education should be?

Obviously, that's not easy to define in a paragraph. Especially since every design school I know of has been struggling with that question since the subject was discovered.

I've heard the term "visual journalist" used from time to time to describe what we do, and I don't think it's a bad description. Not that journalists are very well educated in America, but rather that a large part of design activity consists of informing (or, on the dark side, manipulating) the public through visual means. This suggests, among other things, a strong critical consideration of what this role requires. In addition to the technical and aesthetic considerations that schools already teach, I could imagine a useful course of study that would include linguistics, anthropology, behavior, business (the true religion of the United States), and perhaps most importantly, an understanding of the unique relationship of artists and designers to the culture at large.

Deborah Sussman

Deborah Sussman, graphic, environmental, and industrial designer, is responsible for a wide range of environmental graphic systems, including the signage at Walt Disney World in Orlando, Florida. She studied at Black Mountain College, North Carolina, and the Institute of Design, Chicago.

Were you always interested in art and design?

Yes! My father was an artist who could draw like an angel. For him, it was with watercolor and pencil. To earn a living, he became a brilliant airbrush illustrator. Ever since I can remember, I was drawing alongside him and being encouraged. He also loved the camera, which, much later, I came to love as well. My mother, a natural-born linguist from Warsaw, taught us French even before kindergarten. Together, my parents exposed me (and my younger sister) to every conceivable cultural avenue that New York City afforded. Dance and piano classes, visits to the Metropolitan Museum and MoMA, the Frick, classes at the Brooklyn Museum and the Art Students League, regular and "Young People's Concerts" at Carnegie Hall, theater and ballet were standard fare. I even had preschool classes in movement.

Classical music was always on the radio. For a while there were Hebrew lessons. In addition to all this, I was encouraged and motivated to read. Literature was an integral part of our education. My penchant for performance also got me as far as a Yiddish stage performance with Stella Adler, at about age ten.

Where did you go to school?

I went to P.S. 99 in Brooklyn. We had some amazing teachers; girls took shop, boys took homemaking. I painted murals of medieval life above the storage closets. Eudora Fletcher, the principal, was later immortalized by Woody Allen.

Then, Midwood High School, also in Brooklyn. The art department was wonderful. Maxwell Mandell, the leader, was adored by all. *Patterns* was the art squad publication, and its typography was all in Futura lowercase. Good music, too. During grammar school and high school, I also took classes at Pratt Institute and the Art Students League of

New York. I performed on the All City Radio Workshop, which engaged students to act, light, engineer sound, direct, etc.

For college, I had scholarships to Bard College and the Institute of Design in Chicago, and Black Mountain for a summer.

Black Mountain as run by Josef Albers is a legendary institution, what did you learn there?

Albers was gone by the time I attended Black Mountain College. I went to Black Mountain on a summer scholarship with emerging geniuses—Merce Cunningham, John Cage, Charles Olsen, and students Robert Rauschenberg, Francine Du Plessix Gray, Cy Twombly, Remy Charlip, Viola Farber. The most significant, fortunately for me, was the opportunity to learn from the great abstract expressionist painter Franz Kline. To this day, I remember his counsel, "Paint that door! Don't put stoppers (edges) on those strokes." Also, classes with Merce Cunningham and John Cage were exhilarating. The opportunity to mingle with these extraordinary people on an informal basis in a communal environment—as "cross-disciplinary" as possible—opened creative possibilities beyond what any other school could do. Black Mountain was in every sense avant-garde. We listened to poetry, danced, and, with hardly any money, we all picked okra for dinner and washed dishes. Imagine seeing and participating in early experiments in theater with the then-forming collaboration between Merce, Cage, David Tudor, M. C. Richards, and the students.

Did you have any mentors?

Students can be as important as teachers; there were peers whose ideas and personalities affected me deeply. Many of these people have made important contributions to society and are widely recognized. Some remain good friends today. Among the teachers as mentors was Stef Hirsch, then the head of the arts department at Bard. He knew that design was where I was heading. He had the nerve to suggest that acting, my other love, was perhaps not suited to my personality.

Two faculty members who had a strong impact on me at Bard were the poet James Merrill and the later-to-be-infamous Paul de Man. With him, I read Proust in French—totally unaware of his questionable ethics, yet mesmerized by his insights.

Any others?

In Chicago, lots [were] instructors and students from varying disciplines. A mixture of freedom, exploration, observation. Photographers like Harry Callahan, Aaron Siskind, the painters Hugo Weber, Leon Golub, and June Leaf, as well as two influential students, Norman Laliberte and Mary Anne Dorr. However, my most important mentors were—and continue to be—Charles and Ray Eames. Through them I met Alexander (Sandro) Girard, the Florentine-educated American genius who combined a passion for folk art with a sophisticated new design sensibility. My mentor from the Institute of Design, Konrad Wachsmann (a friend of the Eameses), recommended me for a summer job (six months before graduation) at their Venice studio and BOOM! a lifelong quasi-familial relationship was born. I was very lucky; it was a good fit. Through Charles, Ray, and Sandro, I learned to see the world in altogether fresh terms. The formal abstraction of my New Bauhaus schooling in Chicago morphed into the passion for content and specific cultural expression that is still with me today; the fire in the belly.

The Institute of Design was also a legendary institution. Tell me about studying there.

The Institute of Design (New Bauhaus) had a great premise. Foundation courses acquainted students with the spectrum of design disciplines—taught skills (often very difficult). Later courses enabled students to pursue their own trajectories. For me, the very air sizzled, inside the school and on the streets around it. I was stimulated by the atmosphere of inventiveness, the intensity of the student body, and the rich resources of the post-Bauhaus faculty. I loved living on the Near North side, even its grunge, and found that its intimate scale enabled one to form connections with people in the arts very naturally. Early on, my interest in combining two-and three-dimensional work began to show. Recently, I found a book made in my second or third year that combined my love for theater and graphics: *An Approach to the Design of Sets and Costumes for Maeterlinck's* The Blue Bird. The paper I made for the covers, floating typography, transparent devices, collages, color, simple geometric structures, and choreography presaged the kind of work I continue to do today. And the optimism of the early fifties has not been completely eroded either.

How do you teach?

Lately, I feel like a teacher just about all the time; to my real students, at a minimum, but more so to the staff, collaborators, and especially to clients. Certain clients have overtly asked me to "educate" them regarding ways to develop and/or improve their work in the built/urban environment. Years of travel and photography around the world, with focus on indigenous streetscapes and communal life, enable me to free-associate and leap imaginatively from the challenge of the moment to my library of associations.

How has the field changed since you left school?

The field has changed altogether. First, in the fifties, there were three or four significant design offices and a handful of individual designers. Now there are thousands. Second, until the mid- to late eighties, most tools were physical. It mattered a lot to be able to draw, to have no "edge" between mind, heart, and hand. The difference from then to now is obvious—yet, a new drive is growing. Some curricula emphasize "the old way" before the electronic/digital marriage. That is, to be able to use hands for making things physical.

How have these changes been reflected in education?

All the schools I attended were idealistic, smallish, nonmainstream (even anti-)—tended toward alternative attitudes and solutions—and avant-garde, deeply concerned with social consciousness and intensely involved with the arts, cultural history, and the modern cultural environment. Today, student graduates seem as motivated by money, benefits, and security as they are by achievement and contribution.

What is the perfect design education?

Can there be one? Curiosity is an important ingredient. Also, at the least, a broad background in the arts (intellectual, historical, visual, contemporary), acquaintance with some aspects of science, understanding sociopolitical issues and challenges in the current world, interaction with people from backgrounds that differ from one's own, travel supported by documentation, time for self-examination, and engaging in disciplines that may not come easily. Essential: to learn from and interact with people who matter (the faculty and students are more important than the institution). Be where exploration happens.

Sheila Levrant de Bretteville

Sheila Levrant de Bretteville, graphic and
installation designer, has been an educator for over twenty years and is the chair of the
graduate program in graphic design at Yale University. She is responsible for adding a
sociopolitical component to this celebrated formal program.

Where did you go to school?

My first exposure to graphic design and experience of graphic design education
was at Abraham Lincoln High School where the legendary Leon Friend's pedagogy was
comprised of at least four components:

1. *Examples* Mr. Friend brought in examples of design work he admired. Among
   the images we discussed were Ben Shahn's political commentary; the posters of
   illustrator-designers, including E. McKnight Kauffer, A. M. Cassandre, and
   Savignac; and the letterform design of Jan Tschichold and Paul Renner. The
   work was the focus; I do not remember the specific theories and movements
   mentioned, but there was a sense that somehow graphic design could help
   bring about a democratic society.

2. *Assignments* Some assignments were open in terms of subject matter but
   directed in terms of medium, giving us experience in drawing, painting, and
   engraving, using pen and ink, charcoal, gouache, linoleum cuts. This "artwork" could be seen as less determined by others than the more utilitarian
   projects in design, which included covers for school publications and posters
   for citywide contests.

3. *Competitions* By assigning projects that were in response to citywide competitions, Friend taught us that there was a community of art- and design-making
   folk beyond our school who we should know. The money prizes helped
   economically-challenged immigrant parents. Moreover, it encouraged students
   to believe that we could make viable livings making visual work. I won my
   share of these and learned the lessons as well.

4. *Student-run design organizations* Friend set up the format but did not meddle
   in the workings of such internal organizations as the Art Squad. This group did

what we now call "clinical" work for the school—decorating billboards and designing posters. We also designed "passes."

5. *Interdisciplinary work* In conjunction with the English class, we wrote, illustrated, and designed the covers for the art and literary magazine called *Cargoes.*

Did you learn anything in design school?

Yes. Some of which holds me in good stead now. Other parts I have jettisoned completely.

Did you have mentors?

At Yale University in the mid-sixties, it was assumed that we knew the work of the people who taught us: Alvin Eisenman, Walker Evans, Herbert Matter, Paul Rand, Norman Ives, as well as Poly Lada-Mosarski, who taught bookbinding, and John Hill, who taught photographic techniques. Their lives, their work, their way of teaching were the models I reviewed when I began to teach in 1970.

What stands out as memorable?

In the design school there was support for taking classes in drawing and etching, but there was no overt encouragement for bringing that work into my graphic design work. The content was always provided for us—except in photography. As a result, I enjoyed the photographic essay as a form of communication and expression. Here we focused on formal choices in relationship to content and craft. At the time, I accepted this privilege of having a clean, clear, minimal, and abstract form-language without question because it provided me both with security and a set of skills. What I had not noticed was that the corporate sector was the arena in which those skills and forms were most viable. The connection of those forms to corporate values and concerns was never discussed. I connected the dots much later when in the late 1960s, after graduation, I worked for political movements here and in Italy.

You've been very active in the social sphere. Was this something that emerged in school?

I am not really convinced that a centered involvement in "the social sphere" is taught in school. For me, the social inequities and atrocities of the past are (unfortunately) inextricable in my fiber as they were part of my early childhood. I see hate and greed, which is, at the core, racism and social injustice, as threatening the possibility of a democratic society. But my need to be involved in the creation of visions of other ways to be with each other come from a very personal base. For that reason, I am not sure that caring about others can be taught at the graduate school or college or high school level. That does not mean that we should not try to make this kind of orientation available and attractive, but I do not think it should ever be imposed—imposing a belief in democracy is oxymoronic.

Do you consider yourself a good teacher?

Yes. But I think there are many excellent teachers who teach differently than I do. I think I inspire my students—at least that is what they have told me over the years, so I have come to believe it. I am good at framing a situation for people to acquire their own voice and feel supported in thinking and doing what they believe is worth thinking and doing. I teach well because I genuinely believe in the value of the students and their ability to be agents of their own making. I am impassioned about what I do. This commitment provides social, personal, and professional hope for my students.

What are your weaknesses?

I am less good at breaking down education into the components and use working sessions with other faculty to forge assignments that could teach the components of skills without privileging one aesthetic notion over another. It takes constant vigilance and work!

How would you describe an ideal design education?

This is far too fixed an idea from my perspective. I see our design education constantly evolving and changing, adjusting to the needs of our students, the zeitgeist, the concerns of the scholars in our university, and in the world.

Looking back at your education, how should students be taught today? Differently? The same?

To think critically implies change. I look at how I have been taught and see echoes in how I teach. Of course, what I do in 1998 is not the same as what I did in 1957, 1967, 1977, and 1997!

April Greiman

April Greiman, graphic, video, and multimedia designer, was the chair of design and has taught at CalArts in Los Angeles. She is a pioneer of the New Typography and the integration of multimedia in graphic design.

Where did you go to school?

I was an undergrad at the Kansas City Art Institute (KCAI), in Missouri. Afterward, I went immediately to the Kunstgewerbeschule Basel, now known as the Design School of Basel.

Why did you go to a European school? And, in particular, was there something lacking in American design education?

Frankly, I did not know one thing about an education in graphic design. As a matter of fact, when I applied to Rhode Island School of Design (RISD)—where I was rejected for doing a horrible drawing of a pair of boots, part of its exam—the director of admissions told me I had an incredible portfolio of "graphic design." Since I had never heard this term before, I remained quiet. At that time, he said, RISD really didn't have a strong department in graphic design and that I might want to check out KCAI instead, since it had a very interesting program with visiting European instructors from the Basel school. I flew out to KCAI, where I was accepted on the spot, and just lucked into the Basel school approach.

Did you have any mentors?

My most important mentor (perhaps because she provided my first encounter to "the Basel approach") was Inge Druckery, who is German and was one of the first of the Basel school teachers to come to America—specifically, to KCAI—to teach. With Inge, I learned three main things that turned out to be profound and definitely key to my process: (1) discipline, (2) the constant exploration and evolution of "form," and (3) the commitment to the perceptual.

You also studied with Wolfgang Weingart, correct?

In Basel, I worked closely with Weingart. He was a big inspiration to all of us: his playfulness and availability beyond the call of normal duty/hours. He was the only member of the faculty who hung out with the students. He was very friendly and extremely encouraging in an atmosphere that was quite somber and serious. He taught us (me) to work on a multiple of solutions, probing in all directions. We worked on long "job-cases" in the type shop. Each student had one (approximately twelve-feet long, I'd say). Whenever we worked, we covered the entire table with paper and ideas. Moving subtly and not so subtly from one version to another. He always encouraged and demonstrated, through his own work, the blending of the personal/idiosyncratic with the practical aspects of an assignment. He made us laugh!

And you studied with Armin Hofmann, who is much more of a formalist in the classical modern sense.

As a teacher, Hofmann was quite different. He, too, was an inspiration, of course, but the class was held in silence (my first experience of "Zen"), which was quite a different atmosphere from Weingart's "playschool" approach. I learned to let the work guide me. Looking, looking, and then looking some more. He was a man who was looking for the moment when the intellectual/conceptual merged with the formal. I suppose that was a period known as "fusion" in the arts. Always looking for that "singular" expression—one that integrated all elements into a profoundly simple solution.

And the difference between Hofmann and Weingart?

Weingart represented more of a pluralistic expression; perhaps also an extension of what was going on culturally during more of his and my time—ideas/theories in science, such as "chaos" and "complexity." (This certainly seemed to apply to the work and clientele in Los Angeles when I moved here in 1976.) The Basel "simplifying approach" was key to the process but was not appropriate, or so I thought in my work, to what the final product "looked like."

What was the most important lesson learned in Basel?

To evolve the work from your inner constitution. To integrate ideas (thinking mind) with making and perception (thinking body).

Did you bring back what you learned?

I am, for better or worse, a laboratory for research, experimentation, and discovery.

Sounds like experimentation is not only a school activity.

I am continuously experimenting with photography and image-making tools. I remember getting one of the first digital still, video, and disposable panorama cameras. These and other images taken have been archived here in both digital and transparency form as I produced them. Since the beginning, I have had a strong interest in the low end of technology and did my best to advance both the tools and the software by probing and exploring what was creative and different with them.

What are some of these tools?

I started using video (half-inch industrial quality) in 1982 and incorporating those images into print: for example, a poster for Ron Rezek Lighting and also a Simpson Paper "Sequences" poster. In 1984–85, I started using that video equipment with my 128K Macintosh and then my Mac Plus—all of about 520K! This is what I used on my issue of *Design Quarterly* no. 133 ("If You Give It a Sense It Makes Sense"). Around the same time, I purchased some of the first 8mm "home" video equipment that was available. I was successful at integrating that into my professional work, such as TV spots for Lifetime television and also Esprit's first TV commercials. I always first tried things out for the sheer adventure and thrill of it. First came my own satisfaction, education, and fascination with the potential of these new types of "intelligent" tools.

Are students different today?

I have found them to be somewhat more open, going less for copying and imitating stylistic viewpoints. I have also found them to be very good at generating unique ideas prior to formalizing anything—less predisposed to trends and definitely into pushing boundaries, as am I.

Keep in mind that I use, and am interested in, a vocabulary and visual issues that overlap with what architects might be into—i.e., space relationships, scale, visual hierarchies, and generally the issues of how things feel and are perceived. I am into "reading" a space or articulating a space (even if it is two-dimensional). I like the idea of traveling through a space.

How do you teach today? Do you formulate specific problems or do you allow for experiments to occur at random?

I am quite specific with my problems/assignments.

Graphic design is in a transitional state, moving from static to multiple media and beyond. How can this be best integrated into a student's experience?

I think a good school should provide an environment where the individual is encouraged to pursue whatever he or she feels strong[ly] about. Multimedia is hot now, but it is still just one avenue to pursue creatively. Teachers of design should help a student to find their voice. In other words, not be a templated version of the teacher, but rather to help them [students] unfold what they already know and can bring to the table.

How would you describe the "perfect" design education?

One that integrates the mind and the body. One that fosters true fascination with process and exploration, both external and internal. One that avoids imitation and encourages individual creativity and self-discovery.

Michael Vanderbyl

Michael Vanderbyl, graphic, furniture, and interior designer, is the dean of the California College of Arts and Crafts in San Francisco. He is responsible for the integration of illustration and graphics into a total program.

Where did you go to school?

I studied at the California College of Arts and Crafts (CCAC).

What did you learn in design school?

Among other things, six semesters of art history. More and more, I am convinced of the importance of understanding classical origins, the Academy, and the Renaissance. It's something I refer to in my work every day.

I also learned that Helvetica was not just a typeface, but a lifestyle. It has implications beyond the page.

Did you buy into that lifestyle? If so, how? If not, why?

Swiss design was new and very exciting to me as a student, but it was also a little bit of a disconnect. Growing up as I did in suburbia, the Swiss school was far removed from my experience. It was alluring, but abstract. No, I didn't buy into the Helvetica lifestyle. I appreciate its ideals and elegance, but I was bred in America. I was raised on Disney and electric guitars. America was, and is, a pluralistic and practical culture geared to the consumer, but also materialistic in the best sense of the word. By which I mean, there's a passion for the variety and beauty of the material world.

Still, I did find the intellectual underpinnings of the international style appealing. The idea of casting the essence of a problem in form. In my work, I took the ideas about form and asked, How does this relate to life? You can see the synthesis in a poster I did for public radio. You can see the structure at work—but there's also a use of color, a playfulness that comes from my West Coast background.

Who were your mentors, and what did you learn from them?

Massimo Vignelli, who I admire for his multidisciplinary genius and his longevity. Armin Hofmann, from whom I learned order and simplicity. Push Pin Studios, whose illustrations had great wit. Their work was quirky, expressive, and human.

How does being a full-time practitioner affect your performance and effectiveness as a teacher?

My work in the studio informs my work in the classroom and vice versa. Much of what I do as a designer is intuitive. In teaching, those intuitive leaps have to be made explicit. I have to break it down, to translate a nonverbal thought process into words because I will be talking in detail—and I hope, with clarity—about that process with my students. They will ask questions, so I have to find out how it is that I do what I do. If I can define my way of working, I can teach effectively. The mental exercise of working with students gives me insight that I put to use every day in my practice.

How do you teach? Do you try to gear your students toward the practical world, or do you allow them a chance to experiment in a world free of outside constraints?

At CCAC, we structure assignments around cultural questions rather than taking a trade school approach. In other words, we don't ask students to design a brochure or a letterhead for a company that makes plumbing fixtures. Instead, we might ask them to research a figure from history—Amelia Earhart or Churchill—and to create an identity for that person. The subject matter isn't directly practical, but the students learn to question. They learn the conceptual and formal aspects of the design process, and it forces them to think in terms of the subject's place in history and culture. The students have to reach more to solve the problem.

An interesting example: One of the students decided to do a project that would graphically contrast the life of a design student with that of a homeless person. This immediately raised several questions. We had to question the intention behind the project. We had to ask what is being communicated here. What is the objective? What is the designer's responsibility? It was important that the student did not exploit the person, that there was an attitude of respect and humility. Because there's a fine moral line here.

The student hired a homeless man, gave him a notebook and pencil, and asked him to record his experiences on certain days over a number of weeks. The student kept a diary of his own thoughts on those same days. Huge posters were made from the pages of each, printed on two different colors of paper and placed side by side along the wall. It was a dramatic presentation, and one that challenged us all to think about the role of design.

So, my answer to your question is yes and no. Students do learn that when you design letterhead, it has to function. There are practical concerns, but they don't drive the curriculum. I try to find balance. I try to make students aware of how well a solution will work for a client and to encourage the student to form his or her own vision. Reality sets in soon enough.

I think one thing that sets CCAC apart is that we create a spark of questioning. If we were to include automobile design in our curriculum, the first question we might ask is, Why cars? Rather than accepting our assumptions, we dig into them—and solve the problem only after we've mined the bigger issues. It's more fun, more creative, and, ultimately, it results in good design.

Do you consider yourself a good teacher?

I try, I listen, I question.

How would you describe an ideal design education?

The more that a person brings to design, the better his or her ability to communicate. At CCAC, we attract a large percentage of students with prior degrees and those transferring from a university who have knowledge in one of the sciences or humanities. That knowledge enriches their formal work as designers. Ideally, students would be introduced to the whole theater of history and culture; they would be well versed in another discipline—whether it's art history, literature, or biology—and they would receive solid formal training. Designers today require an understanding of the place and practice of their art in the context of a world that is much more complicated than the one I knew as a student.

Looking back on your education, how should students be taught today? Differently? Or the same?

Technology has changed the way our profession is practiced. Although the basic principles of visual communication have changed little, the medium in which ideas are communicated has changed radically. We design for motion and sound and in three dimensions. We design not only graphic identities for clients, but their actual products. We design interiors. Designers find themselves working in a wider context, and students need to be exposed to a broader world, not just the latest software. As the creators of cultural artifacts, students need to understand the world they work in—how people construct and interpret their lives. And they need to appreciate that their work—design—has an impact on our society, that it can enrich human experience.

How do you plan on making that happen in your own school?

At CCAC, we've structured the environment so that there are no rigid boundaries between the areas of design, industrial design, and architecture. There are no camps. Everyone is working in the same physical space, and there is interaction between all the students. We've also chosen to have open critiques so that an architecture student can sit in on a design crit and vice versa. The students gain an appreciation for each other's work and often end up working as partners or, at the least, contributing ideas to another student's project. What we've tried to do is deconstruct the traditional disciplinary ghettoes. And it works.

With the inclusion of sound and motion media, is the definition of a graphic designer significantly different? Do you, in fact, see a time when your program will no longer be for "graphic designers" but rather all designers?

The two-dimensional frame that the word "graphic" implies no longer applies to what we do. In the Bay Area, designers work on multimedia projects for new electronic media as well as menus for restaurants and annual reports. We passed graphic design a while ago. It belongs to the era of the typewriter, not the Internet. What we do today, really, is to act as agents of communication. And it's interesting that the phrase "communication design" was used before the profession of graphic designer was recognized. It's coming full circle.

Still, I love graphic design, and I think of myself as a graphic designer. I work that way when designing furniture and showrooms—because it's still a visual presentation that requires a certain way of thinking. I also believe that it's important to have one discipline under your belt before you try to become multidisciplinary. The fact is, however, that my work is inclusive. It may begin with an identity, but often expands into a website, a showroom, a multimedia presentation, and so forth.

I would tell design students that designers really do have to live their art in a way. And by that I don't mean putting your career before everything else, but keeping your eyes and your mind open and your passion for design alive.

Krzysztof Lenk

Krzysztof Lenk, graphic designer and information architect, teaches typography at the Rhode Island School of Design (RISD). He has been one of the foremost proponents in the new field of information design.

Where did you go to school?

In Poland. I started my education in 1954 at the Warsaw Academy of Fine Arts. After three years in Warsaw, I transferred to Katowice, to the graphic design department of the Kraków Academy of Fine Arts. I graduated in 1961 with an M.F.A. in graphic design.

At that time, the Warsaw Academy had a six-year curriculum: two years of foundation at the beginning, followed by four years of studies in a major selected by the student. I chose the department of graphic design, which used to be (and is to this day) a combination of graphic print—all with metal, woodcut, and lithography techniques—and graphic design. All students accepted to the department had to complete one year of general introduction to graphic print and graphic design. After the first year in the major program, they applied to the workshop of a master (like Henryk Tomaszewski) where they would study for at least three years.

I remember the program being focused on drawing, painting, sculpture, and strong in lessons of anatomy and perspective, but having no two- and three-dimensional compositions, photography, or typography. The concept of teaching the history of graphic design was also unknown, even the history of Polish design. The program in Katowice was nearly identical.

Did you learn anything in design school?

No and yes. When I was a student, graphic design in Poland was treated as an applied art (and by and large, it still is) rather than an integral discipline including methodology, links to printing, and theory of communication. During the seven years of my studies, I spent a lot of time doing things important for my visual sensitivity, but learned nothing about type and printing or photography.

Looking back from a distance, I think that I can name three important factors from my student years that have determined my life. At the Warsaw Academy I had a very demanding teacher of letterforms—Andrzej Rudzinski. He introduced me to the anatomy of the Latin alphabet, and, more important, he opened my eyes. Instead of passively looking at text, I started to see it as a structure, where strokes and counterform; character, word, and line spacing; printed and nonprinted areas of the page work together as a coherent system of interrelated components. The aim of this system is to develop a desired balance between blackness of the print and whiteness of the paper. This dynamic balance can be consciously controlled by the designer. Being able to perceive the visual form is like an illumination. It can be attained through exercise. Rudzinski was an extremely demanding, almost cruel teacher. I owe him everything.

I was never a student of the two professors who stigmatized me for life. One was Aleksander Kobzdej—a gifted painter, but, more important, a vibrant personality, full of temperament and sense of humor, a great storyteller, dancer, a real model of manhood for us, young students. I met him once around a conference table, in a meeting of a student organization with faculty. Of the fifteen or so people in the room, everybody smoked except for him. It surprised me because I had known him to be a heavy smoker. So I offered him my package of cigarettes over the table.

"Thank you. I don't smoke anymore," he said.

To hear such an announcement from him—a man of all senses—was a shock. Silence fell and everyone around the table looked at him. He had to say something.

"I had pains in my stomach" he said, "and I visited a doctor. The doctor examined me for a long time and finally asked a question: 'Do you smoke?' he asked."

"I do."

"'Do you drink?'"

"'Of course I do.'"

"'So, starting tomorrow, for the rest of your life, you will either drink or smoke. It's your choice, but don't do the two things at once,' said the doctor. I made up my mind quickly. I prefer to stay with drinking. When I left the doctor's office, I bought two packages of cigarettes and chain-smoked them till late night. When I woke up in the morning, my smoking habit was over," the professor said.

I was so impressed by his story, that in the total silence around the table I asked him a question, "Was it difficult for you to quit the habit?"

In the moment I said it, I knew that this is the one question I should not have asked him. He looked at me for a long, long moment of silence and said in a quiet voice:

"Listen, young man," he said. "Either you are a man, or you are not. If you are a man, you don't exaggerate."

It was like a slap on my face. I was young. I wanted to be a man. I shouldn't exaggerate when making a tough decision. Much later in my life, living in the United States, I realized how much of a John Wayne–like advice the professor had given to me. I'll remember it forever.

The other important advice I got came from Professor Henryk Tomaszewski, in an artists' nightclub, over a bottle of vodka. I was nineteen. Together with two of my student friends, we had just gotten paid for our very first design job. With money in our pockets, we went to a famous gathering spot of Warsaw's artist elite where we ran into Tomaszewski and arranged to be introduced to him. He told us in a moving, poetic way about our own unique responsibility to grow and to develop our talents because nobody would do it for us. And to start right away, that night, because time would work against us, and later would be too late. Time runs against me—it was a shocking truth.

Forty years later, I have a feeling that these two stories have shaped my character and put me on my own track as a student and later as a designer. Everything else about graphic design I have learned through practice, by listening carefully to the advice of my older colleagues and looking at them at work over their shoulders.

Mentors? Who were they?

I have only one mentor in my life: Lou Danziger, a designer whom I admire for his enormous talent, wisdom, and integrity and the most modest man I have ever met. He is one who knows more about constructivism in Poland than most Polish art historians. He has been supporting me continuously since the early seventies. He is one who made my American dream possible.

You come out of an Eastern European tradition. How has this influenced your practice in the United States?

I don't know what you mean by "East European tradition." If it is the tradition of the poster, together with its heavy use (or overuse) of metaphors and strong affiliations to art rather than to design—it is not my cup of tea. I am a rational guy, driven by reasoning, and looking for inspiration from Kobro and Stazewski; from Polish constructivism, Shuitema, and Zwart; from Holland; and from Ulm, Maldonado, and Bonsiepe rather than from the Polish poster.

Poland has no modern typography tradition when compared with the German, Czech, or Hungarian heritage. My publication design program at the School of Design in Lodz was the first modern attempt to see newspapers, magazines, textbooks, and railroad timetables as parts of the visual civilization in which we live. The design of modern prints should reflect, and be coordinated with, modern methods of production and distribution, and the aesthetics of design should respond to the changing expectations and frustrations of the society. I developed such a program. Teaching was based on research and experiments, and projects were tested. The program got recognition, and the results were published in many international media. Under communism, an omnipotent state had neither interest nor motivation to invest in such a program, and graduates had to find work abroad rather than in Poland.

When I came to RISD in 1982, my design consciousness was filled by modern standards. What I brought from Eastern Europe are my hands gesturing in conversation, my emotional reactions in discussions, and a thick, East European accent.

How do you define yourself as a teacher?

My pedagogical goal is to help a student in defining his or her frame of mind. This foundation will help the student build his or her own design personality, combining intelligence, stamina, persistence, and various talents. This model of interaction between the instructor and student is based on the assumption that the result of the teaching process is only as good as the student's ability to learn and absorb. My mission is to stimulate, to inspire, and to help the students discover what they already have within themselves. And, of course, to reveal to them some professional methods.

The most difficult concept for the students to understand and approve is the fact that visual communication is foremost *visual*. This visual language has its own grammar and syntax, and plays with colors, shapes, and various contrasts of typography. All these factors influence the meaning of a message, and many of them have no equivalent form in the verbal language. Students have their expectations. By browsing through design magazines and books, they see the world's most recent design. They have design heroes they identify themselves with: Weingart, April Greiman, Neville Brody, Carson. Heroes come and go, serving each generation of students as an example of a rebellious attitude toward the established design. Young people desperately like to adopt the design "look" of an actual hero—his or her style. It takes a long time to persuade students to adopt the *attitude* of a hero, rather than the style.

What makes a good design program?

Design education is a collective activity. We are never alone with a student in a program. We work in a team of instructors, and only as a team are we strong or weak. This is why it takes years to create a well-synchronized program and only a few stupid decisions to ruin it.

How would you describe an ideal design education?

I think that a good design program should help students to self-define the kind of talent with which each of them was born and to shape their design consciousness, teach them how to articulate visually their ideas and give them certain fluency in using a wide range of media—from pencil and X-acto knife to the newest version of Adobe Photoshop, and convince them that design is not only a human but also a humanistic activity. Designers are members of a society and should be ethically responsible for the cultural and environmental consequences of their work.

What is the graphic design discipline today, in the year 1997? How does it compare to what graphic design meant in 1967 and 1957? What will it be in 2007?

Let me use my own example: I was trained as a poster designer. My career, since 1958, was in publication design. I started teaching publication design in Lodz in 1973 and came to RISD to teach at the Department of Graphic Design in 1982. Invited by Tom Ockerse to teach a class on diagrams, charts, and graphs, I became fascinated with the discipline of diagrammatic languages. Results from my diagrams class were published by

Walter Herdeg in *Graphis* 238 (1985). That was the year when the first Macintosh computers arrived to RISD. In 1987, computers and scanners began to replace typesetters and stat cameras in the department, and the faculty started to learn (mostly from our students) what was (or was not) possible in Illustrator 88.

Since that time, I have been introduced to new technology primarily by my students. Being born with a remote control in their hands, and trained in computer games, they have an inherent ability to grasp novelty with little effort. I am learning fast, but I am no longer a "master" for them.

My experience in teaching diagrams (and, in a broader sense, information design) helped me open in 1991, together with two partners, an information design studio, Dynamic Diagrams ("consultants in visual logic"). We do a lot of visual consulting for the computer industry, develop museum kiosks, design prototypes for CD-ROM publications, and corporate Internet and Intranet sites. Today, I am an information architect. What will I do in 2007? I wish I knew.

When I stand in front of my students in the Type I class, on the very first day of their sophomore year, to teach them about the anatomy of letterforms, historical development of printing types, and rules of proper spacing, I like to tell them why they will have to learn all this stuff over the next three years in the program. What is it for? I am less sure of the reason today than I used to be three years ago.

Recently, at the coffee break during the introductory talk, two students came up to me asking if they could show me the Internet home pages they had designed for clients as a student side job. They were much more fluent in HTML than I. How do I convince them to go slowly, step-by-step through the program, digging deep into the visual form and analyzing semantics and semiotics for three years of their lives, and more than $80,000 from their parents' pockets? I don't know.

3. How We Teach What We Teach

Graphic Design as Cognitive Artifact

Meredith Davis

INTRODUCTION

Introduction to course content and expectations.

Introduction to communication models and discussion of the degree to which models acknowledge information perception and processing: Shannon and Weaver (1948), Berlo (1972), Emmert and Donaghy (1981).

Reading: Chapter 2, "Human Communication Perspectives," in Philip Emmert and William Donaghy, *Human Communication: Elements and Contexts* (Reading, Mass.: Addison-Wesley Publishing, 1981).

Introduction to framing design-research projects based on readings from outside the field (problem finding).

Reading: Chapter 2, "Goodness of Fit," in Christopher Alexander, *Notes on the Synthesis of Form* (Cambridge: Harvard University Press, 1964).

WHAT IS A COGNITIVE ARTIFACT?

A discussion of the power of representation and experiential versus reflective cognition.

Readings: Chapters 2 and 3 in Donald Norman, *Things That Make Us Smart* (New York: Addison-Wesley Publishing, 1993). Chapters 1–3 in Donald Norman, *The Design of Everyday Things* (formerly *The Psychology of Everyday Things*) (New York: Doubleday, 1988).

Assignment: Bring to class examples of graphic design artifacts that engage their audiences experientially and/or reflectively. Be prepared to discuss the cognitive consonance or dissonance of such engagement with the learning/interpretation expected of the audience (example: the dissonance of a dialogue box that intrudes reflectively during the expert use of computer software or the expert behavior in response to corporate identities and branding). Also, be prepared to analyze the relevance of particular organizational or visual strategies to these examples of experiential or reflective engagement.

DEFINING AUDIENCES BY COGNITIVE STYLE

A discussion of differences in how individuals perceive and process information (including research on brain dominance and learning types) and how historic perspectives have limited our assumptions about human cognitive behavior. Implications of defining audiences by something other than demographics for the design of information.

Readings: Chapter 3, "The Four-Quadrant Brain Model of Thinking Preferences" (based on the work of Ned Herrmann, David Kolb, and Bernice McCarthy) in Edward and Monika Lumsdaine, *Creative Problem Solving* (New York: McGraw-Hill, 1995). Chapter 2, "A Rounded Version," in Howard Gardner, *Multiple Intelligences: The Theory in Practice* (New York: Basic Books, 1993). Part I, "Learning Styles," in Bernice McCarthy, *The 4MAT System: Teaching to Learning Styles with Right/Left Mode Techniques* (Barrington, Ill.: Excel, Inc., 1987). Chapter 1, "A Taxonomy of Critical Thinking Dispositions and Abilities," Robert Ennis, in *Teaching Thinking Skills: Theory and Practice,* ed. Robert J. Sternberg (New York: W. H. Freeman and Co., 1987). Chapter 9, "An Integrative Framework for Understanding Mind in Context," Robert J. Sternberg, in *Mind in Context,* ed. Robert J. Sternberg and Richard K. Wagner (New York: Cambridge University Press, 1994).

Assignment: In-class work on articulating potential research projects within this broad category of cognitive style. Bring to class five design-research questions related to one or more of these readings. Write each question on a separate piece of paper, large enough to be read from across the room. Be sure to consider the characteristics of researchable problems discussed in our first class. Questions may be variations on the same core design-research problem. Pay close attention to the phrasing of the problem in relation to our list of characteristics of what is researchable.

CATEGORIZATION AND SCHEMAS

Survey of research into how people group concepts and attach meaning based on those groupings. Included in the discussion are "prototypes" (best examples) that represent concept categories within certain contexts, social schemas, and representations that trigger meaning among seemingly unrelated objects, places, or concepts. Greater elaboration on the cognitive basis of stereotyping and identity. Exploration of the mental structuring power of metaphors.

Readings: Chapter 2, "Social Schemas," in Martha Augoustinos and Iain Walker, *Social Cognition: An Integrated Introduction* (London: Sage Publications, 1995). Pages to be assigned from various chapters in George Lakoff, *Women, Fire, and Dangerous Things: What Categories Reveal about the Mind* (Chicago: University of Chicago Press, 1987). Pages to be assigned from various chapters in George Lakoff and Mark Johnson, *Metaphors We Live By* (Chicago: University of Chicago Press, 1980). Chapters 7–10, "Social Schemas and Social Representations," "Attributions and Social Representations," "Stereotypes, Prejudice, and Intergroup Attributions," and "Postmodern Challenges to Social

Cognition," in Martha Augoustinos and Iain Walker, *Social Cognition: An Integrated Introduction* (London: Sage Publications, 1995). Mark Johnson, "The Imaginative Basis of Meaning and Cognition" in *Images of Memory: On Remembering and Representation,* ed. Suzanne Kochler and Walter Melion (Washington, D.C.: Smithsonian Institution Press, 1991).

Assignment: Through a series of images, illustrate the centrality and representation of prototypes for a category. Also explore examples that reside on the periphery of a concept. Through composition and rendering style, demonstrate how visual variables reinforce the prototypical nature of the example. In class, we will discuss how far we can depart from prototypes and still maintain communication value in the selected example.

Assignment: Explore how diagrams representing physical schemas referring to the human body and movement may be used to enhance audience understanding of metaphorical references to the same concept.

COGNITIVE MAPS

Extension of the categorization discussion within the context of cognitive maps and memory. Focus on spatial and wayfinding examples from architecture. Discussion of the cultural origin of various cognitive maps.

Readings: Chapter 1, "Image of the Environment," in Kevin Lynch, *Image of the City* (Boston: MIT Press, 1960). Assigned pages in Christopher Alexander, *The Timeless Way of Building* and *Pattern Language* (New York: Oxford University Press, 1975, 1977).

Assignment: Develop a navigation system (example: computer interface, wayfinding signage, printed map, etc.) that uses orientational or ontological metaphors as the basis for visual organization. Examine the limits of the metaphor and the medium in which it is applied. Be prepared to defend the relationship between the metaphor and the cognitive/behavioral task.

NARRATIVE AND STORYTELLING

A discussion of cognitive predispositions to narrative as a way of explaining and understanding the world. Implications for the structuring of information.

Readings: Chapter 2, "Folk Psychology as an Instrument of Culture," in Jerome Bruner, *Acts of Meaning* (Cambridge: Harvard University Press, 1990). Chapter 5, "Design Principles for Human-Computer Activity," in Brenda Laurel, *Computer as Theatre* (New York: Addison-Wesley Publishing Company, 1991). Abbe Don, "Narrative and the Interface," in *The Art of Human-Computer Interface Design,* ed. Brenda Laurel (New York: Addison-Wesley Publishing, 1990).

INTRINSIC MOTIVATION

The role of intrinsic motivation in learning and the successful completion of cognitive tasks.

Readings: Thomas W. Malone and Mark R. Lepper, "Making Learning Fun: A Taxonomy of Intrinsic Motivation for Learning," in *Aptitude, Learning, and Instruction,* ed. Richard E. Snow, vol. 3, (Lawrence Erlbaum Assoc., 1987). Edward Deci, *Why We Do What We Do* (New York: Putnam's Sons, 1995). R. M. Ryan, J. P. Connell, and E. L. Deci, "A Motivational Analysis of Self-Determination and Self-Regulation in Education," in *Research on Motivation in Education: The Classroom Milieu,* ed. Carole Ames and Russell Ames, vol. 2 (New York: Academic Press, Inc., 1985).

TECHNOLOGICAL AFFORDANCES AND COGNITION

Readings: Selections from Donald Norman, *Things That Make Us Smart* (New York: Addison-Wesley Publishing, 1993). Selections from Derrick de Kerchhove, *Connected Intelligence* (Toronto: Somerville House Publishing, 1997). Lauralee Alben, "Quality of Experience: Defining Criteria for Effective Interaction Design," *Iterations* III (1996) (may substitute criteria developed by Alben's team for *Communication Arts* magazine competition). Chapter 2, "Media Hot and Cold," in Marshall McLuhan, *Understanding Media* (Boston: MIT Press, 1964, 1994).

PICTURE PROCESSING

Brief survey of relevant research in picture processing, speed of recognition, and memory.

Readings: Chapter 7, "Picture Processing and Memory," in Kathryn T. Spoehr and Stephen W. Lehmkuhle, *Visual Information Processing* (San Francisco: W. H. Freeman and Co., 1982). Chapter 7, "On Exploring Visual Knowledge," Allan Paivio, in *Visual Learning, Thinking, and Communication,* ed. Bikkar S. Randhawa and William E. Coffman (1978).

MIDTERM EXAM

Collect and analyze examples of visual communication that rely on prototypes and stereotypes for their interpretation. Using you class readings, describe how these communication examples work.

FINAL EXAM

Student presentations of design assignments during the last two class sessions.

History, Theory, and Undergraduate Education

Ellen Lupton and J. Abbott Miller

Design programs around the United States have come to recognize that history courses are crucial to the education of designers, grounding students in a critical discourse about the origins and future of their discipline. That said, it is a considerable feat to implement such courses, which often are taught as an internal affair of graphic design departments, rather than being offered by formal humanities divisions. As few art historians are equipped to lecture on graphic design, practicing designers are relied on to teach the history of their field, often working from zero, with no established models or visual resources. Meanwhile, many art history departments view design history courses as "service" classes aimed at a particular trade, and thus not worthy of teaching in a purely academic setting.

When we started teaching design history in the late 1980s, the biggest challenge was to create and maintain a slide collection. Over the past eight years, we have shot, labeled, and organized over three thousand slides. This invaluable image bank has supported a range of courses developed for diverse contexts—undergraduate survey courses, lectures series for M.F.A. students in design, seminars for M.A. students specializing in design history, and not-for-credit seminars for working designers. We believe that history and theory should confront students throughout their careers, from the undergraduate level right on into their lives as practicing designers.

The course outlined below aims to integrate history with theory. We view the course as an "intellectual survival kit" for graphic designers, which aims to make them literate about their own discipline as well as to help them understand the overlaps between design and a broader history of ideas. We expose students to landmark texts in modern thought, showing them how concepts from semiotics, politics, and critical theory reverberate through the visual arts. Graphic design is an act of cultural interpretation: it is a form of reading, writing, and editing using words, pictures, symbols, materials, and technologies. Our course reveals the ideological underpinnings and social implications of design practice by immersing students in a wide array of images as well as a broad range of reading materials, including primary texts by designers, major documents of critical theory, and recent essays in design history. Although several excellent surveys of design history are now available, we do not make these required reading, preferring, instead, to draw written documents from various sources.

The following fifteen-week syllabus is aimed at undergraduates in graphic design. The course is divided into three main units: Reform and Revolution, focusing on the European avant-garde movements; Consumption and Mass Culture, looking at design in America and postwar Europe; and Media and Messages, introducing visual literacy through critical interpretations of recent advertising and design.

UNIT I: REFORM AND REVOLUTION

The first unit focuses on the avant-garde movements that form the aesthetic and philosophical basis of modern graphic design. This unit also introduces students to "semiotics," the study of signs. Semiotics provides a theoretical framework that loosely informs the historical lectures in the course.

1. The Critical Object: Arts and Crafts to Art Nouveau

The industrial revolution triggered passionate critiques of the commodity system. Karl Marx developed the theory of "commodity fetishism," arguing that, in a capitalist culture, an object's function or use value is eclipsed by its exchange value. The Arts and Crafts movement applied the socialist critique of factory production to objects, architecture, interiors, and typography. William Morris and others embraced hand techniques and the honest use of materials as a way to demystify objects of daily use. The Arts and Crafts movement, which was followed by the more aesthetically innovative movements of art nouveau and Jugendstil, marked the origins of design as a critical discourse, positioned in opposition to mainstream culture.

Readings: Karl Marx, "Commodities" and "The Fetishism of Commodities and the Secret Thereof," 1867, in *Capital: Volume 1*; William Morris, "Art under Plutocracy," 1884, in *Political Writings of William Morris* (New York: International Publishers, 1973.)

2. Semiotics: Language as Culture

Ferdinand de Saussure was the founder of structuralism, a current of thought that shaped art, philosophy, and anthropology across the twentieth century. Saussure argued that language is a system of differences, not a collection of autonomous, individual signs; thus, the meaning of any sign resides not in the isolated word or mark, but in its relation to other signs in the system. Saussure also argued that language is not a neutral reflection of reality, but a system that describes the world from a cultural point of view. This lecture discusses Saussure's ideas in relation to language, writing, and typography.

Reading: Ferdinand de Saussure, *Course in General Linguistics* (excerpt), 1916.

3. Materialist Typography: Futurism and Dada

Futurism and dada were avant-garde movements that emerged in the 1910s. Although both began as literary movements, they had a profound impact on the visual arts. The poetry of F. T. Marinetti and Tristan Tzara challenged the conventions of literary presentation by borrowing techniques from advertising—from mixing styles and sizes of type to composing letters along conflicting axes. Futurism and dada celebrated the materiality of typography, recognizing it as a sign system with its own meanings and effects.

Readings: Jan Tschichold, "The History of the New Typography," excerpt from *The New Typography*, 1928; Johanna Drucker, "Experimental Typography as a Modern Art Practice," excerpt from *The Visible Word*, 1994.

4. The Technological Eye: Constructivism and Montage

Constructivism built a bridge from the deliberately disruptive experiments of futurism and dada to an accessible public language. After the Russian Revolution, artists in the young Soviet Union sought to bring art into everyday life, creating posters, books, propaganda stands, theater designs, textiles, furniture, and other objects of communication and daily use. Fascinated by new technologies of representation, they mobilized the camera and the printing press as instruments of visual interpretation.

Readings: El Lissitzky, "Topography of Typography," 1923; "Typographical Facts," 1925, and "Our Book," 1926, in *El Lissitzky: Life, Letters, Texts*; Walter Benjamin, "The Work of Art in the Age of Mechanical Reproduction," 1936, in *Illuminations*.

5. Transcendental Grids: De Stijl and Dutch Modernism

The de Stijl movement was spearheaded by Theo van Doesburg, a Dutch painter, poet, and designer. Working with Piet Mondrian, Vilmos Huszar, Gerrit Reitveld, and other artists, he promoted a purified visual language consisting of perpendicular elements and primary colors. While immersed in this transcendental search, van Doesburg eagerly tapped the international network of the avant-garde, crossing wires with dada and constructivism. This lecture traces the origins and development of modernism in the Netherlands, ending with a look at recent Dutch design.

Reading: Kees Broos, "From De Stijl to a New Typography," *De Stijl, 1917–1931: Visions of Utopia*, Walker Art Center.

6. Language of Vision: The Bauhaus and the New Typography

The Bauhaus was founded in Germany in 1919 as a progressive school of art and design, seeking to build creative relationships among art, craft, and industry. Expressionist experiments dominated the early phase of the Bauhaus, while the later years were associated with functionalism and rationalism. Bauhaus graphic designers embraced constructivist theories of design, participating in what came to be known as the New

Typography, which assimilated avant-garde aesthetics into a critical commercial practice and helped consolidate the profession of graphic design.

Readings: Walter Gropius, "The Theory and Organization of the Bauhaus," 1938, in Bayer, Gropius, and Gropius, *Bauhaus, 1919–1928*; and László Moholy-Nagy, "Typophoto," 1927, in *Painting Photography Film*.

UNIT II: CONSUMPTION AND MASS CULTURE

The second unit of the course moves from European modernism to the American context. We begin with Reyner Banham's brilliant critique of functionalism, launched in the late fifties at the birth of the international pop art movement. The following lectures consider how modernism interacted with American consumer culture, and show how contradictions in modernist theory and practice resulted in the dilemmas of postmodernism.

7. Revising the Modern: Beyond the First Machine Age

The dramatic expansion of consumerism and mass culture after World War II was accompanied by a revision of modernist ideals of universality and permanence. The architectural historian Reyner Banham rejected the emphasis placed by his elders on the creation of rational, functional objects; instead, he embraced ideas of disposability, consumption, and speed that he saw in futurism.

Readings: Reyner Banham, *Theory and Design in the First Machine Age*, 1960 (excerpt); Antonio Sant'Elia and F. T. Marinetti, "Futurist Architecture," 1914; and Le Corbusier, *Towards a New Architecture*, 1931 (excerpt).

8. The Aesthetics of Waste: Streamlining and Industrial Design

In the United States, industrial design emerged alongside advertising and packaging in the 1920s and 1930s as a technique of "consumer engineering" designed to hasten the movement of goods through a cycle of purchase and disposal. This lecture looks at how industrial designers transformed middle-class American life by creating a vibrant style and a commercial ideology suited to American consumer culture.

Readings: Harold van Doren, *Industrial Design*, 1940 (excerpt); Henry Dreyfuss, *Designing for People*, 1955 (excerpt).

9. Graphic Design in America: From Popular Modernism to Corporate Modernism

European modernism moved across the Atlantic in the 1930s and 1940s, where it interacted with the commercial culture of the United States. Designers including Herbert Bayer, Walter Gropius, Ladislav Sutnar, and Will Burtin emigrated to the United States.

American designers such as Alvin Lustig and Lester Beall were influenced by émigrés as well as by publications and exhibitions of European art and design, while designers such as W. A. Dwiggins already had forged an American approach to modernism.

Readings: T. H. Robsjohn-Gibbings, "Do You Know the Difference between Modern and Modernistic?" *House Beautiful*, October 1946; Herbert Bayer, "Design, Designer, and Industry," 1951, in *Herbert Bayer: The Complete Work*.

10. Swiss Design: From System to Subjectivity

Avant-garde typography was rationalized into a coherent design methodology in Switzerland after World War II by Armin Hofmann, Karl Gerstner, Josef Müller-Brockmann, and others who favored the use of rational grid systems, objective photography, carefully abstracted symbols, and sans serif letterforms. In the late 1960s, the young Swiss designer Wolfgang Weingart subverted this rational language, using it to construct complex, overtly subjective compositions. Swiss modernism had a profound impact on design education and practice in the United States, giving rise to the new New Typography in the 1970s and 1980s.

Reading: Emil Ruder, *Typographie/Typography*, 1967 (excerpt).

11. Design as Sign: Pop and Postmodernism

An international pop art movement emerged in the 1950s that celebrated consumption, promoting image over structure, communication over function, and ephemerality over permanence. Working in New York, Herb Lubalin and the Push Pin Studios exerted a worldwide influence on design by using popular imagery, historical typefaces, and bold humor. Andy Warhol, who began his career as an illustrator, became notorious for appropriating commercial imagery. Pop movements also emerged in England, Italy, and Japan. In the 1970s, Robert Venturi and Denise Scott Brown turned to the electric lights and parking lots of Las Vegas as a source of architectural inspiration.

Readings: Robert Venturi, Denise Scott Brown, and Steven Izenour, *Learning from Las Vegas*, 1972 (excerpt); Gillo Dorfles and Vittorio Gregotti, *Kitsch: The World of Bad Taste*, 1968 (excerpt).

UNIT III: MEDIA AND MESSAGES

The course ends with a series of lectures and discussions devoted to interpreting design and media. Returning to the theory of semiotics introduced at the beginning of the course, the readings include texts by Roland Barthes and Jacques Derrida, who carried Saussure's study of verbal language into the domain of visual communication. These lectures are based on essays from our book *Design Writing Research: Writing on Graphic Design* (New York: Kiosk, 1996).

12. Mythologies: Reading Visual Culture

Scholars and critics became increasingly interested in popular culture in the 1950s and 1960s. Roland Barthes used the structural linguistics of Saussure to analyze artifacts of popular culture, showing how signs feed on one another in ravenous chains of appropriation to create the "mythologies" of modern life. In this class meeting, we discuss Barthes's ideas in relation to advertisements and objects from recent culture.

Reading: Roland Barthes, *Mythologies*, 1957 (excerpts).

13. White and Black on Gray: Race and Advertising

The Civil Rights movement of the 1960s compelled progressive art directors to introduce images of black men into mainstream "white" media. A common theme in advertising and editorial design was to impose white paint or makeup on the face of the black man. This lecture reviews the history of the New Advertising from the point of view of race relations, and shows how "separate but equal" advertising campaigns directed at black consumers remained the norm. Recent advertising issues also are discussed.

Reading: Miller and Lupton, "White and Black on Gray," in *Design Writing Research: Writing on Graphic Design*, 1996.

14. Low and High: Design and the Vernacular

As graphic design asserted itself as a legitimate profession in the United States in the 1970s and 1980s, many designers reacted against the polished forms and corporate values that occupied the center of the field. Designers looked outside the aesthetic and cultural ideologies of the profession in search of more direct and innocent forms of expression. Charles Anderson produced a richly nostalgic style based on the commercial arts of the 1940s and 1950s; Tibor Kalman created a blunt, clever aesthetic of nondesign; and club kids appropriated logos from supermarket packages.

Reading: Lupton and Miller, "Low and High: Design in Everyday Life," in *Design Writing Research: Writing on Graphic Design*, 1996.

15. Deconstruction: Examining the Structure of Style

The term "deconstruction" was coined by the philosopher Jacques Derrida in the 1960s, referring to the critique of such culturally entrenched oppositions as nature/culture, inside/outside, and speech/writing. After sweeping literary studies in the United States in the 1970s and 1980s, the term "deconstruction" entered design culture as a stylistic category applied to architecture, products, and graphics. This final lecture in the course looks at deconstruction both as a popular phenomenon and as a philosophical idea with profound links to design and typography.

Readings: Ferdinand de Saussure, *Course in General Linguistics*, 1916, (excerpt); Jacques Derrida, *Of Grammatology*, 1967 (excerpt); Lupton and Miller, "Graphic Design and Deconstruction," in *Design Writing Research: Writing on Graphic Design*, 1996.

Hyperarchitexture: Marked Typography and the Hypertextual Landscape

Katie Salen

BLUE SKY SYLLABUS: PREMISE

Communication lines are replacing transportation lines (roads, tracks, air links) to create an environment in which movement of information supplants the movement of bodies. As a result, simultaneous redefinitions of space, personal identity, and civic legibility are emerging as the network grows. How we interact with these new and constantly transforming definitions reflects the values that our society attaches to social structures such as race, sex, and class. With the change in the character of public space and the development and articulation of particular kinds of private space within sites of electronic orality, such as MUDs, MOOs, chatrooms, and e-mail, we can begin to question the identities that emerge from these interactions. Furthermore, as designers, we can hypothesize about the future role of typography in the (re)construction of these fragmented and complex identities.

HYPERARCHITEXTURE AS TYPOGRAPHIC LANDSCAPE

Typography on the Net enters the space of performance. Because it has no inherent physicality or integrity of form in the virtual textscape, typography has the potential to become "intelligent" or responsive to a variety of conditions present in the information structure it is representing. "Intelligent typography or behavioral graphics are endowed with their own inherent, but adjustable, physical attributes, such as gravity and bounce, for animation purposes—physical characteristics that the computer can model, but that cannot actually be produced in the 'real world'" (Muriel Cooper, MIT Media Lab). The flexibility of such an environment extends typography into the realms of architecture and composition. Such a consideration of typography as hyperarchitexture allows for an understanding of not only text, but the markers of that text (letterforms) as potential gateways for embedded structure. Furthermore, hyperarchitexts are multidimensional. Figurelike, they can carry on an argument at several levels simultaneously. As a result, it is proposed that in virtually constructed sites, typography can assume the "voice" of its author (or speaker/writer) so that as a form of communication it begins to move beyond syntactic form into the semantic realm of cultural and gendered identity.

OBJECTIVE

Part I of this course will examine the concept of typography as a culturally "marked" visible language system, exploring the potential for a typographically based representation of cultural identity. Part II will situate this work within sites of electronic orality and the hypertextual landscape, creating a relationship between oral gesture, or dialect, and typographic form as an expression of identity. A series of typographic and hypertextual prototypes and studies will be developed, and results may offer suggestions for possible applications within future telecommunication structures.

Conclusions will be drawn as to:

- the extent to which cultural identity can be "made visible" through typographic form
- the way in which bodies are being represented in sites of electronic orality
- the extent to which identity is being constructed through these representations
- the potential role of typographic form as visual agents of identity in sites of electronic orality
- the degree to which hypertextual typefaces can be constructed as gateways to personal visual/verbal vocabularies that are both expandable and self-authored

METHOD

The structure of this course will be based on the relationship between the exploratory (process), the experimental (prototype), and the speculative (theoretical). We will begin with a two-tiered set of questions and then move into the development of exploratory prototypes:

1. Marked typography: culture and identity
   a. Can character or cultural identity be made visible through typographic form?
2. The hypertextual landscape: typography, gesture, and context
   a. How is identity, on the level of ethnicity and gender, constructed and communicated within sites of electronic orality?
   b. Can typographic form function as a potential gateway for embedded structures connotative of a unique social and cultural identity?
   c. Can hypertextual typefaces be designed that reflect these structures of identity?

PROJECT MATRIX

We will be utilizing a matrix based upon a point, line, and plane structure. This matrix will allow for investigation of isolated concepts while maintaining a clearly identified set of relationships among constituent parts:

- Point (the level of the letterform)
- Line (the level of joinery)
- Plane (the level of reference)

Supplemental readings and assigned writings will support inquiry and discussion. We will be using Anna Deavere Smith's book *Fires in the Mirror* as a case study for course projects. Her work in the investigation of linguistic "character" and identity sets an excellent precedent for the goals of this course and will provide a richly textured context for the application of your work.

COURSE SEQUENCE

Part 1: Culture and Identity (weeks 1–4)

I. LEVEL OF THE LETTERFORM (*three weeks*) Question: Can letterforms be designed to be marked in terms of gender or ethnicity? What historical and contemporary precedents exist?

PROJECT 1—POINT: SPOKEN WORD TRANSLATIONS (*the object*)
Language reflects what is unseen in an individual. Can character or identity be made visible through typographic form, specifically at the level of letterforms? Select one character from the text *Fires in the Mirror*. Develop a "typographic portrait" for the character using Deavere Smith's interview with the individual as a source for content. Your objective is to develop a cultural voice for the individual through the design and application of a typographic syntax that visually expresses the identity of the individual within the context of the Crown Heights uprising.

Part 2: Electronic Orality and the Hypertextual Landscape (weeks 5–16)

II. LEVEL OF JOINERY (*five weeks*) Question: How can the issue of vocal gesture be addressed typographically to reference cultural identity through a material expression of dialect (dialect of the body, dialect of the voice)? This component focuses on the manipulation of the spacing between letters, words, and paragraphs to reference specific patterns and rhythms of speech and physical gesture.

PROJECT 2—LINE: TYPOGRAPHIC JOINERY AND GESTURE (*the animated object*)
This investigation focuses on the relationship between writing and design found in electronic orality or telewriting. You will be making both visual and conceptual proposals for the design of "behavioral typefaces" that reflect the physical and vocal qualities of their user. Excerpts from *Fires in the Mirror* will again be used as points of departure for the design of these typefaces. Extend the letterform syntax developed in Project 1 into an investigation of the way these forms connect over time. Focus on the physical and vocal dialect of the individual, using typographic joinery as the basis for the study. You will also be asked to address the relationship between the user (speaker/writer), the keyboard (interface), and the representation of the electronically mediated speech act (typeface). Consider what kind of mediation occurs between the keyboard and the output of the

letterforms—this mediation relates directly back to gestures (oral and physical) of the speaker.

Design the behavior of the typography as well as its visual form:

- Construct an appropriate representation of the alphabet (consider uppercase, lowercase, numerals, punctuation). Apply results of Project 1.
- Design a system for how the typeface "behaves" over time, using typographic joinery as the basis for the study (consider spacing, scale, color, consistency, baseline, etc.)
- Visualize the interaction between the user, interface, and representation in the format of a type specimen "page."

III. LEVEL OF REFERENCE (*seven weeks*) Question: Can a hypertextual typeface be developed that uses letterforms as gateways to personal visual/verbal vocabularies that are both expandable and self-authored?

PROJECT 3—PLANE: HYPERTEXTUAL TYPEFACES (*the situated object*)

This investigation into hypertextually based, architecturally based, body-based, data-based constructions of typographic language and self seeks to visually explore the subtleties of links between patterns of identity, gesture, and context. Application of this research will result in the design of a typographic interface focusing on the intrusion and juxtaposition of alternate self-authored perspectives voiced from within the hypertextual link. Integrating the concept of culturally marked typographic structures with an investigation into situating narrative structures, this "typeface" will contain embedded structures or hypertextual links alluding to the cultural identity of the user.

Applying the research from Projects 1 and 2, investigate possible models for hypertextual typefaces that express the identity of the user through form, behavior, and navigation. These prototypes should be speculative and experimental, posing questions about the role of typographic form and meaning in the hypertextual landscape.

READING LIST

Project 1

Anna Deavere Smith, *Fires in the Mirror* (New York: Anchor Books, 1993).

Johanna Drucker, *The Visible Word: Experimental Typography and Modern Art, 1909–1923*, (Chicago: University of Chicago Press, 1994).

Andrew Blauvelt, "In and Around: Cultures of Design and the Design of Cultures," *Emigre*, no. 33: 2–23.

Mark Skiles, "Margaret Crawford's Greatness Close to Home: My Daily Trip Down La Brea," *Offramp* 1, no. 6, SciArc, (1996).

Project 2

Jessica Helfand, *Six Essays on Design and New Media* (New York: William Drenttel, 1995).

Phil Baines, "Clear Enough to Read," *Emigre* no. 18.

Frances Butler, "Punctuation, or the Dream of Legibility: From Vision to Substance," *Emigre* no. 40: 56–64.

Andrea Codrington, "Invasion of the Copy Snatchers," *Eye* 23, vol. 6 (winter 1996): 66–69

Ursula Held, "Read this Aloud," *Eye* 23, vol. 6 (winter 1996): 36–46.

Johanna Drucker, "The Future of Writing," *Emigre* no. 35.

Project 3

Eduardo Kac, guest editor, "New Media Poetry: Poetic Innovation and New Technologies," *Visible Language* 30.2 (1996).

J. Abbott Miller, *Dimensional Typography: Case Studies on the Shape of Letters in Virtual Environments* (Princeton: Princeton Architectural Press, 1996).

William Owen, "Experiments in Hypertype," *Eye* 21, vol. 6 (summer 1996): 6–7.

Teal Triggs, ":-{ } She Wears Lipstick" in Katie Salen, ed., *Zed.2 Real World Design: The Role of the Experimental,* Center for Design Studies (1995): 39–48

Katie Salen and Sharyn O'Mara, "Dis[appearances]: Operational Strategies and Representational Needs in Codexspace and Cyberspace," in Dietmar Winkler, ed., *Visible Language* (1998): 260–85.

Visual Literacy

Judith Wilde and Richard Wilde

- Required class for all graphic design majors
- Weeks: 12
- Texts: *Visual Literacy*, Judith Wilde and Richard Wilde; *Design Literacy*, Steven Heller and Karen Pomeroy
- Method of teaching: Lectures, slides, and weekly critiques on all assignments

This course is designed to foster a personal approach to conceptual problem solving while investigating the classical principles of graphic design and developing a visual vocabulary through experimentation that sets the groundwork that reinforces one's critical, analytical, and perceptual skills.

Each assignment creates conditions where one discovers the language of graphic design and encourages conceptual thinking through exploration that results in original and personal imagery.

WEEK 1: BLACK SQUARE ASSIGNMENT

By using four black squares of the same dimension, students are to create a graphic image in the eight rectangles indicated on a given assignment sheet to express the meaning of each of the following six words: "order," "increase," "bold," "congested," "tension," and "playful."

This problem serves as an introduction toward the development of a geometric idiom through the discovery of various two-dimensional design principles needed to extend the limited graphic vocabulary where only four black squares are utilized in expressing the intended message. The principles to be explored include framal reference; touching; overlapping; intersecting; cropping; illusory space; contrast in terms of size, direction, position; and the dynamics of negative-positive relationships.

WEEK 2: ALTERED PAGE ASSIGNMENT

Using the three mechanically drawn linear images that appear on the assignment sheet, which depict an interior wall with a socket, a brick wall, and a window, "defamiliarize the familiar" by altering, changing, rearranging, and/or redesigning the given images.

The intention of this assignment is to develop a way of appropriating an image, yet transcending its original form by making it one's own through a personal approach to narrative storytelling. This provides an opportunity to play, which minimizes fear of failure. Playing, fooling around, and experimenting are the keys to this assignment.

WEEK 3: HOMAGE TO ANDRÉ BRETON ASSIGNMENT

Using the gridlike dot patterns printed on the assignment sheet, students are asked to experiment with the phenomenon of automatic writing, in terms of image making and doodling as a spontaneous experimental exercise in discovering one's own voice.

The intention of this assignment is to first familiarize students with the work of the French surrealist poet André Breton and to expand the creative process to discover subconscious and intuitive problem-solving impulses.

WEEK 4: CIRCLE, SQUARE, TRIANGLE ASSIGNMENT

Using the geometric shapes of circles, squares, and triangles that appear on the assignment sheet as focal points, students are to create identifiable images by adding other elements while maintaining the integrity of the original geometric shapes.

The intention of this assignment is to make use of the reductive nature of geometry as a basis for a visual language, which, in turn, sets the foundation for a formalistic approach to design that readily encompasses corporate identity, signage, trademark, logos, and pictograms.

WEEK 5: SOUND ASSIGNMENT

Students are given an assignment sheet with nine blank four-by-four-inch square areas with titles printed beneath them, such as car crash, busy diner, jazz band, bumblebees making love, clock, striking a match, and conversation between a tuba and a flute. Students are asked to visually represent the sounds of these specific subjects. For each of the nine solutions required for this assignment, they are reminded to consider the character of the sound in terms of tempo, volume, duration, context, and color.

The intention of this assignment is to expand one's graphic vocabulary beyond the simple narrative voice by moving students beyond the literal problem-solving arena into the less familiar area of conceptual problem solving through the use of metaphor, symbolism, and abstraction.

WEEK 6: "A LINE IS A DOT THAT WENT FOR A WALK" ASSIGNMENT

Students are given an assignment sheet printed with the following eighteen descriptive qualities that are often associated with human behavior: anxious, embarrassed, bizarre, exhausted, fragile, systematic, lyrical, turbulent, nonsensical, psychotic, ambiguous, distracted, slovenly, sensual, spontaneous, aggressive, awkward, and indecisive. In the given area next to each word, students are asked to graphically interpret the subjects by using line as a point of departure.

The intention of this assignment is to familiarize students with Paul Klee's famous expression, to develop sensitivity to the expressive quality of line, and to explore the descriptive nature of line as a multipurpose medium for the expression of emotional qualities. Students have an opportunity to discover the vast properties of line, ranging from thick, thin, rigid, blurred, broken, curved, soft, and angular, while experimenting with different media and color.

WEEK 7: GRAPHIC DESIGN 101 ASSIGNMENT

Students are given an assignment sheet with one hundred small rectangles and one larger rectangle printed on it. They are asked to choose one of the following subjects and visually interpret it one hundred different ways: paper bag, frog, sneaker, gumball machine, manhole cover, sun, ant, dandelion, or apple. Students are asked to consider various graphic design principles including cropping, touching, overlapping and intersecting of forms, negative and positive relationships, composition, texture, scale, and color. The combining of these principles gives rise to an enormous variety of solutions. Upon completion of the one hundred solutions, students are then asked to select their best solution and execute it in the larger rectangle on the assignment sheet.

The intention of this assignment is threefold. First, it challenges a student's endurance and resourcefulness by demanding such a multiproblem-solving task. Second, it encourages playing, risk taking, and experimentation while it reinforces previously taught graphic design principles. Lastly, it enforces the critical skill of editing, which is an important aspect of the design process that requires students to develop an inner sense or understanding—a barometer for assessing the impact of their work. The completion of this assignment is empowering.

WEEK 8: THE NOTEBOOK ASSIGNMENT

Using the twenty-one rectangles on the assignment sheet, students are to depict the physical or emotional characteristics, or specific personalities, of twenty different grade-school pupils and one teacher by utilizing the basic elements that a notebook page is comprised of: many horizontal blue lines and two vertical red lines on a white background. In the redesigning of the notebook page, students may alter the space between lines, increase or decrease the thickness of the line, or change the direction of the lines. The only limitation is to maintain the basic identity of the notebook page.

The intention of this assignment is to offer students an abstract vehicle where successful solutions do not rely on drawing skills, but on a pure graphic design idiom and the employment of graphic design principles. Students are encouraged to develop a more conceptual approach to problem solving because of the constraints and parameters of the assignment.

WEEK 9: UPC ASSIGNMENT

Using the eight rectangles on the assignment sheet, students are asked to alter the UPC (Universal Price Code) symbol by interpreting it in a personal, political, or social statement, then to select the best solution and execute it in the larger rectangle on the assignment sheet.

The intention of this assignment is to offer an opportunity for playful problem solving, which can produce satirical, comical, and witty solutions for a designer's graphic vocabulary. The inherent familiarity of the subject gives a certain tangibility to the problem, but the success of the solutions ultimately lie in the articulation of the graphic execution and formalistic concerns. The UPC mark is one of the most widely used symbols in the world, appearing on packaged goods, magazines, book jackets, and other mass-produced products. It is the nemesis of graphic designers because its placement often conflicts with one's design solution. Therefore, having this opportunity for revenge is widely appreciated.

WEEK 10: ROAD SIGN ASSIGNMENT

Students are given an assignment sheet printed with twelve blank yellow road signs. The following topics are listed beneath each of the signs: ant farm, red-light district, nuclear power plant, quicksand, running of the bulls, lovers' lane, fortune-teller, target range, paratrooper landing, shark crossing, alien sighting area, and hole in the ozone. Students are asked to depict the given subjects by keeping immediacy in mind, which is the primary function of a road sign.

This assignment encourages simplicity and personalization while keeping immediate communication in mind as the primary function of the road sign. Although the familiar context of a road sign encourages a traditional solution, the nonsensical topics allow for uninhibited experimentation and the opportunity to play.

WEEK 11: LIFE-AND-DEATH ASSIGNMENT

Students are given an assignment sheet with six small and one large truck printed on it. They are asked to create a life-and-death image to be executed in two parts on the rear panels of each truck, with the left panel representing any subject, object, or situation, while the right panel must show its destruction or transformation. The solutions should be personal rather than functional (e.g., instructing motorists is not the primary goal—as trucks having "pass/do not pass" written on their back panels).

The intention of this assignment is for students to transcend their automatic responses to the concept of life and death, and to discover that the alteration of anything is its death. Personal responses allow for more meaningful participation in the problem-solving process and to accomplish this, at the onset, students are asked to write lists of ideas that help develop concepts. This process may be applied to a broad range of conceptual problem-solving situations.

WEEK 12: TYPOGRAPHIC PORTRAIT ASSIGNMENT

A specific type of personality, characteristic, or subject is described in each of the twelve rectangles on the assignment sheet. They are as follows: chameleon, acrobat, amphibian, linebacker for the New York Giants, taxi driver, TV evangelist, allergy, Chernobyl, hiccups, accident prone, magician, and one's self. Students are asked to choose an appropriate typeface that best expresses the characteristics of each subject, then render their whole name, part of their name, or their nickname, considering the typeface style, letter spacing, and use of upper- and lowercase characters.

Learning to work expressively with typography is the intention of this assignment. Typography is the definitive tool of the graphic designer. Most problems can be solved within the confines of this expressive form. This assignment encourages the initial problem-solving impulse to be pushed beyond the literal toward a more conceptual approach. The use of one's own name adds a more personal element, which engages students to work expressively, giving a deeper meaning to the project.

Designing with Self-Authored Text

Paula J. Curran

COURSE OVERVIEW

How do writing and design implicate each other? What place does self-initiated, non–client-driven design have in the life of a graphic designer? Historically, graphic designers have been mediators rather than creators of the text. To challenge this paradigm, this course examines the consequences of the student/designer inventing text, form, and audience. Through a series of creative writing exercises and typography problems, the student will investigate verbal and symbolic visual language and meaning from within a conceptual framework. In addition, this topic will be examined through readings, lectures, and analyzing artists' books.

CONTENT AREAS

The two major content areas for this course are writing and design, with each of the four projects involving both. The expectation is that knowledge and concepts will be abstracted and translated in the next project area. Lectures will clarify and expand the concepts and objectives of the problem statements. Each student is responsible for the completion of each assignment, which includes developmental and exploration work and a final solution to the verbal and visual communication problem.

WRITING PROCESS

The process of writing is similar to the design process in that writing involves research, creative thinking, writing drafts, and refinement. Like the design process, it is not reasonable to expect to write a successful piece by sitting down, putting fingers to keyboard, and finishing it in one sitting. To aid in the writing process, writing assignments will be workshopped in class. Workshopping allows for feedback and suggestions from the professor and classmates.

Most of the projects will begin by writing the content (words) followed by designing the form. In rare instances, form may precede design, but students will be required, unless specified, to concentrate on the written component first.

DESIGN PROCESS

The next step in the process is the design. Each student is expected to take each project to a creative and highly innovative solution. This can be achieved by understanding and following the guidelines of good design process and spending the necessary time on each assignment. It is not reasonable to expect successful solutions to complex problems with one or two quickly executed ideas. It is important to generate many ideas for each visual solution to the assignment. Each stage of a visual solution must be thoroughly investigated. The professor will provide guidelines for the appropriate quantity of sketches that should be completed.

Each assignment requires a well-organized notebook of both the writing and design processes that lead to the solution. These notebooks are usually in the form of a plastic folder with clear pages to insert the work. The brand name is ITOYA® and they are available at bookstores and commercial copy centers around campus. Each assignment will require a different notebook.

WORKSHOPPING

Workshopping writing is similar to the critique process in graphic design. We will spend approximately two class periods for each project workshopping written work.

To ensure proper workshopping, students must have—at the beginning of class, on the date due—their completed written work and nineteen copies. No excuses, please. The student will then pass out a copy of their work to each student—two copies will go to the professor. Workshopping will take place during the next two classes. To prepare for the workshops, each student must read everyone's work and make critical comments, either in the margins or typed on a separate page.

During the workshop, each student will read his or her piece out loud (or have someone else read it). The class will then spend ten to twelve minutes discussing and commenting on the work. It is vital to the progress of each writer that he or she receives critical feedback from all students. At the end of the workshop, each writer will collect all comments. Sign your comments and please avoid unkind or irresponsible comments. They serve no one.

TEXTS

Robin Williams, *Beyond the Mac Is Not a Typewriter: More Typographic Insights and Secrets* (Berkeley: Peachpit Press, 1996). Required.

Anne Lamott, *Bird by Bird: Some Instructions on Writing and Life* (New York: Pantheon Books, 1994). Required.

Carol Burke and Molly Best Tinsley, *The Creative Process* (New York: St. Martin's Press, 1993). Recommended.

Robin Behn and Chase Twichell, eds., *The Practice of Poetry: Writing Exercises from Poets Who Teach* (New York: Harper Perennial, 1992). Recommended.

Anne Bernays and Pamela Painter. *What If? Writing Exercises for Fiction Writers* (New York: HarperCollins, 1995). Recommended.

Rob Carter, Ben Day, and Philip Meggs, *Typographic Design: Form and Communication*, 2d ed. (New York: Van Nostrand Reinhold, 1993). Recommended.

Wucius Wong, *Principles of Form and Design* (New York: Van Nostrand Reinhold, 1993). (Textbook used in ArtGR 270/271.) Recommended.

Rob Carter and Philip Meggs, *Typographic Specimens: The Great Typefaces* (New York: Van Nostrand Reinhold, 1993). (Excellent reference. Used in ArtGR 270/271.) Recommended.

Erik Spiekermann and E. M. Ginger, *Stop Stealing Sheep and Find Out How Type Works* (Mountain View, Calif.: Adobe Press, 1993). (Excellent type specimen reference. Brief, but informative examples of how typography is used. Useful, always. Used in ArtGR 270/271.) Recommended.

BIBLIOGRAPHY: DESIGN

Philip Meggs, *Type and Image: The Language of Graphic Design* (New York: Van Nostrand Reinhold, 1992).

Keith Smith, *Text in the Book Format: Book NR. 120* (Rochester, N.Y.: Sigma Foundation, 1989).

Keith Smith, *The Structure of the Visual Book: Book 95* (Rochester, N.Y.: Keith Smith, 1984).

Anne Burdick (guest editor) and Rudy VanderLans (publisher), "Mouthpiece 1," *Emigre*, no. 35 (1995); and "Mouthpiece 2," *Emigre* no. 36 (1995).

Rob Carter. *American Typography Today* (New York: Van Nostrand Reinhold, 1989).

Kim Elam, *Expressive Typography: The Word as Image* (New York: Van Nostrand Reinhold, 1990).

Jasia Reichardt, "Joshua Reichart, "Typography as Visual Poetry" in *The Liberated Page: A* Typographica *Anthology*, Herbert Spencer, ed. (San Francisco: Bedford Press, 1987).

Christine Celano, "A Typographic Visualization of the Narrative Structure of On the Road," *Design Issues* IX, no. 1 (fall 1992).

Steven Heller, "The Shock Is Gone," *I.D.* 35, no. 2 (March–April 1988): 62.

John Morgan and Peter Welton, *See What I Mean* (London: Edward Arnold, 1992).

Kenneth J. Hiebert, *Graphic Design Processes: Universal to Unique* (New York: Van Nostrand Reinhold, 1992).

SOFTWARE

Bill Parsons, *Graphic Design with PageMaker 6.0* (Delmar Publishers, 1996). Information on the Web: *www.delmar.com/delmar.html*; e-mail: *info@delmar.com*; phone: (800) 347-7707

Robin Williams, *The Mac Is Not a Typewriter* (Berkeley: Peachpit Press, 1989).

Paula J. Curran, *Me and Jackie O.* (Ames, Iowa: self-published, 1995).

Warren Lehrer, *Nicky D. from L.I.C.: The Portrait Series: A Narrative Portrait of Nicholas Detommaso* (Seattle: Bay Press, 1995).

Warren Lehrer, *The Portrait Series: A Narrative Portrait of Charles Lang* (Seattle: Bay Press, 1995).

Art Spiegelman, *Maus: A Survivor's Tale I: My Father Bleeds History* (New York: Pantheon Books, 1986).

Art Spiegelman, *Maus: A Survivor's Tale II: And Here My Troubles Began* (New York: Pantheon Books, 1991).

Nick Bantock, *Sabine's Notebook* (San Francisco: Chronicle Books, 1992).

Nick Bantock, *Griffin and Sabine* (San Francisco: Chronicle Books, 1992).

WRITING

William Zinsser, *Writing to Learn* (New York: Harper & Row, 1988).

Robin Behn and Chase Twichell, eds., *The Practice of Poetry: Writing Exercises from Poets Who Teach* (New York: Harper Perennial, 1992).

GRADING

Each project will be evaluated and graded for both design and writing, based on the criteria established in the problem statement and problem objectives. Projects will be weighted in importance based on the complexity of the concepts and the solutions required. Each project will be given a letter grade based on a system of points for each assignment. You will receive both written and verbal evaluations for each assignment. The verbal evaluation will take place during the critiques that are scheduled for the assignment due dates. These critiques may last the entire class period or they may not. Be prepared to stay for the whole critique. Each project will be given a letter grade based on the + or – system. Projects will be graded and returned by the due date for the next project.

- A: *Excellent* This is usually work done by a highly motivated student meeting all or most of the performance criteria as set forth by the problem. In order to earn an A in the course, a student must earn an A consistently on every writing/design project.
- B: *Good* This work is above average but lacks the qualities that give it the stamp of excellence. It shows better-than-average design sensitivity.
- C: *Satisfactory* This work is merely average. Work is handed in on time and has fulfilled the requirements for the project, but it lacks strong writing and/or visual interest and thoughtful and imaginative resolution.
- D: *Poor* Below Average. This work is handed in on time, but lacks many or most areas that show any understanding of design or design print production.

- F: *Unacceptable* Work that is not handed in on time or is so despicable as to be an affront to design sensibilities. Makes printers moan in anguish.

GRAPHIC DESIGN AREA ARCHIVES

Each student will be required to submit a copy of one piece from this course (in both print and digital form) for the Graphic Design Area Archives. This piece will be selected by your course instructor, and must be turned in at the time of your final project submission for this semester. Your instructor will also ask for specific works to be photographed for the Graphic Design Area Archives, which may be more than one project.

DUE DATES AND PROJECT SUBMISSION

In the working world of design, deadlines must be met, period! All assignments will have due dates. Late projects will be marked down one letter grade (+ or –) for each day they are late. This includes nonclass days and weekends. Projects are due at the beginning of class. No excuses, please. Your client is interested in results, not excuses. As with any rule, there are exceptions. A written doctor's explanation is required if a due date is missed due to illness. Discuss problems with instructors in advance to anticipate a problem and offer solutions. Organize your time and plan ahead! Finally, a project may not be redone for a higher grade. Students are encouraged to try the assignment again if they did not do well—for the purpose of making their portfolio better. However, the project will not be regraded.

PROJECT DUE DATES

The following are the dates each project is due. Each project, including final print product, disk, and ITOYA® are due at the beginning of class. Critiques will be on the due date, unless otherwise specified.
- Tuesday, February 4: Project 1
- Tuesday, March 4: Project 2
- Tuesday, April 3: Project 3
- Thursday, April 24: Project 4

Off the Page and into the Streets:
Communication and Activism

Sharyn O'Mara

Bill Newkirk writes:

Art and design: some definitions. . . . I can't see one without seeing the other.
Take either the heart or the mind out of the body and what do you have left?

Design is external, in that its forms and applications extend basic human
functions and needs. These pertain to three primary areas—messages, as in our need
to communicate with each other; products, which enable us to extend the mechanical
functions of the body; and environment, or control of conditions around us.

Art is internal, in that its forms affect the senses and thereby influence the
psyche, the emotions, the spirit. The fine arts emanate from the area of human
messages. They involve the individual, the one whose forming is a singular act.
And they involve the individual who may or may not elect to correspond with the
maker of that form. This does not rule out the human need on both sides. . . .
The design profession is a problem-solving activity. The problem or task most
often originates with someone other than the designer. This is the client. . . .
Design is well done if it does its job. Design becomes an art when it elevates the
task to touch the spirit as well. ("Art and/or Design," *Spirals* 91)

DESCRIPTION

"Off the Page and into the Streets" provides a forum for students from any
discipline to consider and expand their roles as members of a community, residents of an
urban environment, and participants in our culture. This course is an immersion in the
social, political, historical, and economic issues that guide and divide our city and our
country, and offers the opportunity for students to take a public stand on issues of importance ranging from the personal to the political. Students are required to read the *New
York Times* daily.

There are three main components to the course.

I. PUBLIC ART AND/OR DESIGN: AN OVERVIEW

Looking at historical and contemporary examples of communication and activism, we will investigate the methods and materials for achieving a particular aim, and the impact/effectiveness of each work. This component takes place during the first nine weeks of the course and involves slide lectures, discussions, and assigned readings.

Context for Inquiry

In Linda Burnham's article "What Price Social Art?" (*High Performance*, no. 35, 1986) she states that "the effectiveness of a social artwork is bound up in its context, framed in its time zone. Can any social spectacle be effective in 1986?" More than a decade later, the question looms large. As we navigate each day, we cannot help but be confronted by evidence of the vastness of societal ills—homelessness and poverty, war and famine, issues in race, gender, sexuality, cultural identity, human rights, education, healthcare, and politics—newspapers and city streets alike scream at us and the sound is overwhelming; inaction, however, is deafening. Artists and designers, as communicators, are uniquely positioned to act upon these issues within the realms of both the poetic and the pragmatic. But making issue-oriented work is not without challenges, and many of these arise from the efforts of those who have gone before. Burnham points out that issue-oriented works "must adopt a truly fresh approach. So many have tried so hard, and the problems are still with us. We are psychologically worn out with the effort to solve them, and perhaps this leads us to steel against ourselves. . . . Has this tool lost its cutting edge?"

Week One: Tours

Tour One: Trolley Tour with MTSI. We will see the city the way that tourists see it. Consider for discussion next week: What do we see/not see? Who is visible/invisible? What areas are deemed acceptable/unacceptable? Which cultures are represented/not represented? What is the percentage of retail to living space that we see, and how does that correspond to percentages for the entire city? Where are the homeless, the poor, the margins? Consulting the map of the City of Kansas City, Missouri, what percentage of the city is viewed in these tours? How accurate a view is this? Document this experience through visual and verbal notations; bring a camera and film, videocamera, sketchbook.

Tour Two: Car Tour with class. We will take a driving tour of the City of Kansas City, Missouri, using the city map to determine our route. Consider this in light of the earlier tour. Document this experience.

Week Two: Memorial and Place

Krzysztof Wodijko: Projections
Maya Lin: Vietnam Veterans' Memorial

Jenny Holzer: Survival Series
Biddy Mason and Experience of Place
Sheila Levrant de Bretteville
Susan King
Betye Saar

Precedents:
Diego Rivera
Picasso: *Guernica*
Francisco Goya
Kathe Kollwitz

Discussion and Analysis: Discussion of tours and analysis of information gathered; discuss readings. Discuss assignment one: KCAI campus. Proposals due and concept presentations: week 6. Conversation with Director of Exhibitions (installation procedures, proposal preparation); campus tour (with maps) to identify potential sites; documenting campus for reference.

Week Three: Culture in Action

Carrie Mae Weems
Krzysztof Wodijko: Homeless Vehicle Project
Trinh T. Minh-ha: *Surname Viet, Given Name Nam*
Adrienne Piper: Business Card
Sculpture Chicago: Daniel Martinez, *Consequences of a Gesture*
Suzanne Lacy: *Full Circle*
Kate Ericson and Mel Ziegler: *Eminent Domain*
Robert Peters: *Naming Others, Manufacturing Yourself*
Mark Dion: Chicago Urban Ecology Action Group
Iñigo Manglano-Ovalle: *Tele-Vecindario* (a street-level video project)
Haha Flood: A volunteer network for active participation in healthcare

Week Four: Activism Through Ideology

Dada
Constructivsim
Bauhaus
Situationist International
Punk
Fluxus

Jan van Toorn
Spike Lee
John Heartfield
Robbie Conal
Ralph Nadar

Protest Posters:
Revolutionary Posters: Central and Eastern Europe
Suffragettes: U.S. and Britain
Keith Haring
Grapus

Week Seven: Advocates for Change

Greenpeace
Habitat for Humanity
Amnesty International
Humanity magazine

Collectives and Collaborations:
Guerilla Girls
Act Up
Bureau
WAC
Gran Fury
Tim Rollings: KOS (Kids of Survival)
Suzanne Lacy: *The Dark Madonna, The Crystal Quilt*
AIDS Quilt

Designers Take Action:
Class Action
WD+RU (Women's Design and Research Unit)
Liberation Graphics
Jerry Mander: The nation's first not-for-profit ad agency

Week Nine: Methods of Dissemination

Jenny Holzer
Barbara Kruger
Shepherd Ferry: *Andre the Giant Has a Posse*
WWW Sites: political and social

Private Firms Take Public Action . . . for a Profit:
The Body Shop
Espirit
Ben and Jerry's
Buddy Shapiro: Social Tees

Texts: Cultural Memory
"Introduction" in Marita Sturken, *Tangled Memories* (Berkeley and London: University of
California Press, 1997).

Texts: Place
"City: Visions and Revisions" in Brian Wallis, ed. *If You Lived Here: The City in Art,
Theory and Social Activism, A Project by Martha Rosler* (Seattle: Bay Press,
1991).
"Claiming Urban Landscapes as Public History" in Dolores Hayden, *The Power of Place:
Urban Landscapes as Public History* (Cambridge: MIT Press, 1995).
"Experiencing Cities" in Tony Hiss, *The Experience of Place* (New York: Vintage Books,
1990).

Texts: Into the Streets
Arlene Raven, "Introduction" in Arlene Raven, ed. *Art in Public Places* (Ann Arbor and
London: UMI Research Press, 1989).
"Introduction" in Lis McQuiston, *Graphic Agitation: Social and Political Graphics Since
the Sixties* (London: Phaidon Press, 1993).

II. PUBLIC SERVICE

Individual

Each student is required to perform three hours of community service per week at
a community organization of their choosing from the list provided; a variety of different
issues are addressed by the organizations ranging from homelessness and poverty to
literacy and arts education. (Community service will take place during the Thursday
session from 2 to 5 P.M. for the first ten weeks of the semester.) I will assist with the
arrangements for your volunteer work.

Rationale: As a part of learning about issues in our community, it is imperative
that we invest ourselves in that community through active participation. This experience
will provide valuable insight into the day-to-day realities—both triumph and failure—of
organizations working to improve the human condition.

Group

During the last four weeks of the semester (with the exception of critique week) we will work as a group for a variety of causes (preparing meals for the homeless, painting houses for the elderly, teaching art to young children).

Rationale: The ability to work as a team member, collaborating toward a mutual goal, is critical to designers and artists in the expanding global market. In addition, since there is power in numbers, we can positively impact various elements of our community.

III. STUDIO

Objective: The studio component allows students to synthesize their experience in the community, knowledge gained from lectures, and individual research to develop a point of view and then act upon it. Through critique and discussion we will consider content, audience, intended and perceived meaning, and we will ask how designers and artists position themselves in their communities: What is their responsibility within this arena? How can we challenge the status quo and provoke thought in a way that causes resonance and perhaps inspires action? What is the role of the commercial media in communication? When should we and how do we take a stand? What are the benefits of taking design off of the page, art off of the walls, and taking to the streets? You are required to keep a sketchbook as a part of the studio component. Use this for taking notes, working out ideas, sketching, and documenting your experience as a resident of this city.

Project 1: KCAI Campus

As you know, many students on campus do not take the time to stay connected to the community around them or make themselves aware of larger issues in our city and in society as a whole. Choose an issue that you feel is important to communicate and "install" or "act" it on campus. Proposals are due week five for review and approval by the director of exhibitions; all proposals must be approved before proceeding. Of course, you may not do anything illegal for any part of your project. You are required to document your event and submit ten to twenty slides and video clips.

Project 2: Kansas City

Choose an issue or issues of importance in relation to your research about and experience in Kansas City, and develop a work or works that address this issue in an active manner. Again, you may not do anything illegal as any part of your project. Appropriate permits must be obtained for certain types of actions; I will assist you with this process.

Green Graphic Design Seminar

Lisa Fontaine

The goal of this green design seminar is to develop informed decision makers, able to weigh conflicting data and set personal and professional priorities. This ability will be achieved through the three primary learning objectives outlined below. The interrelationship of these objectives will become evident as you progress through the course.

1.

You will focus your attention on the ecological concerns of graphic designers. Through an examination of the destructive consequences of paper manufacturing, printing, and packaging on the environment, you will develop skills to consider ways to minimize this impact. You will also consider the many ways that designers can have a positive impact on the environment through their problem-solving and innovative thinking skills. In response to the interdisciplinary nature of green design, your study will include issues facing the design community as a whole.

2.

In addition to studying published information, you will conduct original qualitative research on green design. The cross-disciplinary aspects of ecology and the contradictory nature of the information sources make this topic an ideal introduction to critical thinking. Your original research will provide you with experience in thinking and writing critically, preparing you for the eventual task of thesis development for your M.F.A. degree. In preparation for this research, you will study the basic principles of logic, argument, and the scientific method.

3.

You will use your expanding knowledge of green design to develop new ideas for integrating ecology into design education. These curricular prototypes will be included in the Green Design Curricular Initiative currently being organized through ICOGRADA Education.

Please note: It is not the intention of this course to create or enforce an eco-correct doctrine. Your personal beliefs and questions are important and welcome in all discussions.

PRIMARY READING LIST

Starting Research by Roy Preece
The Research Paper Workbook by Ellen Strenski and Madge Manfred
The Art of Creative Critical Thinking by John C. S. Kim
The Designers Guide to Eco-friendly Design by Poppy Evans
Recycled Papers by Claudia Thompson
The Green Imperative by Victor Papanek
How Much Is Enough? by David Durning
Green Design by Dorothy Mackenzie
The Great Printers Project published by the Environmental Defense Fund
The Graphic Designer's Greenbook by Anne Chick
Packaging and the Environment by Susan E. M. Selke
Design for Society by Nigel Whitely

ASSIGNMENT 1: PRESENTATION OF GREEN DESIGN ISSUES

Objective: To incorporate assigned readings into a coherent presentation of green design issues.

Procedure: You will be assigned a specific section of the readings to use in the development of a fifteen-minute presentation. Your objective will be to bring the readings to life by presenting additional material or participatory exercises that enhance the group's understanding and interest in the topic. Your objective is *not* to rehash the readings. Prepare your presentation with the assumption that everyone has done the reading; your task is to make it more memorable for them, or show them how it relates to comparable or broader issues.

An effective presentation will be innovative, coherent, and manageable within the fifteen-minute limitation.

ASSIGNMENT 2: LIFE-CYCLE ASSESSMENT

Objective: To develop an understanding of the concept of extended producer responsibility through examination of the cradle-to-grave impact of printed materials.

Procedure: Conduct a life-cycle analysis of an existing piece of printed graphic design. This entails examining all aspects of the product's life, including manufacturing of the paper, printing, distribution, disposal, recyclability, and de-inking prospects. You will need to interview the designer of the piece to learn the specifics about the paper and printing process used. Present alternatives for each of the phases of the life cycle that you feel could be more eco-friendly. Be specific with your suggestions.

You will be graded on the thoroughness and accuracy of the information you gather, as well as the appropriateness of your suggested alternatives. Keep in mind that some special-interest groups have intentionally presented misinformation on the topics of paper, ink, and printing; therefore, you will need to develop your investigative abilities— i.e., your ability to sift through the "green-washing" to find the most accurate and unbiased information.

ASSIGNMENT 3: HYPOTHESIS DEVELOPMENT EXERCISE

Objective: To learn the principles of the scientific method of inquiry, the basic elements of logic, in preparation for developing original research in green design.

Procedure: This exercise will allow you to test the basic research methods identified in your texts

(The Art of Creative Critical Thinking, Starting Research, and The Research Paper Workbook). In this preliminary exercise, you will *not* be expected to develop each research idea in-depth, instead, your focus should be on developing hypotheses and outlining the processes that would be necessary to test them.

Begin with a topic about which you have both knowledge and opinions. Based on the combination of data and opinion, develop a hypothesis. Consider how you would need to test such a hypothesis, and what information or discovery would disprove it. Your opinions will help in developing ideas; however, they can also be problematic. Consider how your hypothesis and/or methodology might be biased or compromised by your current opinions.

Although your hypothesis proposals will never be carried through to a final paper, you will be required to present them as though they would actually be pursued. Structure your proposal according to the following categories:

- Title: Your title must be accurate and unambiguous. This is not as easy as it seems.
- Abstract: Synthesis of the problem definition and hypothesis that clarifies your intentions.
- Problem Definition: Background on the topic: existing literature, in what academic disciplines the topic is being studied; unexplored links, etc. Cite sources.
- Hypothesis: The new assertion you are making, based on your study of existing data and your opinions, which is worded in a way that is clearly testable.
- Investigation of the Hypothesis: Explain the intended methodology for testing the hypothesis.
- Potential Limitations of the Methodology: Describe limitations of time, funding, or other variables that will make it impossible to fully test the hypothesis or achieve conclusive results.

Your proposals should be a maximum of two to three pages. Brevity will force you to think and write with greater clarity.

ASSIGNMENT 4: GREEN DESIGN PEDAGOGY

Objectives: To develop new and innovative ways to present green design issues to design students and to contribute to the development of a prototype curriculum for the ICOGRADA Education Green Design Initiative.

Procedure: You will develop a curricular proposal for design students that would increase their awareness and understanding of green design issues. Each student will be assigned a specific subtopic within green design that must be addressed by their prototype.

Within your assigned topic, develop one assignment or educational component that accomplishes the following:

- Clearly states its learning objective and pedagogical rationale
- Demonstrates its potential to meet this objective
- Clearly identifies the recommended process for students to follow
- Directs the students toward meaningful, in-depth research
- Assigns appropriate readings
- Is innovative in its approach to the topic
- Cannot be achieved through superficial solutions
- Could be supervised by an instructor with no expertise in green design

Prepare a draft proposal of the assignment. Structure your proposal as follows:
- Project Title
- Learning Objective: what students will learn, not what they will do
- Target Audience: design discipline, education level, etc.
- Rationale: why it's needed, why it's structured the way it is
- Methodology: lecture content, discussion groups, research method, ideation process
- Anticipated Outcomes: what they have created or done by the end of the assignment

These proposals will be sent to graphic design educators at other schools for feedback and critique. Additionally, these proposals will be presented to an environmental education professor for interdisciplinary critique. Your final proposal should be revised in response to the feedback you receive from all reviewers.

ASSIGNMENT 5: RESEARCH PAPER

Objectives: To increase your knowledge of green design through in-depth research of a related subtopic and to further your understanding of the scientific method and learn to apply it toward the development and investigation of an original hypothesis.

Procedure: This paper will be developed and evaluated in three phases. Each phase will be presented for peer review in class. The topic for your research will be assigned from the following list:

- environmental education
- solid-waste reduction
- papermaking
- chlorine bleaching of paper
- recycling
- ecophilosophy
- nontree papers
- client education
- life-cycle analysis
- packaging design
- printing and ink technology

Structure each phase of your research paper according to the categories used in Assignment 3. Note the following clarifications regarding expectations at each phase:

- *Phase One*
  - Title: Consider how different wordings of the title help or hinder the clarity of your intentions.
  - Abstract: This is extremely important at this phase, as it helps to clarify your approach.
  - Problem Definition: This will be in its early stages in phase one. Describe the background of the problem in terms of both past and present situations. Also, clarify the need for your investigation. It is not expected that you have completed your literature review at this point, but sources should be identified.
  - Hypothesis: This is also extremely important at this phase, as it determines the direction of both your literature review and your methodology.
  - Investigation of the Hypothesis: Describe your intended methodology. How will new data be collected? How will Internet resources be used? Will there be surveys and interviews?
  - Identify the known experts in this topic. What assumptions are you making? What results would nullify your hypothesis?
  - Potential Limitations of the Methodology: Describe gaps in this methodology, or other limitations that will make it impossible to test the hypothesis.
- *Phase Two* Review the critical responses to your phase-one submission. Rework the paper as follows:
  - Title: Clarify as necessary.
  - Abstract: Clarify ambiguous issues; correct errors in reasoning.
  - Problem Definition: Show evidence of continued progress. Document sources here (and throughout the paper) with footnotes as you would a research paper.

- Hypothesis: Clarify as necessary.
- Investigation of the Hypothesis: Show evidence of continued progress. Document your research interactions, both passive and active. Prepare prototypes of any surveys or tests you will conduct. List the questions you are asking, and why you think they are pertinent questions. How was your survey audience selected? Identify your opinions, and follow up with a methodology for investigating the validity of those opinions. Identify assumptions you are making.
- Potential Limitations of the Methodology: Acknowledge any newly considered limitations that have been identified by you or your reviewers, along with possible solutions.

- *Phase Three* This phase of the paper should have resolved all problems that were identified in phase-two feedback. The final paper should make a unique contribution to the body of knowledge in the area of green design, and should show evidence of an understanding and appreciation of the principles of argument (such as inductive and deductive reasoning) that you have been studying.

ASSIGNMENT 6: PEER REVIEW OF IN-PROGRESS RESEARCH

Objectives: To continue dissecting written arguments in order to evaluate their validity and clarity; to assist peers in their own research progress.

Procedure: You will be given a draft of another student's research proposal (phase one). Study the proposal critically. Respond to each section with comments about clarity, validity, uniqueness, verifiability, sources, etc. Is there faulty reasoning used? If so, describe. What assumptions are being made that were not identified by the author? Is the author making an assertion that has already been proven, or is already well documented in existing literature? What recommendations can you make about revisions in each section? Your evaluation and analysis should be two to three pages.

Designing with Movement and Sound/ Designing in Time and Space

Jay Chapman

INTRODUCTION

From numerous exercises and workshops I developed as a creative consultant to the interactive multimedia/motion graphics/digital design community, I adapted and organized a selection into a two-part new media foundation course designed to meet the needs of students who are trying to find, nourish, and enrich their own "voice" and sensibilities.

What emerged is a heightened-awareness, enhanced-stimuli, multidisciplined (and, I might add, extremely successful) approach to turning traditional (static-based) designers into new media (movement-based) designers.

DESIGNING WITH MOVEMENT AND SOUND

(The first part of a two-course foundation sequence for all new media)

A design class where you use the computer as a tool in a series of short dynamic divertissements emphasizing expressive movement and sound, combined at the end of the term into your own multimedia circus.

Major/term: Open to students of all majors in any term (working on any platform).

Prerequisites: Fascination with movement and/or sound. Willingness to expand your perceptions and sensibility. Ability to generate movement in any computer program on any platform (no computer programs are taught in this class). Ability to record sound. Excitement at the thought of a circus. A sense of humor.

Raison d'être: Life is movement/movement is not necessarily life. Just as an eye can be developed to see more, a body's awareness of internal and external movement and sound can be expanded. Enriched awareness of movement and sound is the key to more vital and dynamic expression. To nourish an expanded sensibility, you must have constant experimentation, exploration, and reinforcement, one small bit at a time. Once any design incorporates movement and sound, they have to become the foundation for the design. In fully communicative multimedia, movement becomes the primary expressive force and main compositional element. Movement must be used expressively in order to effectively communicate a concept. Sound must be designed as an integral part of the overall concept, rather than mere accompaniment to the visual material.

Focus: Expressive movement and sound.

Aim: To develop greater sensitivity to movement and sound dynamics as a way of infusing computer-generated work with more "life," energy, and feeling.

Method: Short weekly exercises exploring the expressive potential of movement and sound.

Teaching tools: Lectures, demonstrations, body-awareness exercises, environmental-awareness exercises, film and video screenings, slides, analytical frame-by-frame film examinations, in-class analysis of student and other work.

Result: A series of "acts" and "environments" sequentially arranged around the concept of a circus/sideshow/carnival, which will document the creator's experiments with and facility for employing movement and sound in an expressive, dynamic manner.

DESIGNING WITH MOVEMENT AND SOUND: SYLLABUS

Each weekly assignment functions as both an "act" or "environment" in your circus/sideshow/carnival and a formal exercise. Assignments are due on the weeks specified, but may be reworked for the final presentation.

- Week 1
  - Introduction
  - Movement analysis and discussion
  - Linear representation of movement/feeling exercise (by hand, on five sheets of paper, record with a single continuous line the feeling generated by the way five different people are moving)
  - Character personality/naming exercise (to prepare for first assignment)
  - Body-awareness exercises and assignment
- Week 2
  - Discuss body-awareness exercises assigned
  - Assignment due: the headliner (one line) (Animate a line so that the movement of the line expresses the dominant personality trait of the "character" you have created, and name it appropriately. No color/grays, sound, backgrounds, 3-D, recognizable forms.)
- Week 3
  - Assignment due: the troupe (group of lines) (Animate a group of similar lines so that their interaction expresses the dominant personality characteristic of the "group," and name it appropriately. No color/grays, sound, backgrounds, 3-D, recognizable forms.)
- Week 4
  - Assignment due: the star animal (one shape) (Animate an amorphous shape so that the movement of the shape expresses the dominant personality trait of the "animal" you have created, and name it appropriately. No color/grays, sound, backgrounds, 3-D, recognizable forms.)

- Week 5
  - Assignment due: the animal act (group of shapes) (Animate a group of similar amorphous shapes so that their interaction expresses the dominant personality characteristic of the "group," and name it appropriately. No color/grays, sound, backgrounds, 3-D, recognizable forms.)
  - Environmental-awareness exercises and assignment
  - Spatial-dynamics discussion and in-class computer exercise
- Week 6
  - Discuss environmental-awareness exercises assigned
  - Assignment due: the house/room/tent (a consistent space) (Develop an abstract, nonspecific, moving environment with a definite feeling through the movement of lines and shapes, and name it appropriately. No color/grays, sound, recognizable forms.)
  - Spatial-dynamics discussion and in-class computer exercise
- Week 7
  - Assignment due: the ride (an evolving space) (Develop an abstract, nonspecific series of moving environments that evolve from one to the next—each with a different specific feeling—through the movement of lines and shapes, and name it appropriately. No color/grays, sound, recognizable forms.)
  - Introduction to sound
  - Sound-awareness exercises
  - Sound-creation exercises
- Week 8
  - Discuss sound-awareness exercises
  - Assignment due: intermission (sound collage) (Create a sound collage that evokes a definite feeling. No recorded music, use of words in phrases or sentences.)
  - In-class computer exercise
- Week 9
  - Assignment due: the playroom/divertissement (lines and sound) (Create a divertissement evoking a specific feeling through the play of lines and sound, and name it appropriately. No color/grays, backgrounds, 3-D; can be representational, but not recommended.)
  - In-class computer exercise
- Week 10
  - Assignment due: "animals" in their native habitat (shapes and sound in space) (Through the play of shapes and sound in an environment, evoke the feeling of specific imaginary "animals" at play in their "native habitat," and name appropriately. Use grays/no color; can be representational, but not recommended.)
  - In-class computer exercise

- Week 11
  - Assignment rough: finale (anything/everything) (Create a final act for your circus/sideshow/carnival, integrating what you have learned into a "finale" of your choice, and name appropriately. No restrictions.)
- Week 12
  - Assignment due: finale (anything/everything)
  - Discussion of ways to connect all "acts"/exercises
- Week 13
  - Preview of entire show (connections) (All "acts"/exercises arranged into your own circus/sideshow/carnival.)
- Week 14
  - Opening night (bravo!) (Your complete circus/sideshow/carnival, named appropriately.)

In-class, computer-based exercises are determined by students' particular needs, and are always executed by pairs of students working together.

Each class session concludes with a screening of short films, film clips, and/or videos chosen from the 1920s through the 1990s—to serve as examples of points made and sources of inspiration and stimulation. Slide and sound presentations are determined by students' needs and interests.

DESIGNING IN TIME AND SPACE

(The second part of a two-course foundation sequence for all new media)

A design class where you use the computer as a tool to continue to "play" with movement and sound in a more sophisticated, complex manner emphasizing rhythm, spatial dynamics, and principles of continuity, in order to help you to further develop your own new media "voice."

Prerequisite: Designing with Movement and Sound

Raison d'être: In fully communicative new media, movement becomes the primary expressive force and main binding element, supplanting customary notions of (static) "composition" in classic graphic design.

Once you have acquired sufficient experience through experimentation with movement and sound as expressive forces (the main focus of Designing with Movement and Sound), you are now ready to progress to the next level: movement and sound as the basis for a new, active/dynamic form of "composition."

In order for this new, active/dynamic form of "composition" to communicate in a clear, coherent manner, concepts of rhythm and spatial dynamics must be explored and mastered. When putting these concepts into practice in more complex projects, an understanding of the principles of continuity is essential.

Focus: Rhythm, spatial dynamics, and elements/principles of continuity.

Aim: To have you acquire a facility for using rhythm and spatial dynamics to enhance your movement and sound skills in order to communicate more complex concepts in a more sophisticated manner. To give you an opportunity to demonstrate the extent of your newly expanded sensibilities in projects of your devising directly related to your new media concerns.

Method: Four simple, one-week, computer-based exercises during the first third of the course focus on using rhythm and spatial dynamics as expressive tools to evoke feeling, sound, environment, and situation. After an introduction to the elements and principles of continuity, three more complex, two-week, computer-based exercises and a final three-week student-conceived project give you an opportunity to develop more sophisticated design solutions employing all the resources available to you.

Teaching tools: Lectures, demonstrations, body-awareness exercises, environmental-awareness exercises, film rhythm-recognition exercises, film and video screenings, slides, analytical frame-by-frame film examinations, in-class analysis of student work, analysis of other new media work.

Result: A series of exercises and brief final project that will document the creator's experiments with and facility for employing rhythm, spatial dynamics, and elements of continuity with sophistication in order to communicate complex concepts.

DESIGNING IN TIME AND SPACE: SYLLABUS

The overall theme/context for the exercises and brief final project is determined by each student, in order to integrate individual experiments into your own specific directions/goals in new media. Exercises are due on the weeks specified, but may be reworked for the final presentation.

- Week 1
  - Introduction
  - Review of previous class
  - Body rhythm-awareness exercises and assignment
  - Environmental rhythm-awareness exercises and assignment
  - Film rhythm-recognition exercises and assignment
  - Assignment: next week bring in five different music examples (three-minute excerpts)
- Week 2
  - Exercise due: use of purely visual rhythms to evoke a specific feeling (No sound, color/grays, backgrounds, 3-D, recognizable forms.)
  - Rhythm discussion and in-class computer exercise
  - Music rhythm-recognition exercises
- Week 3
  - Exercise due: use of purely visual rhythms to evoke sound (No sound, color/grays, backgrounds, 3-D, recognizable forms.)
  - Spatial-awareness exercises and assignment

- Spatial-dynamics discussion and in-class computer exercise
- Week 4
  - Exercise due: use of rhythm and space to evoke a feelingful environment (Use grays/no color; can be representational; sound: complementary.)
  - Counterpoint discussion and in-class computer exercise
- Week 5
  - Exercise due: use of rhythm and space to evoke the "feel" of a situation (Use grays/no color; can be representational; sound: counterpoint.)
  - Elements/principles of continuity and in-class computer exercise
- Week 6
  - Exercise rough: visual/sound essay using series of still photos/images (point of view) (No type/spoken words.)
  - Elements/principles of continuity
- Week 7
  - Exercise due: visual/sound essay (still photos/images)
  - Elements/principles of continuity
- Week 8
  - Exercise rough: visual/sound narrative (expressing emotional content of situation) (No dialogue/narration; sound must develop the narrative as much as visuals.)
- Week 9
  - Exercise due: visual/sound narrative
- Week 10
  - Exercise rough: expression of a point of view (You must use still and moving images, animation, type and sound.)
- Week 11
  - Exercise due: expression of a point of view
- Week 12
  - Final project rough: anything student wants, using all skills mastered in the course
- Week 13
  - Final project refinement
- Week 14
  - Final project due
  - Final presentation of all exercises

In-class, computer-based exercises are determined by students' particular needs. Each class session concludes with a screening of short films, film clips and/or videos chosen from the 1920s through the 1990s—to serve as examples of points made and sources of inspiration and stimulation. Slide and sound presentations are determined by students' needs and interests.

Contributors

Roy R. Behrens, who teaches graphic design and design history at the University of Northern Iowa, is editor of *Ballast Quarterly Review* and contributing editor of *Print*. In 1995, he received the Donald McKay Research Award, and, in 1996, the Faculty Excellence Award from the Iowa Board of Regents. Among his publications are two design textbooks, *Design in the Visual Arts* and *Illustration as an Art*.

Andrew Blauvelt is head of the department of graphic design and director of the graduate program at North Carolina State University, Raleigh.

Max Bruinsma is editor of *Eye*, the international review of graphic design. He was trained as an art historian, and as a cultural critic has written extensively on the visual arts, architecture, and graphic design. As an educator, he taught design history at the Rietveld Academy in Amsterdam.

Jay Chapman has been teaching at the Art Center College of Design in Pasadena for the past twenty years. He teaches: new media design (interactive multimedia and motion graphics); graphic design history, theory, aesthetics, criticism; and film history, theory, aesthetics, criticism. He is principal of movementsoundspacetime: creative consultants to the interactive multimedia/motion graphics/digital design community.

Moira Cullen is an internationally published design writer, educator, and strategist whose career spans the worlds of dance, photography, fashion, marketing, and design. She currently chairs the department of communication arts at Otis College of Art and Design in Los Angeles and is president of the Los Angeles chapter of the American Institute of Graphic Arts.

Paula J. Curran teaches graphic design at Iowa State University and lives in Ames with Louie, her blind Australian shepherd. When Paula clutters the living-room floor with *HOW*, *Print*, *Step-by-Step Graphics*, *American Center for Design*, *Type Directors Club*, and other annuals in which her client- and self-initiated projects have appeared, Louie is not impressed. He would rather she not rearrange the furniture.

Louis Danziger, graphic designer, art director, and design consultant, is on the faculty of Art Center College of Design in Pasadena, California. An educator since 1956, he is one of the pioneers of graphic design pedagogy.

Meredith Davis is a professor and director of the graduate program in the department of graphic design at North Carolina State University; president of the American Center for Design; a member of the board of directors of the American Institute of Graphic Arts for which she chairs the NASAD accreditation task force; and was founding president of the Graphic Design Education Association.

Sheila Levrant de Bretteville has been an educator for over twenty years and is the chair of the graduate program in graphic design at Yale University.

Johanna Drucker has published several books on the theory and history of typography including *The Alphabetic Labyrinth* (Thames and Hudson, 1995) and *The Visible Word* (University of Chicago, 1994). She has taught art history at Yale, Harvard, and Columbia, and is now directing a master's program in twentieth-century art historical, visual, and critical studies at SUNY Purchase where she is professor of art history.

Lisa Fontaine is an associate professor of graphic design at Iowa State University. She is the project director for ICOGRADA Education's Green Graphic Design Initiative, an international collaboration developing curricular strategies to bring environmental education into graphic design. She has lectured across the United States and internationally on the ecological impact of graphic design.

Geoffry Fried is a graphic designer and educator. He is currently chair of the design department at the Art Institute of Boston, and has also taught at Boston University, Northeastern University, and Rhode Island School of Design.

Milton Glaser, illustrator, graphic designer, and cofounder of Push Pin Studios, has taught for over thirty years at the School of Visual Arts in New York City.

Michael Golec received his M.A. in art history from the University of Illinois, Chicago. He is currently pursuing a Ph.D. in art history at Northwestern University. He lives and works in Chicago.

April Greiman, graphic, video, and multimedia designer, was the chair of design and has taught at CalArts in Los Angeles. She is a pioneer of the New Typography and the integration of multimedia in graphic design.

Sylvia Harris is a consultant and educator who specializes in the planning and design of user-centered information services for diverse audiences. From 1980 to 1993,

Harris was a cofounder and principal of Two Twelve Associates, Inc., a New York City graphic design firm specializing in the design of communications for large public audiences. She is currently a critic at the Yale University School of Art and is on the board of the American Institute of Graphic Arts. She has traveled worldwide and writes on culture and "design for diversity."

Lorraine Justice is an associate professor of visual communication and acting chair of the department of industrial, interior, and visual communication design at Ohio State University. She is the recipient of a team award in education from the Smithsonian Institution, and of a National Endowment for the Arts grant in design and technology. Professor Justice has worked in the area of interactive media for the past fifteen years.

Jeffery Keedy is on the faculty of the program in graphic design at CalArts. He received an M.F.A. from Cranbrook Academy of Art and is known as an educator, writer, and type designer.

Julie Lasky is a freelance arts journalist and editor in New York City.

Krzysztof Lenk, graphic designer and information architect, teaches typography at the Rhode Island School of Design. He has been one of the foremost proponents in the new field of information design.

Ellen Lupton is cochair of visual communications at Maryland Institute, College of Art, in Baltimore, with J. Abbott Miller. She is adjunct curator of contemporary design at the Cooper-Hewitt, National Design Museum in New York City.

Victor Margolin, founding editor and now a coeditor of the journal *Design Issues,* is associate professor of design history at the University of Illinois, Chicago. He is editor of *Design Discourse: History Theory Criticism,* coeditor of *Discovering Design: Explorations in Design Studies* and *The Idea of Design,* and author of *The Struggle for Utopia: Rodchenko, Lissitzky, Moholy-Nagy, 1917–1946.*

Katherine McCoy is a senior lecturer at Illinois Institute of Technology's Institute of Design and a visiting professor of the Royal College of Art in London. She was cochair of design at Cranbrook Academy of Art for twenty-three years. As partner of McCoy & McCoy, her design practice includes graphic design and design marketing for an international range of cultural, educational, and corporate clients. She is an elected member of the Alliance Graphique Internationale, a Fellow and past president of the Industrial Designers Society of America, and has served as president of the American Center for Design.

Ellen McMahon teaches typography and graphic design theory at the University of Arizona where she directs the visual communications program and cochairs the studio division of the art deparment. Her research explores the cultural representations and lived experience of motherhood.

J. Abbott Miller is director of Design Writing Research, a multidisciplinary studio in New York City. Projects include the award-winning cultural journal *Twice*, of which Miller is editor and art director. He is cochair, with Ellen Lupton, of graphic design at Maryland Institute, College of Art, in Baltimore.

Sharyn O'Mara is an assistant professor in the foundation department at Kansas City Art Institute. Previously, she taught at Rhode Island School of Design and was head of the Design Program at KCAI. In keeping with her belief that designers should take an active role in their community and culture, she does pro bono projects for women's organizations, including a shelter for survivors of domestic violence and sexual assault and the local Planned Parenthood affiliate. A writer and installation artist, O'Mara's passion for language inspires much of her three-dimensional work. She has also pursued a two-year study of glassblowing as a means to articulate her ideas.

Rick Poynor founded *Eye,* the international review of graphic communication, and edited it from 1990 to 1997. His books include *Typography Now: The Next Wave, The Graphic Edge,* and *Design without Boundaries: Visual Communication in Transition.* He lectures widely in Europe and the United States, and is a visiting professor in the school of communications at the Royal College of Art, London.

Chris Pullman is vice president for design at WGBH Boston, which produces about a third of the PBS prime-time schedule. His staff works in all media, including print, video, and the Internet. He has taught in the graduate design program at Yale for over thirty years and lectures widely to schools and professional organizations.

Michael Rock is an associate professor at the Yale School of Art and partner in the graphic design firm 2 × 4.

Katie Salen is an assistant professor of design at the University of Texas at Austin and the editor/designer of the design journal *Zed.* Her research focuses on utilizing a broad design practice to investigate ideas about the dynamic relationship between cultural identities and their expression through visual language.

Douglass Scott is a senior designer at the WGBH Educational Foundation, public television and radio in Boston. He teaches graphic design, typography, and design history at the Rhode Island School of Design and Yale University School of Art. Since 1978, Scott has given over one hundred lectures on the history of design and printing at various colleges, universities, and symposia.

Steven Skaggs is professor of design at the University of Louisville. Author of *Logos: The Development of Visual Symbols* (Crisp, 1994), his articles on design theory and semiotics have appeared in many publications, including the *AIGA Journal of Graphic Design, Journal of American Semiotics, Hi-Fives: A Trip to Semiotics* (Lang, 1999), and *Letter Arts Review*. His calligraphy has been exhibited around the world, and he is currently working on a book about improvisatory calligraphy, *Jazz Writing*, expected to be available in 2000.

Virginia Smith's biography of a graphic icon, titled *The Funny Little Man*, was reviewed internationally as a work of "graphic archeology." Her book on typgraphy and forms, *Visual Set: Typography and the Design Arts*, will be published in spring 2000. A graduate of Wellesley College and Yale University, she is a professor of art at Baruch College of the City University of New York.

Deborah Sussman, graphic, environmental, and industrial designer, is responsible for a wide range of environmental graphic systems, including the signage at Walt Disney World in Orlando, Florida.

Gunnar Swanson teaches in the design program at the University of California, Davis. He formerly headed the graphic design program at the University of Minnesota, Duluth, and taught at Otis College of Art and Design and other schools in the Los Angeles area.

Ellen Mazur Thomson is the author of *American Graphic Design: A Guide to the Literature* (1992) and *The Origins of Graphic Design in America, 1870–1920* (1997).

Michael Vanderbyl, graphic, furniture, and interior designer, is the dean of the California College of Arts and Crafts in San Francisco. He is responsible for the integration of illustration and graphics into a total program.

Karen White teaches design and computer graphics at the University of Arizona. Her courses explore two-dimensional and time-based design and include theoretical, conceptual, and critical issues. Her current research examines the relationship between design, culture, and technology.

Lorraine Wild is a designer and educator. She has been teaching at CalArts for ten years and also serves as a project tutor at the Jan van Eyck Akademie in Maastricht, The Netherlands.

Judith Wilde is a poet, author, copywriter, illustrator, graphic designer, fine artist, a principal at Wilde Design, professor of graphic design and illustration and director of the

A.A.S. degree program in graphic design and illustration at Kingsborough Community College. She has co-authored *Visual Literacy* (Watson-Guptill) and *101 Ways to Stay Young* (Warner Books).

Richard Wilde is the chair of the graphic design and advertising departments at the School of Visual Arts, senior vice president at Ryan Drossman and Partners, and a principal at Wilde Design. He has written *Problems: Solutions* (Van Nostrand Reinhold) and co-authored *Visual Literacy* (Watson-Guptill) and *101 Ways to Stay Young* (Warner Books). He has won over one hundred awards and has given creativity workshops on five continents.

Michael Worthington is the director of the graphic design program at CalArts, teaching typography and design for print and screen. His work has been published in design books and magazines, nationally and internationally, and he has lectured at various schools in the United States as well as in Holland and England.

Credits

Index

Books from Allworth Press

Design Dialogues *by Steven Heller and Elinor Pettit* (softcover, 6¾ × 10, 256 pages, $18.95)

Design Culture: An Anthology of Writing from the AIGA Journal of Graphic Design *edited by Steven Heller and Marie Finamore* (softcover, 6¾ × 10, 320 pages, $19.95)

AIGA Professional Practices in Graphic Design *by the American Institute of Graphic Arts, edited by Tad Crawford* (softcover, 6¾ × 10, 320 pages, $24.95)

Design Literacy: Understanding Graphic Design *by Steven Heller and Karen Pomeroy* (softcover, 6¾ × 10, 288 pages, $19.95)

Looking Closer: Critical Writings on Graphic Design *edited by Michael Bierut, William Drenttel, Steven Heller, and DK Holland* (softcover, 6¾ × 10, 256 pages, $18.95)

Looking Closer 2: Critical Writings on Graphic Design *edited by Michael Bierut, William Drenttel, Steven Heller, and DK Holland* (softcover, 6¾ × 10, 288 pages, $18.95)

Careers by Design: A Headhunter's Secrets for Success and Survival in Graphic Design, Revised Edition *by Roz Goldfarb* (softcover, 6¾ × 10, 224 pages, $18.95)

The New Business of Design *by the International Design Conference in Aspen* (softcover, 6¾ × 10, 256 pages, $19.95)

Licensing Art & Design, Revised Edition *by Caryn R. Leland* (softcover, 6 × 9, 128 pages, $16.95)

Business and Legal Forms for Graphic Designers, Revised Edition *by Tad Crawford* (softcover, 8½ × 11, 208 pages, $22.95)

Legal Guide for the Visual Artist, Third Edition *by Tad Crawford* (softcover, 8½ × 11, 256 pages, $19.95)

Electronic Design and Publishing: Business Practices, Second Edition *by Liane Sebastian* (softcover, 6¾ × 10, 216 pages, $19.95)

Selling Graphic Design *by Don Sparkman, foreword by Ed Gold* (softcover, 6 × 9, 256 pages, $18.95)

Uncontrollable Beauty: Toward a New Aesthetics *edited by Bill Beckley with David Shapiro* (hardcover, 6 × 9, 448 pages, $24.95)

Please write to request our free catalog. To order by credit card, call 800-491-2808 or send a check or money order to Allworth Press, 10 East 23rd Street, Suite 210, New York, NY 10010. Include $5 for shipping and handling for the first book ordered and $1 for each additional book. Ten dollars plus $1 for each additional book if ordering from Canada. New York State residents must add sales tax.

If you would like to see our complete catalog on the World Wide Web, you can find us at *www.allworth.com*